ORIGINAL NARRATIVES
OF EARLY AMERICAN HISTORY

REPRODUCED UNDER THE AUSPICES OF THE
AMERICAN HISTORICAL ASSOCIATION

GENERAL EDITOR, J. FRANKLIN JAMESON, PH.D., LL.D.

DIRECTOR OF THE DEPARTMENT OF HISTORICAL RESEARCH IN THE
CARNEGIE INSTITUTION OF WASHINGTON

JOHNSON'S
WONDER-WORKING PROVIDENCE

1628 — 1651

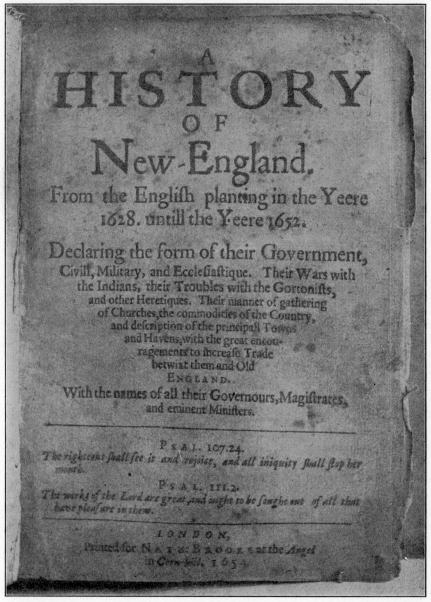

A

HISTORY

OF

New-England.

From the English planting in the Yeere
1628. untill the Yeere 1652.

Declaring the form of their Government,
Civill, Military, and Ecclesiastique. Their Wars with
the Indians, their Troubles with the Gortonists,
and other Heretiques. Their manner of gathering
of Churches, the commodities of the Country,
and description of the principall Towns
and Havens, with the great encouragements to increase Trade
betwixt them and Old
ENGLAND.

With the names of all their Governours, Magistrates,
and eminent Ministers.

PSAL. 107. 24.
The righteous shall see it and rejoice, and all iniquity shall stop her
mouth.

PSAL. 111. 2.
The works of the Lord are great, and ought to be sought out of all that
have pleasure in them.

LONDON,
Printed for NATH. BROOKE at the Angel
in Corn-hill. 1654.

TITLE-PAGE OF THE "WONDER-WORKING PROVIDENCE"
From a copy of the original in the Woburn Public Library

JOHNSON'S
WONDER - WORKING
PROVIDENCE

1628–1651

EDITED BY

J. FRANKLIN JAMESON, Ph.D., LL.D.

DIRECTOR OF THE DEPARTMENT OF HISTORICAL RESEARCH IN THE CARNEGIE INSTITUTION
OF WASHINGTON

WITH A MAP AND TWO FACSIMILES

CHARLES SCRIBNER'S SONS
NEW YORK

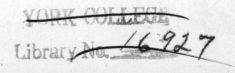

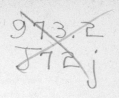

CONTENTS

JOHNSON'S WONDER-WORKING PROVIDENCE OF SIONS SAVIOUR IN NEW ENGLAND —"HISTORY OF NEW ENGLAND"

Edited by J. Franklin Jameson

	PAGE
INTRODUCTION	3
To the Reader	21
Book I. The Sad Condition of Old England	23
The Call of Christ's People to New England; their Churches	25
The Demeanor of their Church Officers	26
The Demeanor of the People	28
Their Civil Government; the Maintenance of the First Table	30
Their Care for Warlike Discipline	33
Their Liberty; their Charter; their Means	36
The Massachusetts Indians	39
The Pestilence	40
The Men of Plymouth and the Indians	42
John Endicott	44
The Settlement of Salem	45
The Founding of the Salem Church; Mr. Higginson and Mr. Skelton	46
The Glorious Beginnings of a Thorough Church Reformation	49
The Farewell to England	50
The Cost of the Peopling of New England	54
God's Providence in Transporting his People Safely	56
An Exhortation to the Advancing of the Kingdom of Christ	58
Providences in Deliverance from Perils of Waters	61
The Arrival of Winthrop's Fleet; the Old Planters	63
The First Elections, 1630; the Death of Isaac Johnson and Others	65
The Gathering of the Church of Charlestown-Boston; Mr. Wilson	67
The Church and Town of Dorchester; Mr. Maverick	69
The Church and Town of Boston	70
The Church and Town of Roxbury; Mr. Eliot	71
The Church and Town of Lynn; Mr. Batchellor	73
The Church and Town of Watertown; Mr. Phillips	74
The Trials of the Wilderness; Governor John Winthrop re-elected, 1631	75
The Lord's Protection of his People from the Indians; the Small Pox	78

PAGE

The Elections of 1632; Deputy Governor Thomas Dudley . . 81
Mr. James of Charlestown 82
Mr. Weld of Roxbury 83
Mr. Wilson of Boston; his Return 84
The Elections of 1633; Mr. Increase Nowell 85
Supplies in Time of Need 86
Arrival of Mr. Haynes, Mr. Stone, and Mr. John Cotton . . . 87
The Church and Town of Newtown or Cambridge; Mr. Hooker . 90
The Elections of 1634; Mr. Stone 93
The Escape of Mr. Norton and Mr. Shepard from England . . 94
The Church and Town of Ipswich; Mr. Nathaniel Ward . . . 95
The Arrival of Mr. Bellingham and Mr. Lothrop 97
The Church and Town of Newbury; Mr. Noyes and Mr. Parker . 98
The Arrival of Mr. Symmes 100
The Elections of 1635 101
The Arrival of Sir Henry Vane and Sir Richard Saltonstall . . 102
Of Mr. Harlakenden and of Eleven Ministers; Mr. Norton . . 103
Mr. Richard Mather 105
The Founding of Connecticut 105
The Gathering of the Second Cambridge Church; Mr. Shepard . 107
The Arrival of Mr. Hugh Peters 109
The Church and Town of Concord; Mr. Bulkley 110
The Laborious Work of Planting it; Mr. Jones 111
The Church and Town of Hingham; Mr. Hobart 115
The Arrival of Mr. Thomas Flint, Mr. Carter, and others . . . 117
The Elections of 1636; Mr. Fenwick's Plantation 118
Mr. Partridge of Duxbury; Mr. Nathaniel Rogers of Ipswich . . 119
Mr. Whiting of Lynn 120
Satan raises Enemies against Christ's People 121
Justification by Faith; Mr. Cotton 125
The Magnifying of Free Grace 126
The Gainsaying of Mrs. Hutchinson 127
The Shallowness of the Erronists 128
They slight the Ordinances of Christ 129
They disturb the Churches 131
The Distress of a Poor Soul landing at this Time 133
The New England Churches prone neither to Heresy nor to Tyranny 136
The Elections of 1637 139
The Form of Civil Government in New England 140
Mr. Simon Bradstreet 141
The Principal Deputies 143

BOOK II. The Beginning of the Pequot War 147
The Lord delivers his People from Error; the Calling of the Synod . 152
Prosperity in Outward Things 153
The Lord Preserves his People from Morton and the Bishops . . 154
The Malignancy of the English Prelates and their Downfall . . 157
The Embassy to Canonicus 161

CONTENTS

PAGE

The Insolence of the Pequots 164
The March against them; the Ministers' Exhortations . . . 165
The Destruction of the Pequots 167
The Assemblage of the Synod 170
Four Sorts of Men who might profitably have Attended . . . 171
The Disarming of Dangerous Heretics; Excommunication of Some . 175
The Planting of the Colony of New Haven 176
Mr. John Davenport 177
Mr. Theophilus Eaton; Mr. Hopkins 178
The Church and Town of Dedham; Mr. Allen 179
The Church and Town of Weymouth 181
The Elections of 1638 182
The Establishment of a Printing Press 183
The Church and Town of Rowley; Mr. Ezekiel Rogers and Mr.
    Miller 183
The Earthquake; the Banishment of the Erronists 185
Their Bad End 186
Mr. John Harvard and Harvard College 187
The Elections of 1639; the Church and Town of Hampton; Mr. Dalton 188
The Church and Town of Salisbury; Mr. Worcester 189
Mr. Knowles added to the Church of Watertown 190
Sad Accident at Boston 191
The Elections of 1640; the Arrival of Mr. Burr and Mr. Rayner . 192
Of other Ministers 193
The Planting of Long Island 195
The Church and Town of Sudbury; Mr. Brown 195
The Church and Town of Braintree; Mr. Thompson and Mr. Flint . 197
The Desire for the Promotion of Learning 198
The Founding of Harvard College 200
Hopeful Plants raised up therein 202
President Dunster 204
The Elections of 1641 205
The Church and Town of Gloucester; Mr. Blinman 205
The Church and Town of Dover 206
Sundry Misguided Persons sail for the Isle of Providence . . . 207
The Elections of 1642; the Fall in the Price of Cattle . . . 209
The Prosperity of New England 210
The Founding of the Town of Woburn 212
The Gathering of the Church 214
The Church Covenant 216
The Ordination of Mr. Thomas Carter 217
The Elections of 1643; the New England Confederation . . . 219
The Struggle between Miantonomoh and Uncas 220
The Death of Miantonomoh 222
The Outrageous Conduct of the Gortonists 222
Their Punishment 224
The Elections of 1644; The Church and Town of Reading; Mr.
    Green 225

                                                                    PAGE
The Church and Town of Wenham; Mr. Fisk 226
Military Precautions and Arrangements 227
The Military Commanders 229
The Fortifications 231

BOOK III. The Elections of 1645 234
The Church and Town of Haverhill; Mr. John Ward . . . 234
The Sons of Canonicus overawed 235
The Church and Town of Springfield; Mr. Moxon 236
Fasting and Prayer for the Brethren in England 238
The Elections of 1646; the Petition of Dr. Child and others . . 240
The Mission of Winslow 241
The Second Synod of Cambridge; the Cambridge Platform . . 242
The Images of the Sun 243
The Compiling of the Laws of 1648 244
The Elections of 1647; the Rise of Manufactures 245
The Elections of 1648; the Church and Town of Andover . . 249
The Church and Town of Malden 250
The North Church of Boston 251
The Death of Winthrop and other Eminent Persons . . . 251
Other Disasters 253
The Elections of 1650 254
Of 1651; Special Providences 255
Verses on God's Dealings with His New England People . . . 257
The Preaching of Christ to the Indians 261
Ministers sent to the Godly in Virginia 265
Judgments following their Expulsion 266
The Church in the Bermudas 267
The Time of the Fall of Antichrist 268
Concluding Verses on God's Wonder-working Providence . . . 272
INDEX 277

MAP AND FACSIMILE REPRODUCTIONS

TITLE-PAGE OF THE "WONDER-WORKING PROVIDENCE." From a copy of the original in the Woburn Public Library . . . *Frontispiece*

PAGE

MAP OF NEW ENGLAND IN 1628–1651. From Palfrey's "History of New England" 64

FIRST PAGE OF THE RECORDS OF THE TOWN OF WOBURN. Handwriting of Major William Johnson, son of Captain Edward Johnson . . . 213

WONDER-WORKING PROVIDENCE
OF SIONS SAVIOUR IN NEW ENGLAND
1628-1651

INTRODUCTION

LATE in the year 1653, but under date of 1654, Nathaniel Brooke, a London publisher, "at the Angel in Cornhill," brought out a small octavo book of two hundred and thirty-six pages, entitled *A History of New-England, from the English planting in the Yeere* 1628 *untill the Yeere* 1652, etc. The title, inexact in any case, for the book is rather a history of Massachusetts than of all New England, was evidently affixed by the publisher. His advertisements show that at one time he thought of giving the book the title *Historicall Relation of the First Planting of the English in New England in the Year* 1628 *to the Year* 1653 *and all the Materiall Passages happening there.* But many reiterations in the text of the book show that the author's own title for his production was that which appears in the running headlines of the printed book, and by which it has been generally known, *The Wonder-working Providence of Sion's Saviour in New England.* The author's name nowhere appears in the book.

Five years later the publisher took advantage of this latter fact, since the sale of the work had been so disappointing as to leave many copies on his hands, to utilize the sheets in another of his ventures. He had in hand a book entitled *America Painted to the Life.* Of the four parts of which he composed it, the first and fourth were apparently written by Ferdinando Gorges, Esquire, grandson of the celebrated patentee Sir Ferdinando Gorges, while the second was by that knight himself. Brooke impudently sandwiched-in the unsold sheets of *Wonder-working Providence* as Part III., "Written by Sir Ferdinando Gorges Knight" (the grandfather), and

3

"Publisht since his decease by his Grandchild Ferdinando Gorges Esquire, who hath much enlarged it and added severall accurate Descriptions of his owne."

The reader who has any remembrance of the relations between Sir Ferdinando Gorges and the Massachusetts colony, and of the diametrical difference between his state of mind and that which breathes through every page of the *Wonder-working Providence*, will say that imposture could hardly be more shameless. The younger Gorges protested publicly. In the newspaper called *Mercurius Politicus* for September 13, 1660, appeared the following advertisement:

> I, Ferdinando Gorges, the entituled Author of a late Book, called *America Painted to the Life*, am injured in that additional Part, called *Sion's Saviour in New England* (as written by Sir Ferdinando Gorges;) that being none of his, and formerly printed in another name, the true owner.

The last statement is erroneous. So far as is known, no copies of the original book were issued with the author's name. In New England it has been known for more than two hundred years that it was written by Captain Edward Johnson of Woburn, Massachusetts. The accurate Thomas Prince, in the preface to his *Chronological History of New England* (Boston, 1736), after speaking of the false attribution of the book to Gorges, says: "But the true Author was Mr. Johnson of Woburn in New England, as the late Judge Sewall assur'd me, as of a Thing familliarly known among the Fathers of the Massachusetts Colony." In Prince's own copy of the *Wonder-working Providence*, now preserved in the library of the American Antiquarian Society at Worcester, is a manuscript note which is still more explicit:

> Judg Sewall tells me, this Book was known to have been written by Captain   Johnson of Woburn, Father to Hon[bl] W[m] Johnson Esq[r] of Woburn, w° was chosen assistant in 1684 at the same time wth Judg Sewall Himself, and as it was commonly known th[t]

Capt. Johnson was the author of this Book; so the Judg was intimately acquainted wth his son the assistant, and had conferred wth Him about it. This the Judg tells me this [symbol for Friday] aug. 23, 1728.

There are also various internal evidences which point to this authorship. The foundation of the town and church of Woburn are related at much greater length than is the case with any of the other Massachusetts towns, some of them much more important. Other transactions in which Captain Johnson is known to have had an official part are likewise narrated with especial fulness. In chapter XXVI. of the second book, in which the author names the other officers of the military companies of the colony, he says, "The band of Concord is led by Capt. Simon Willard, being a Kentish souldier, as is Capt. Goggin [Gookin], . . . the band of Woburn led by another Kentish Captain." Now we know that the unnamed trainband captain of Woburn was Captain Edward Johnson, and that he came from the county of Kent in England.

The editor of this volume, a descendant of Captain Johnson, takes pleasure in remembering that by a little simple investigation in Canterbury, some years ago, he established with practical certainty the captain's genealogy and local position. The will of one of his sons, who died in Maryland, had recently disclosed the fact that the captain came from Canterbury. It now appeared that he was of the parish of St. George, that he was christened September 16 or 17, 1598 (born therefore in all probability a few days earlier), and that the future town clerk of Woburn was son of William Johnson, parish clerk of St. George's parish. He was married about 1618, and had five sons and two daughters, all born in England and christened in St. George's Church, the last three in 1631, 1633, and 1635, after their father's first voyage to New England. He was possessed of a considerable estate in Canterbury and elsewhere in Kent, and on his first appearance in New England is among the moderate number of those whom the official records of the colony call "Mr."

Edward Johnson came over to New England in 1630 with Winthrop, probably in the *Arbella*. He was licensed by Governor Winthrop to trade with the Indians along the Merrimac River, and in May, 1631, was admitted a freeman of the colony; but he returned to England, probably in that year, and remained there till the spring of 1636, when he came out again, this time bringing his family. This absence accounts for some of the meagreness and vagueness of his information respecting the events of the years 1631–1635. In an official list of passengers sailing from Sandwich, England, in 1636, for America, we find the entry, "Edward Johnson, of Canterbury, joiner, and Susan, his wife, seven children, three servants." Data respecting the occupations of emigrants were often given in a form intended to mislead the royal officers; but the records of St. George's parish also call him a joiner, and two of his sons were shipwrights and carpenters.

Arriving in Massachusetts at the height of the Antinomian excitement, of which he gives a vivid though prejudiced account, Johnson threw himself heart and soul into the life of the colony and of its orthodox party. Settling in Charlestown, where we find him in 1638 in the possession of considerable land-grants, he found abundant opportunity for his active and optimistic spirit in the "wilderness work" of founding a new town, that process so typical in American history. The General Court in May, 1640, on the petition of Charlestown, made a grant, enlarged a few months later to four miles square, for a new town to the northward, called at first Charlestown Village, but after incorporation Woburn. Of this new town Johnson was the leading man. For thirty years, from its incorporation in 1642 to his death in 1672, he was almost constantly one of its "selectmen" or executive committeemen, the captain of its trainband, its town clerk, and its representative in the General Court, and a great part of his time was given to its business. To his deep interest in its affairs we owe it that in *Wonder-working Providence*, book II., chapter XXII., he gives an exceptionally full account of the successive steps in the founding of this new town and church—the appointing of a committee of seven by Charlestown, the committee's careful scrutiny of would-be settlers, its arrangements for village sites and the allotment of outlying farming lands, the engaging of a minister, the gathering of a covenanted church, the minister's ordination by the democratic methods of the new Congregationalism—an account so full and so interesting that it has been one of the classical passages for the student of the origins of town and church government in New England. At the first meeting of the persons chosen by the Charlestown church to manage the new settlement, Edward Johnson was chosen as their recorder or town clerk. Accordingly the first pages of the town records, preserved in a copy in his son's handwriting, furnish a parallel narrative, of all these transactions, to that which he gives in his book. Characteristically, he opens the town records with a rude "copy of verses," which are worth quoting (with clarified punctuation) for their exhibition of the writer's spirit and for their relation to the verses which so thickly bestrew the pages of his printed book.

Records for the Towne of Woburne
ffrom the year 1640 *the* 8 *day of th* 10 *month*
Paulisper Fui
In peniles age I woburne Towne began;
Charls Towne first moved the Court my lins to span.
To vewe my land place, compild body Reare,
Nowell, Sims, Sedgwick, thes my paterons were.[1]
Sum fearing Ile grow great upon these grownds,
Poor I wase putt to nurs among the Clownes,

[1] Increase Nowell, Rev. Zachary Symmes, Robert Sedgwick, in compliment to whom the town was named; see notes on their names, on pp. 85, 100, 212. *post.*

Who being taken with such mighty things
As had bin work of Noble Qeeins and Kings,
Till Babe gan crye and great disturbance make;
Nurses Repent they did har undertake.
One leaves her quite; an other hee doth hie
To foren lands, free from the Babys Crye;
To [two] more of seaven, seing nursing provd soe thwarte,
Thought it more ease in following of the Carte.
A naighbour by,[1] hopeing the Babe wold bee
A pritty Girle, to Rocking har went hee.
Too [two] nurses less undanted [danted ?] then [than] the rest,
ffirst howses ffinish; thus the Girle gane drest.
Its Rare to see how this poore Towne did rise
By weakest means, two [too] weake in great ons [ones'] eys.
And sure it is that mettells cleere exstraction
Had never share in this Poore Towns erextion;
Without which metall and sum fresh suplys
Patrons conclud she never upp wold rise.
If ever she mongst ladys have a station,
Say twas ffrom Parentes, not har education,
And now conclud the lords owne hand it wase
That with weak means did bring this work to pass,
Not only Towne but Sistor church to ade
Which out of dust and Ashes now is had.
Then all Inhabit woburne Towne, stay make
The lord, not means, of all you undertake.[2]

Greatly as Captain Johnson was interested in the affairs of the town of Woburn, yet from the time of his entrance into the legislature or General Court as representative of that town we find his practical talents largely employed in the concerns of the colony at large. He was placed on nearly every military committee, and in 1659 became surveyor-

[1] Johnson himself. Under the designation of nurses he alludes to the seven members of the managing committee appointed by Charlestown.

[2] The meaning is, "Then all who inhabit Woburn town, make the Lord, not the mere means or instrumentalities, the chief stay of all that you undertake." See these verses in the fac-simile opposite p. 213. The most important extracts from the early town records of Woburn are printed in the introduction to Poole's edition of the *Wonder-working Providence*, pp. lxxx-lxxxix. The full text of them, with notes by Hon. Edward F. Johnson and Mr. William R. Cutter, was printed in the *Woburn Journal* newspaper in 1888.

general of the arms and munitions of the colony. He took part in the arrest of Gorton in 1643. In 1645–1647 he served on some of the important committees for the codification of the laws. He had apparently especial skill in surveying, and often had duties in that field assigned to him by the General Court. Thus it will be seen that when he undertook the writing of a history of the colony, he had had good opportunities of knowing its towns, by personal visits or through their representatives, and that he was familiar with many portions of its public business, by reason of several years of active participation, in a subordinate but still influential capacity. This participation he continued for many years after the composition of the book, and indeed until his death, which took place on April 23, 1672.

A systematic attempt to discover from internal evidence the date at which Captain Johnson wrote the *Wonder-working Providence*, shows that it was not all the product of one time. Various passages would seem to show that it was written, not only after the deaths of Winthrop and Shepard in March and August, 1649 (pp. 108, 251, 252), but also after the fourth election of Dudley as governor in May, 1650 (p. 81), yet before the third election of Endicott in May, 1651 (p. 44). Also the reference on p. 247 to Boston's soon-defeated hopes of being made a city would seem to fix the date between June, 1650, and May, 1651. But on another page (p. 255) Endicott's election in May, 1651, is recorded, and the account on p. 202 of the Harvard Commencement of August 12, 1651, and the graduation of Seaborn Cotton, compels a later date, though on p. 63 the latter is referred to as still "a young student in a Colledge." The truth no doubt is, that the book was mostly written in 1650, or before May of the next year, but that additions and amendments were made later in 1651. The numerous descriptions given of the various towns seem to refer to their condition at about that date.

The motive for the composition of the book appears from several passages. The author was convinced in every fibre that there had been set up in New England an ecclesiastical and civil polity more closely according with the Word of God than any other which the world had seen, and that the Lord had manifested His approval by doing marvellous things in the wilderness for these His chosen people. Persons disaffected to this holy experiment, lewd fellows like Morton and Gardiner, presumptuous heretics like Gorton, had spread in England reports injurious to the Massachusetts plantation, and these ought to be combated by any one who cared for the material and political welfare of the colony, or who valued intelligent English opinion. What was perhaps still more grievous, there had been bitter criticism even from a portion of the godly in England, for in the recent debates, in and out of the West-minster Assembly, on the reforming of the ecclesiastical polity of England, the Presbyterian party, dominant in Parliament, had hotly assailed the "New England Way," the principles and practices of Congregationalism. One to whom those principles were as clear as the sun, those practices invested with the absolute warrant of Scripture, could not rest easy without exhibiting to all English readers the marvellous providences, the gracious and evident mercies, by which Jehovah had proclaimed to every attentive ear His approval of New England methods.

So came into existence the first published history of Massachusetts, a book which, whatever its shortcomings, represented the honest attempt of a Puritan man of affairs to set forth to his fellow-Englishmen the first twenty-three years' history of the great Puritan colony. A book on that subject, we may be sure, met a real want in the Puritan England of 1653 and 1654, although in the changed atmosphere of 1659 Nathaniel Brooke might find it slow of sale. But, printed as it was with the author three thousand miles away, it appeared with many typographical defects, and with vagaries of punctuation which must have made many passages difficult of comprehension even at the time of its appearance, and are still greater hindrances now.   Printer's punctuation, executed under such circumstances, cannot be regarded as sacred.   The editor of the present volume has by no means attempted to systematize the punctuation; even a pointing that may appear eccentric has in most cases not been altered if after all it leaves the sense clear.   But where a stupid compositor has given to the punctuation of the original a form which perverts or obscures the sense, yet the meaning intended is to an experienced eye perfectly clear, the needful alteration has been made without compunction.   A good example occurs in the beginning of chapter xx. of the first book, where the author is made to say that Boston is "invironed with the Brinish flouds, saving one small Istmos, which gives free accesse to the Neighbour Townes; by Land on the South side, on the North west, and North East, two constant Faires are kept for daily traffique thereunto."   Since "Faires" is obviously a misprint for "Ferries," to retain a punctuation which represents two ferries as operating in three different directions, and one of them by land, would be a Chinese fidelity for which the editor sees no occasion. Printing "Faires" but adding "Ferries" in square brackets, he silently alters the reading above to "Istmos, which gives free accesse to the Neighbour Townes by Land on the South side; on the North west," etc.   But such alterations of punctuation have not been made save where the sense is indubitable.   Brooke's printer's italics have been deemed no more sacred than his punctuation.

With whatever helps an editor may supply, the *Wonder-working Providence* remains hard reading.   Though the author can tell plain facts in a plain way when he chooses to do so, and gives us many valuable details respecting business matters, his enthusiasm for the great cause of militant Puritanism frequently leads him astray into rhetorical flights which, though often vigorous and imaginative, are turgid, bombastic, and tedious. Hardest of all to peruse are the labored verses which, with excellent motives and a pathetic patience, he has hammered out whenever he has felt that an eminent leader in the upbuilding of his Zion calls for especial commemoration. Yet the prose style has picturesque imagination and a certain manly vigor, and though the diction of the rhetorical passages is all borrowed from the one Book the author knew well, a diction borrowed from that source will never wholly lack beauty and elevation. Even among the verses, one may discriminate. There are worse verses than those in the ninth chapter of the third book, beginning,

"From silent night, true Register of moans."

Johnson's habit of "dropping into poetry" has been so much commented on by those who have in any way written of him, that it is natural to ask the question what models he followed, in the three varieties of metre which we see in his work. On this point the editor has consulted his friend Professor R. E. Neil Dodge, of the University of Wisconsin, an accomplished student of Elizabethan verse. Of the metre of which Johnson's first two "poems," those in honor of Cradock and Endicott, are specimens, he says: "The measure as a whole, the fourteen-syllable couplet ('fourteeners' or, more learnedly, 'septenars'), would in its general swing be familiar to every good Puritan in the metrical Psalms of Sternhold and Hopkins, e. g., Ps. xxii.:

'O God my God, wherefore doest thou
    forsake me utterly:
And helpest not, when I do make
    my great complaint and cry.'

Sometimes, by rhyming the half-lines, these versifiers make of the original couplet a fully rhymed quatrain, *e. g.*, Ps. xcv.:

> 'O come let us lift up our voyce,
>   and sing unto the Lord:
> In him our rock of health rejoyce
>   let us with one accord.'

The double ending is rare in these Psalms, as is also internal rhyme except in the quatrain arrangement given above. See, however, Ps. xxii., stanza 21:

> 'And from the Lyons mouth, that would
>   me all in sunder shiver:
> And from the hornes of unicornes,
>   Lord safely me deliver.'

The particular arrangement of internal, or sectional, rhymes which you say is characteristic of his verse may be found in *Tottel's Miscellany* (*v.* Arber's *English Reprints*), a book very popular with the Elizabethans under its title of *Songs and Sonnets*, which Master Slender wished he had with him when he set eyes on Mistress Anne Page (*Merry Wives of Windsor*); see p. 62 of Arber's edition:

> 'O Goodly hand
> Wherein doth stand
> My heart distract in pain:
> Dear hand, alas!
> In little space
> My life thou dost restrain.'

Write this out as a septenar couplet and you have exactly the measure with sectional rhymes used by Captain Johnson. It was common, but I cannot say just how common."

The variety next seen, in the verses on Higginson, is the elegiac quatrain, that of Gray's *Elegy*. It had been used, says Professor Dodge, by Wyatt, Surrey, Sir John Davies, and

Spenser (*Colin Clout's Come Home Again*). All the verses in the book are in one of these two measures, except the poem alluded to above, beginning,

"From silent night, true Register of moans,"

and that with which the volume closes. Of this six-line stanza, Professor Dodge says that it is "used by Spenser in *January* and *December* of the *Shepherd's Calendar*, in *The Tears of the Muses*, and elsewhere. It is to be found also in Shakespeare's *Venus and Adonis*, in Drayton's *Legend of Gaveston* and in several of his *Eclogues*, in fact in poetry about 1600 very often." He adds:

All these measures were sufficiently common to make specific investigation of the good Captain's models needless. He may have had his favorite poets and may have imitated them, but to decide who they were would require the reading of all his verse, and even by that process one would probably not arrive at any very exact conclusions, for it takes a man of artistic temperament to imitate style recognizably, whereas a man of ordinary facility with the pen may turn out verse according to familiar measures readily enough.

However crabbed the style of the *Wonder-working Providence*, he that reads it through will be profited. It is little to say that it is the first published history of New England, and the most important work on its history brought out before Cotton Mather's *Magnalia* (1702). This is only to say that Winthrop's *Journal* did not see the light of publication till 1790, nor Bradford's *History of Plymouth Plantation* till 1856. The *Wonder-working Providence* is far from ranking in the same class with those incomparable narratives. It is the work of a much inferior mind; it is disfigured, as may be seen from the foot-notes of the present edition, by many errors and inaccuracies; and the thought and arrangement are often sadly confused. Yet it gives us, what neither Bradford nor Winthrop could supply, the history, or at any rate the essential spirit, of the Massachusetts colony depicted from the point of view of the rank and file.

Captain Edward Johnson, though superior to the average man in intelligence, education, abilities, and influence, may fairly be regarded as typical of the mass of Puritan settlers. He is by nature an "organization man," a stalwart, a member of the majority, an upholder of constituted authority in political life. In religion, quite incapable of understanding the subtilties of theology, he adheres instinctively to the orthodox side. It is his nature to venerate his file-leaders, and to follow them enthusiastically and without a shadow of doubt that their beliefs and positions are alone correct.

To see, displayed before us, the mind of such a Puritan, is no small privilege. The founders of Massachusetts, we know, were distinguished above most founders of colonies in the fact that they definitely intended to found a great state, on principles marked indeed by narrowness, but also by elevation. It is good to be permitted to see how far their notions prevailed in the minds of their less exalted followers, with what ardor of enthusiasm the austere programme of the leaders was maintained in the ranks. The foremost principle of the Puritan régime in Massachusetts was that the will and the interests of the individual should be rigidly subordinated to those of the community. It bred intolerance and persecution in the seventeenth century, but it bred solidarity and public spirit in the eighteenth and nineteenth. Democracy being fated to prevail in a new country, it is good to be enabled to see the early workings of that spirit of union and solidarity in the mind of the common man, captain or private in the village trainband. Captain Johnson explains to us Hosea Biglow. He helps us to understand the formation of that extraordinary body, the like of which the world has seldom seen, the Massachusetts population of 1840, so homogeneous, so resentful of contamination, yet so intelligent and capable and so infused with public spirit and the social sense that it could perform to a marvel the task which awaited it in the next half-century, the wholesale digesting of the alien.

If we turn to the more personal qualities of Johnson as an historian, we must admit that we have in him a striking example of the hot zealotry, the narrow partisanship, the confident dogmatism, which characterized so much of Puritanism. All his opinions are self-evident to him. If for want of apter phrases one may repeat what one has already said of him elsewhere: "He is full of that narrow Hebraism which, when it prayed, kept open its windows toward Jerusalem, but closed every other avenue to the soul. To hew Agag in pieces before the Lord is to his mind not the least attractive of religious duties. With him the Church militant is more than a metaphor. The life of the colony appears to him most frequently in the guise of an armed conflict; he hears in its story the noise of battle, the thunder of the captains and the shouting, and in vehement canticles summons the Israel of New England to the help of the Lord against the mighty." To the Puritan zeal he adds the Puritan superstition, and his pages bristle with special providences.

Yet, however severe his creed, Johnson was a kindly man. This will be especially apparent to any one who, reading between the lines, sees how gently he deals with erring brethren. His spirit, though narrow, is far from ignoble. He has those virtues which spring from confidence in a high purpose and a mission felt to be momentous and sacred. It is impossible not to admire the exaltation, the fervent enthusiasm with which, in such passages for instance as the fifth chapter of the second book, he glories in the success of militant Puritanism in old England, and which invests his hortatory passages, partisan harangues though they are, with a certain rugged eloquence.

The original edition of the *Wonder-working Providence* is now a rare book, not to be obtained for less than a hundred dollars. There are copies, however, in the British Museum, the Boston Public Library, the Woburn Public Library, the Congregational Library in Boston, those of the Massachusetts Historical Society, the Boston Athenæum, the American Antiquarian Society, and Brown University, the John Carter Brown Library, the Pequot Library, that of the State of New York in Albany, the Lenox Branch of the New York Public Library, the Library of Congress, and the libraries of Mr. E. E. Ayer, the late Mr. E. D. Church, and the late Mr. L. Z. Leiter. The copy in the Woburn Public Library, which formerly belonged to Dr. Abiel Holmes (and was "bought in London in the year 1810 for 7 *s.* sterling"), has, pasted on the inside of the cover, an advertisement clipped from a newspaper, unknown but of date between 1736 and 1762, in which John Draper, the Boston printer, proposes the reprinting of the work by subscriptions; but it was not done. In 1814–1819 the Massachusetts Historical Society reprinted it in portions scattered through volumes II., III., IV., VII., and VIII. of its second series of *Collections*, volumes reprinted in 1846 and 1826. The text was seen through the press by the accurate James Savage, but there were no annotations. In 1867 a reprint, almost a fac-simile, was brought out in a small edition of 260 copies by Dr. William F. Poole. This also was without annotations, but it has a long introduction on Johnson and his work which is a model of thorough investigation, and to which all subsequent writers who have touched on Johnson, including the present editor, have been deeply indebted. The present is the first edition supplied with foot-notes, which the *Wonder-working Providence* seems particularly to require.

The frontispiece to the present volume is a reproduction of the title-page of the original work, which, by the courtesy of Mr. William R. Cutter of the Woburn Public Library, we were permitted to make from the volume in his custody. The map of New England, showing the settlements founded within the period covered by the book, is taken from the first volume of Dr. John G. Palfrey's *History of New England,* by permission of Messrs. Little, Brown & Co., publishers of that work. The second fac-simile represents the first page of the town records of Woburn, consisting of the verses by Captain Edward Johnson, town clerk, which have been quoted above, on pp. 7 and 8. The handwriting, however, is not that of the captain, but that of his son, Major William Johnson. For permission to photograph the document we are indebted to the present city clerk of Woburn, Mr. John H. Finn.

J. FRANKLIN JAMESON.

WONDER-WORKING PROVIDENCE
OF SIONS SAVIOUR IN NEW-ENGLAND
1628–1651

A HISTORY OF NEW-ENGLAND

From the English planting in the Yeere 1628. untill the Yeere 1652.

Declaring the form of their Government, Civill, Military, and Ecclesiastique. Their Wars with the Indians, their Troubles with the Gortonists, and other Heretiques. Their manner of gathering of Churches, the commodities of the Country, and description of the principall Towns and Havens, with the great encouragements to increase Trade betwixt them and Old England. With the names of all their Governours, Magistrates, and Eminent Ministers.

Psal. 107.24. The righteous shall see it and rejoice, and all iniquity shall stop her mouth.

Psal. 111.2. The works of the Lord are great, and ought to be sought out of all that have pleasure in them.

London, Printed for Nath: Brooke at the Angel in Corn-hill. 1654.[1]

TO THE READER

Good Reader,

As large Gates to small Edifices, so are long Prefaces to little Bookes; therefore I will breifly informe thee, that here thou shalt find, the time when, the manner how, the cause why, and the great successe which it hath pleased the Lord to give, to this handfull of his praysing Saints in N. Engl., and it will be clearly demonstrated, if thou compare them with any other people, who have left their countryes, as the Gothes, Vandals, etc. to possesse a fatter, as Italy, or warmer, as Spaine, etc. But these forsooke a fruitfull Land, stately Buildings, goodly Gardens, Orchards, yea, deare Friends, and neere relations, to goe to a desart Wildernesse, thousands of leagues

---

[1] This, as explained in the Introduction, is the publisher's title for the book, not the author's.

by Sea, both turbulent and dangerous; also many have trav-elled to see famous Cities, strong Fortifications, etc. or in hope to enjoy a setled habitation, where riches are attained with ease. But here the onely encouragements were the laborious breaking up of bushy ground, with the continued toyl of erecting houses, for themselves and cattell, in this howling desart; all which they underwent, with much cheerfulnesse, that they might enjoy Christ and his Ordinances in their primitive purity.

And now, you, my honoured Countrey-men, who have with indefatigable paines, and expence of a great part of your Estates, furthered this blessed work: Behold how the Lord of Hosts hath carried it on in despight of all opposition from his and their enemies, in planting of his Churches in this New World, with the excellent frame of their Government, both civil and military, already established; but why stop I you at the Threshold? go in, and seriously consider this *Wonder-working Providence of Sions Saviour.* In the perusing of which, if thou receivest profit or delight, and God may have glory thereby, he hath attained the end that he aimed at, and full satisfaction for all his paynes, who heartily wishes thee all the good, both of this life, and a better life, in him who is a Christians all in all.

T. H.[1]

[1] Who T. H. was is not known.

WONDER-WORKING PROVIDENCE OF SIONS SAVIOUR

BEING A RELATION OF THE FIRST PLANTING IN NEW ENGLAND, IN THE YEARE, 1628

[Book I.]

CHAP. I.

The sad Condition of England, when this People removed.

WHEN England began to decline in Religion, like luke-warme Laodicea, and instead of purging out Popery, a farther compliance was sought not onely in vaine Idolatrous Cere-monies, but also in prophaning the Sabbath, and by Procla-mation throughout their Parish churches, exasperating lewd and prophane persons to celebrate a Sabbath like the Heathen to Venus, Baccus and Ceres;[1] in so much that the multitude of irreligious lascivious and popish affected persons spred the whole land like Grashoppers, in this very time Christ the glorious King of his Churches, raises an Army out of our English Nation, for freeing his people from their long servi-tude under usurping Prelacy; and because every corner of England was filled with the fury of malignant adversaries, Christ creates a New England to muster up the first of his Forces in; Whose low condition, little number, and remote-nesse of place made these adversaries triumph, despising this day of small things, but in this hight of their pride the Lord Christ brought sudden, and unexpected destruction upon them. Thus have you a touch of the time when this worke began.

[1] An allusion to the Declaration concerning Sports, promulgated in 1617 by James I., and repeated by Charles I. in 1633, which permitted and indeed encour-aged the practice of playing games on Sundays, after church service.

Christ Jesus intending to manifest his Kingly Office toward his Churches more fully than ever yet the Sons of men saw, even to the uniting of Jew and Gentile Churches in one Faith, begins with our English Nation (whose former reformation being vere imperfect) doth now resolve to cast down their false foundation of Prelacy, even in the hight of their domineering dignity. And therefore in the yeere 1628, he stirres up his servants as the Heralds of a King to make this proclamation for Voluntiers, as followeth.

"Oh yes! oh yes! oh yes! All you the people of Christ that are here Oppressed, Imprisoned and scurrilously derided, gather yourselves together, your Wives and little ones, and answer to your severall Names as you shall be shipped for his service, in the Westerne World, and more especially for planting the united Collonies of new England; Where you are to attend the service of the King of Kings."

Upon the divulging of this Proclamation by his Herralds at Armes, many (although otherwise willing for this service) began to object as followeth:

"Can it possible be the mind of Christ, (who formerly inabled so many Souldiers of his to keepe their station unto the death here) that now so many brave Souldiers disciplined by Christ himselfe the Captaine of our salvation, should turne their backs to the disheartning of their Fellow-Souldiers, and losse of further opportunity in gaining a greater number of Subjects to Christs Kingdome?"

Notwithstanding this Objection, It was further proclaimed as followeth: "What, Creature, wilt not know that Christ thy King crusheth with a rod of Iron, the Pompe and Pride of man, and must he like man cast and contrive to take his enemies at advantage? No, of purpose hee causeth such instruments to retreate as hee hath made strong for himselfe: that so his adversaries glorying in the pride of their power, insulting over the little remnant remaining, Christ causeth them to be cast downe suddenly forever, and wee find in stories reported, Earths Princes have passed their Armies at need over Seas and deepe Torrents. Could Cæsar so suddenly fetch over fresh forces from Europe to Asia, Pompy to foyle? How much more shall Christ who createth all power, call over this 900 league Ocean at his pleasure, such instruments as he thinks meete to make use of in this place, from whence you are now to depart, but further that you may not delay the Voyage intended, for your full satisfaction, know this is the place where the Lord will create a new Heaven, and a new Earth in, new Churches, and a new Common-wealth together; Wherefore,

CHAP. II.

The Commission of the People of Christ shipped for New England, and first of their gathering into Churches.

"Attend to your Commission, all you that are or shall hereafter be shipped for this service, yee are with all possible speed to imbarque your selves, and as for all such Worthies who are hunted after as David was by Saul and his Courtiers, you may change your habit and ship you with what secrecy you can, carrying all things most needfull for the Voyage and service you are to be imployed in after your landing. But as soone as you shall be exposed to danger of tempestious Seas, you shall forthwith shew whose servants you are by calling on the Name of your God, sometimes by extraordinary seeking his pleasing Face in times of deepe distresse, and publishing your Masters will, and pleasure to all that Voyage with you, and that is his minde to have purity in Religion preferred above all dignity in the world; your Christ hath commanded the Seas they shall not swallow you, nor Pyrates imprison your persons, or possesse your goods. At your landing see you observe the Rule of his Word, for neither larger nor stricter Commission can hce give by any, and therefore at first filling the Land whither you are sent, with diligence, search out the mind of God both in planting and continuing Church and civill Government, but be sure they be distinct, yet agreeing and helping the one to the other; Let the matter and forme of your Churches be such as were in the Primitive Times (before Antichrists Kingdome prevailed) plainly poynted out by Christ and his Apostles, in most of their Epistles, to be neither Nationall nor Provinciall, but gathered together in Covenant of such a number as might ordinarily meete together in one place, and built of such living stones as outwardly appeare Saints by calling.[1] You are also to ordaine Elders in every Church, make you use of such as Christ hath indued with the best gifts for that end, their call to Office shall be mediate from you, but their authority and commission shall be immediate from Christ revealed in his word; which, if you shall slight, despise or contemne, hee will soone frustrate your call by taking the most able among you to honour with an everlasting Crown; whom you neglected to honour on Earth double as their due, or he will carry them remote from you to more infant Churches. You are not to put them upon anxious Cares for their daily Bread, for assuredly (although it may now seeme strange) you shall be fed in this Wildernesse, whither you are to goe, with the flower of Wheate, and Wine shall be plentifull among you (but be sure you abuse it not). These Doctrines delivered from the Word of God imbrace, and let not Satan delude you by perswading their learned skill is unnecessary, soone then will the Word of God be slighted as translated by such, and you shall be left wildred with strange Revelations of every phantastick brain; which to prevent here are to be shipped among you many both Godly, Juditious and Learned, who

CHAP. III.

Of the Demeanor of their Church Officers.

"Being called to Office arc in all humility to feed the flock of Christ, and not for lucre to admit mostly of such sheepe, whose faire fleeces allure much: nor yet for filling the flocks to crowd in infectious sheepe, or rather wolves in sheepes cloathing, assuredly it will prove bitternesse in the end: neither shall you, for feare your allowance will fall short, hinder the

[1] That is, the ecclesiastical polity of New England was to be the Independent or Congregational polity—each local church, composed of converted Christians only, to be in nearly all particulars independent of other churches, and to be bound together by a covenant framed for and adopted by the individual church. But it would be quite erroneous to maintain, as Johnson's metaphorical language might lead one to suppose, that the Puritans who planned the great migration to New England had it in mind from the beginning to put in force there the Congregational polity. They regarded themselves as members of the Church of England till the force of circumstances led the Salem men into Independency.

increase of Churches, that so your fellow brethren indued
with like gifts fall short of all; But above all beware of any
love selfe-conceited Opinion, stopping your ears from hearing
the Counsell of an Orthodox Synod,[1] but by daily communication one with another impart Christs minde each to other,
that you may all speake one and the same things; heale not
lightly the wounds that Wolves make, lest from their fester-
ing Teeth a Gangrin grow; and further for compleating the
Churches of Christ as well in matters as in Doctrine, there are
ancient experienced godly Christians shipped among you (but
be sure you make choise of such, for feare they be despised)
and let them not be led by favor or affection (as naturally men
are) to Administer in your Office partially, for unworthy the
name of a Ruling Elder is hee, who loses his Lyon-like courage,
when the sound and wholesome Doctrines delivered by Pastor
or Teacher are spoken against by any;[2] unseemely behaviour
and sleepy hearing by private exhortation prevent (if possible)
lest publick example in open professors stumble some and
hinder the operation of his word, especially in the hearts of
those who have bin long time led away with the inventions of
man in the worship of God.   Be sure you contradict not but
confirme with trienall love the Doctrines of Christ, delivered
by your Teaching Elders, which will be a great means to make
it prevaile, for a three-fold cord is not easily broken, trust not
to your own gifts for preventing error, but use all helpes that

---

[1] In Congregational theory the local churches were not absolutely independent one of another. They were to help each other in several ways, one of
which was that of admonition of an erring church by one of its neighbors, or by
several in concert. It was also contemplated that general synods of all the
churches should occasionally be called, though in practice Massachusetts had
but four, the Cambridge Synod of 1637, dealing with the Antinomians (see *post*,
bk. ii., ch. vii.), the Cambridge Synod of 1646–1648 (bk. iii., ch. iv.), that of
1662, and that of 1679–1680.

[2] At the beginning, the Congregational polity divided between three officers
the functions performed by the pastor of a modern church. Each church was to
ordain for itself a pastor, whose duty was that of exhortation; a teacher, charged
with exposition of the Scriptures and of theological doctrine (either of these two
could administer the sacraments); and a ruling elder, charged with discipline and
ecclesiastical administration. The system was founded on what was judged to
be that of the primitive church, but was found difficult to maintain, and soon
decayed. Deacons, spoken of below, had charge of the treasury of the church,
provision for the sacraments, and the care of the poor.

Christ may bless his own meanes, cast not away as incorrigible such as at first receive not the word in all points, but wait with patience if at any time the Lord will be pleased to give them a heart to turne unto him.   Beware of a proud censorious spirit, and should Christ be pleased to place in his building more pollished stones than thy selfe, make it matter of rejoycing and not of envy.   And further, because the Preaching of the word is to be continued with all diligence, here are likewise imbarked with you faithful servants of Christ to attend on the Tables of the Churches, plaine-dealing men, yea, indued with wisdome from above, by which they are inabled to manage and improve the Churches Treasury, not greedily given to hoord up for themselves, but by their own example leading others to liberality, and hospitality, having the Earth in low esteeme, and Faith in exercise when Cattell and Corne fayle, not given to magnifie their own gifts, but boldly maintayning such sound truths as their Teaching Elders have cleared up from the word of God.   And,

Chap. IV.

How the People in Christs Churches are to behave themselves.

Now you his People, who are pickt out by his provide[ence] to passe this Westerne Ocean for this honourable service, beware you call not weake ones to Office in this honorable Army, nor Novices, lest they be lifted up with pride.   You see how full you are furnished for the worke, give no eare to any Braggadociaes, who to extoll themselves will weaken the hands of those whom Christ hath made strong for himselfe. Yea, such will be the phantasticall madnesse of some (if you take not heed) that silly Women laden with diverse lusts, will be had in higher esteeme with them, then those honoured of Christ, indued with power and authority from him to Preach; [1] Abuse not the free and full liberty Christ hath given you in making choyce of your own Officers, and consent in admitting into his Churches, and casting out such Members as walke

---

[1] An allusion to the subsequent popularity of Mrs. Anne Hutchinson, whose gainsaying is described from the point of view of an orthodox upholder of the standing order, in chapters xxxix.–xliv. of book i., *post.*

disorderly; you are to walke in all humility, lest in injoyment of such freedoms as you formerly have not exercised, you exceede the bounds of modesty, and instead of having your moderation knowne to all, your imbecility, and selfe-exaltation bee discovered by many. In admission of others into Church society, remember your selves were once Aliens from the Covenant of Grace, and in Excommunication, consider how your selves have been also tempted: in sincerity and singlenesse of heart, let your words be few, do nothing [to] be had in high esteeme among men; And think it no imputation of a weake discerning to be followe[r]s of those are set over you in the Lord as they follow Christ; Let your Profession outstrip your Confession, for seeing you are to be set as lights upon a Hill more obvious than the highest Mountaine in the World, keepe close to Christ that you may shine full of his glory, who imployes you, and grub not continually in the Earth, like blind Moles, but by your amiable Conversation seeke the winning of many to your Masters service. Beware of a proud censorious spirit, make it no part of your Christian communication to be in continuall discourse of others faults; Let all things be done in love, and looke not for more smoothnesse in stones as yet unplaced in Christs building then [1] is in thy selfe, who hast been long layd therein: wait with patience and cast not off as Reprobates such as cannot presently joyne with you in every poynt of Discipline, and yet hold fast to sound and wholesome Doctrine. If you will be a people to his prayse, who hath called you, seeke the turning of many to Righteousnesse, purge out all the sowre Leven of unsound Doctrine, for the minde of Christ is to build up his Churches, and breake them down no more; And therefore be sure there be none to hurt or destroy in all his holy Mountaine, and as he hath pressed you for his service, that by passing through the Flouds of Persecution you should be set at liberty, and have power put into your hands, Then let none wrest it from you under pretence of liberty of Conscience. Men of perverse judgements will draw Disciples after them, but let your consciences be pure, and Christs Churches free from all Doctrines that deceive. And all you, who are or shall be shipped for

---

[1] It is the constant practice of the book to use *then* for *than*.

this worke, thinke it not enough that you injoy the truth, but
you must hate every false way and know you are called to be
faithful Souldiers of Christ, not onely to assist in building up
his Churches, but also in pulling downe the Kingdome of
Anti-Christ, then sure you are not set up for tollerating times,
nor shall any of you be content with this that you are set at
liberty, but take up your Armes, and march manfully on till
all opposers of Christs Kingly power be abolished: and as for
you who are called to sound forth his silver Trumpets, blow
lowd and shrill, to this chiefest treble tune; For the Armies
of the great Jehovah are at hand. See you not his Enemies
stretched out on tiptoe, proudly daring on their thresholds, a
certaine signe of their sudden overthrow? be not danted at
your small number, for every common Souldier in Christs
Campe shall be as David, who slew the great Goliah, and his
Davids shall be as the Angels of the Lord, who slew 185000.
in the Assyrian Army.[1]

Finally, all you who are now sent forth by Christ your
Jehovah to enter upon a Blessed Reformation, if ever you
will have the honours to be provokers of his ancient People
Israel (who are againe suddenly to be honoured by him
in believing) kindle the fire of jealousy in their brests by
your Holy, Heavenly and humble walking, have you not
the most blessedest opertunity put into your hands that
ever people had? then

CHAP. V.

*What Civill Government the People of Christ ought to set up,
and submit unto in New England.*

Fayle not in prosecution of the Worke, for your Lord
Christ hath furnished you with able Pilots, to steere the Helme
in a godly peaceable, Civill Government also, then see you
make choyce of such as are sound both in Profession and
Confession, men fearing God and hating bribes; whose
Commission is not onely limitted with the commands of the
second Table, but they are to looke to the Rules of the first

---

[1] An allusion to II Kings xix. 35.

also,[1] and let them be sure to put on Joshuas resolution, and courage, never to make League with any of these seven Sectaries.[2]

First, the Gortonists, who deny the Humanity of Christ, and most blaphemously and proudly professe themselves to be personally Christ.

Secondly, the Papist, who with (almost) equall blasphemy and pride prefer their own Merits and Workes of Supererogation as equall with Christs unvaluable Death, and Sufferings.

Thirdly, the Familist, who depend upon rare Revelations, and forsake the sure revealed Word of Christ.

Fourthly, Seekers, who deny the Churches and Ordinances of Christ.

Fifthly, Antinomians, who deny the Morrall Law to be the Rule of Christ.

Sixtly, Anabaptists, who deny Civill Government to be proved of Christ.

Seventhly, The Prelacy, who will have their own Injunctions submitted unto in the Churches of Christ. These and

---

[1] The "First Table" comprised the first four of the Ten Commandments, those dealing with duties to God; the "Second Table" the last six, dealing with duties to one's fellow men. The doctrine of the Massachusetts government, as evinced, *e. g.*, in the case of Roger Williams, was that the civil power had the right to enforce obedience to the commandments of the First Table.

[2] No one will suppose that these are serenely impartial characterizations of these various religious bodies. The theology of Samuel Gorton, of Shawomet, and his followers (on whose secular history and relations to Massachusetts, see bk. II., chs. XXIII., XXIV., *post*) is not easy to grasp, Gorton being a somewhat incoherent prophet; but he seems to have taught that Christ was simply a manifestation of God, and that God is in a similar sense manifested in the true believer. The Familists were a sixteenth-century sect in Holland and England, called the Family of Love, from the love they professed for all human beings however wicked; orthodox Puritans were wont to speak of them as unsettlers of morality. The Seekers, with whom Roger Williams had become identified as early as 1638, were men who had come to doubt or to deny that there were, or had been since the apostles' day, any true church, divine sacraments, or valid ordinances, and who waited for more light. Antinomian was, as is well known, a term of reproach unjustly applied to the followers of Wheelwright and Mrs. Hutchinson, their doctrine that "sanctification was no evidence of justification," conduct no evidence of divine grace indwelling in one of the elect, being travestied into a denial of the obligations of morality. Finally, Johnson's accusation against the Anabaptists is founded on the fact that the early Anabaptists or Mennonites refused the taking of oaths, the acceptance of magisterial position, and the bearing of arms.

the like your Civill Censors shall reach unto, that the people
of and under your Government, may live a quiet and peaceable
life in all godlinesse and honesty, and to the end that you may
provoke Kings, Princes, and all that are in authority to cast
downe their Crownes at the Feet of Christ, and take them up
againe at his command to serve under his Standard as nursing
Fathers, and nursing Mothers to the Churches and people of
Christ; when your feete are once safely set on the shores of
America, you shall set up and establish civill Government,
and pray for the prosperity thereof, as you love the peace of
his Churches, who hath called you to this service, he hath for
that end shipped among you, some learned in the Law of God,
and practised in rules of good reason or common Lawes proper
to our English Nation.   Be sure you make choyce of the right,
that all people, Nations and Languages, who are soonly to
submit to Christs Kingdome, may be followers of you herein,
as you follow the Rule of Christ; your Magistrates shall not
but open [1] the Gates for all sorts.   But know, they are Eyes
of Restraint set up for Walles and Bulworks, to surround the
Sion of God; Oh for Jerusalem her peace, see that you mind it
altogether, you know right well that the Churches of Christ
have not thrived under the tolerating Government of Holland,
from whence the Lord hath translated one Church already to
the place whither you are now to goe; [2] and further it is well
known, loose liberty cannot indure to looke Majesticall authority in the face.   And also you shall finde erronious persons
will contend with authority for upholding truth irrationally,
denying it any power to condemne deceiveable Doctrines, and
that upon this very ground, because Tyranny hath inforced
error heretofore; be not borne downe with a multitude,
neither let any flatter for preferment, which to prevent,
honour shall be very chargeable among you; yet let not any
deny to beare the burden and cumber of governing this people
of Christ; for assuredly, although their recompence fall short
from man, it shall not be forgotten with the Lord.   Lastly,

[1] Misprint for "put open," probably.
[2] A note in the margin explains: "The Church of Christ at Plimoth was
planted in New England 8 Yeares before any others."

CHAP. VI.

How the People of Christ ought to behave themselves in War-like Discipline.

You shall with all diligence provide against the Malignant adversaries of the truth, for assure your selves the time is at hand wherein Antichrist will muster up all his Forces, and make war with the People of God: but it shall be to his utter overthrow. See then you store your selves with all sorts of weapons for war, furbrish up your Swords, Rapiers, and all other piercing weapons. As for great Artillery, seeing present meanes falls short, waite on the Lord Christ, and hee will stir up friends to provide for you:[1] and in the meane time spare not to lay out your coyne for Powder, Bullets, Match, Armes of all sorts, and all kinde of Instruments for War: and although it may now seeme a thing incredible, you shall see in that Wildernesse, whither you are going, Troopes of stout Horsemen marshalled, and therefore fayle not to ship lusty Mares along with you, and see that with all dilligence you incourage every Souldier-like Spirit among you, for the Lord Christ intends to atchieve greater matters by this little handfull then the World is aware of; wherefore you shall seeke and set up men of valour to lead and direct every Souldier among you, and with all diligence to instruct them from time to time.

Feare not the misse of men to fill your Townes, and compleat your companies; for although at first struglings for truths advance there may but a small number appeare of sound judgement: yet shall you not prefer any to Office, whose zeale is not strong for the truth, for now the minde of Christ is to put out the Name of Ammaleck from under Heaven (I meane such as have persecuted the Churches and People of Christ in their low condition) and assuredly unsound Saules will spare such as should not be saved from destruction.[2]

---

[1] Another marginal note says: "Doctor Wilson gave 1000*l.* to New England, with which they stored them with great Guns." We find the gift acknowledged by the General Court in September, 1634, when the fortification of Castle Island in Boston harbor was begun on account of alarming news from England.

[2] An allusion to I Samuel xv.

Then be strong and of a good courage (all you that are to
fight the Lords Battaile) that your Faith faile not at sight of
the great Armies of Gog and Magog: and as for you, who shall
be preferred to highest places in his New England Regiments,
cause your Captaine and other inferior Officers to be diligent
in their severall places, that you may lend helpe to your
Countreymen, that ere long be will see a necessity of contending for the truth, as well as your selves in choyce of Military
Officers; Let faithfulnesse to the cause in hand, courage,
activity and skill have the prehemency of honours; for although it may seeme a meane thing to be a New England
Souldier, yet some of you shall have the battering and beating
down, scaling, winning and wasting the over-topping Towers
of the Hierarchy; Lieutenants, Ensigne and Serjeants, exceed not your places, till Experience, Skill and true Valour
promote you to higher honour, to which you shall be daily
aspiring.   As the worthy incouragement of a Souldiers labour,
let Military discipline be had in high esteeme among you.
Gentlemen, Corporalls, and fellow-Souldiers, keepe your
weapons in continuall readinesse, seeing you are called to fight
the Battails of your Lord Christ; who must raigne till hee
hath put all his enemies under his Feet, his glorious Victories
cver Antichrist are at hand, never yet did any Souldier rejoyce in dividing the spoyle after Victory, as all the Souldiers
cf Christ shall, to see his judgement executed upon the great
Whore,[1] and withall the Lambs bride prepared for him, who
comes Skipping over and trampling down the great Mountaines of the Earth, whose universall Government will then
appeare glorious, when not onely the Assyrian, Babilonian,
Persian, Grecian and Roman Monarchies shall subject themselves unto him, but also all other new upstart Kingdomes,
Dukedomes, or what else can be named, shall fall before him;
Not that he shall come personally to Reigne upon Earth (as
some vainly imagine) but his powerfull Presence and Glorious
brightnesse of his Gospell both to Jew and Gentile, shall not
onely spiritually cause the Churches of Christ to grow beyond
number, but also the whole civill Government of people upon
Earth shall become his, so that there shall not be any to move

---

[1] An allusion to Revelation xvii., xviii.

the hand, nor dog his tongue against his chosen, And then shall the time be of breaking Speares into Mattocks, and Swords into Sithes; and this to remaine to his last comming, which will be personally to overcome the last enemies of his Saints, even death, which hee will doe by the word of his Mouth, audibly spoken the World throughout.

Then all you, who are now, or shall hereafter be shipped for this Voyage, minde the worke of Christ, and not some following raigne [vain?], titles of honour, others eying the best Grasse-platts and best Situation for Farmes and large Accommodations, crouding out Gods people from sitting down among you. Wherefore above all beware of covetousnesse; all you that will be admitted into these select Bands of Christ Jesus, remember Achan,[1] whereas Rams Hornes could overthrow the high and strong walles of Jericho, before his theft committed, after it the little number of the men of Ai could put the Host of the living God to flight. See then you stand upon your watch continually in the strength of Christ, for assuredly instead of casting downe the enemies of Christ, this sin will cast down you utterly, disinable you for striking one stroke in the cause of Christ; and whereas he hath purposely pickt out this People for a patterne of purity and soundnesse of Doctrine, as well as Discipline, that all such may finde a refuge among you, and let not any Merchants, Inkeepers, Taverners and men of Trade in hope of gaine, fling open the gates so wide, as that by letting in all sorts you mar the worke of Christ intended: neither shall such labourers as hee hath pickt out to be pyoneers in this Campe of his, drinke up like Spunges such meanes as hee hath sent to maintaine both Officers, and private Souldiers. Lastly, let not such as fight, set foote on Land[2] to compose Townes for Habitations, take up large accommodations for sale, to inrich themselves with others goods, who are to follow them, but freely as you have received, so give out to others: for so soone as you shall seeke to ingrosse the Lords wast into your hands, he will ease you of your burden by making stay of any farther resort unto you, and then be sure you shall have wast Land enough.

[1] See Joshua vii.
[2] Apparently a misprint for "such as first set foot on land."

To this Commission was added a strong motive to this work as followeth: Namely, the great enmity betweene that one truth as it is in Jesus, and all other unsound and undeceiveable Doctrines, together with the persons that hold them; insomuch, that they cannot stand in one Common-wealth long together, as sixteene hundred yeares experience will testifie, the which Moses layes down as one maine reason, why he might not admit of a toleration to worship God in Egypt.[1] And therefore all you that believe the Scriptures, which so plainly prophecy the destruction of Antichrist and all Antichristian Doctrines; Pray, pray, pray, pray continually with that valiant worthy Joshua that the Sun may stand still in Gibeon, and the Moone in the vally of Aijalon, for assuredly although some small battailes may be fought against the enemies of Christ, yet the great day of their finall overthrow shall not come till the bright Sonne of that one cleare truth of Christ, stand still in the Gentile Churches, that those who fight the Lords Battells may plainly discerne his enemies in all places, where they finde them, as also such as will continue fighting must have the World kept low in their eyes, as the Moon in the valley of Aijalon.

Chap. VII.

Of the goodnesse of God in helping his People to a large liberty in Spirituall things, under the hopes of gaine in Earthly things.

This Proclamation being audibly published through the Ile of Great Brittaine by sundry Herraulds, which Christ had prepared for that end: the rumour ran through Cities, Townes and Villages; when those that were opposites heard it, some cried one thing, and some another, much like the tumult in the Townhall at Ephesus,[2] some said let them goe, others cryed, sweare them first, others said let no Subsidy men passe, others would have strict search made for non-conformants, and that none of the late silenced Ministers might passe into

---

[1] Exodus viii. 25-27.   [2] Acts xix. 32-34.

the Ships; [1] Amidst this great hurry the sincere servants of Christ humbly seeke the Lords assistance in days of Humiliation, taking up some serious cogitations, how to begin this worthy worke, upon which it was thought meete a patterne [2] should be procured, comprised after the manner of a Corporation-company or Brotherhood, with as large liberty for government of this Association, as could be got under the Broad Seale of England, which accordingly was done by advise of one Mr. White an honest Counsellor at Law, as also furthered by the honoured Mr. Richard Belinham, and under the name of many worthy personages, as Governour, Dep. Gov., Assistant[s] and Freemen, etc. Granted, Ingrossed and Sealed as holding of the manner of East Greenwitch, [3] yeelding by way of homage the sixth part of all such Ore of Gold or Silver, as might for after time be found within the Limits of the said

[1] In 1634 the Commissioners of Plantations had issued orders to the customs officers at the seaports prohibiting the promiscuous passing of His Majesty's subjects to the American plantations. No subsidy men were to pass without a license, nor other persons without the attestation of two justices; while the statutes already provided that none should go forth without taking the oath of allegiance.

[2] Patent. Johnson passes over, as an unimportant step in the proceedings, the patent granted March 19, 1628, by the Council for New England to six patentees, for this same territory, and comes directly to the essential document, the royal charter of Charles I. to the Massachusetts Company, of March 4, 1629. The Mr. White he mentions, John White, was not the eminent Puritan rector of Trinity Church, Dorchester, the founder of the Cape Ann settlement, but a prominent Puritan lawyer in London and member of Parliament. Bellingham, afterward governor of Massachusetts, was at this time recorder (municipal judge) of Boston, in Lincolnshire. The great movement of 1629–1630 toward Puritan emigration to New England was the result of contributory streams from Dorsetshire, London, and Lincolnshire.

[3] "Manner" for "manor." For explanation of this phrase, frequent in charters, see an article by Professor Edward P. Cheyney in the *American Historical Review*, XI. 29–35. For "sixth part of all such Ore" read "fifth part." For "one mile" below, read "three miles." This last error might seem a strange one for Johnson to commit, for when Massachusetts, maintaining a strict interpretation of this phrase despite the northward turn of the upper course of the Merrimac, laid claim to all New Hampshire and Maine up to 43° 43' N., Johnson was one of her commissioners who in 1652 surveyed and located "the most northerly part" of the river, the place where it issues from Lake Winnipiseogee; an inscription they cut there, on "Endicott Rock," is still legible. Our author must have known well in 1652 how the charter read. But he probably wrote his book before that year; or the printer may have made the error.

Grant bounded on the North, with the most Northerly part of the pleasant River of Merimech, one mile beyond, and on the South with the most Southern part of that oft frequented River commonly called Charles, one mile beyond, with power to rule and govern in all those parts both by Sea and Land; To elect and set up all sorts of Officers, as well Superior as Inferior; to point out their power and places, to defend and maintaine the said Land, and Inhabitants thereof with all their lawfull liberties (against all such as at any time should Invade, Molest or Disturbe the same) as well by offensive as defensive War, as also to constitute and ordaine Lawes, etc. Thus these Souldiers of Jesus Christ prepared to advance his Kingly Government, much like Samuel, when he went to annoynt David, took up another errant, withall that the Malignant spirit of Saul might not hinder the worke, so those Worthies of Christ joyning themselves with Merchants and others, who had an eye at a profitable Plantation, who had not herein been deceived would they have stayed their time, but surely such mist not their marke, whose ayme was at the durable interest, unlesse the fault were their owne, neither let any man thinke Christ will not recompense those one way or other, who have been any way helpfull to his people in this his work; amongst whom the Author will not misse that good Gentleman, Matthew Craddock.[1] By the way of thankfullnesse to him, Mr. Goff and others this Verse is tendred:

For richest Jems and gainfull things most Merchants wisely venter:
  Deride not then New England men, this Corporation enter;
Christ calls for Trade shall never fade, come Craddock factors send:
  Let Mayhew go and other more, spare not thy coyne to spend;
Such Trades advance did never chance, in all thy Trading yet:
  Though some deride thy losse, abide, her[e]'s gaine beyond mans wit.

[1] Matthew Cradock, a rich London merchant, had in the charter of the Massachusetts Company been appointed by King Charles governor (in modern American parlance, president) of the company. It was he who, in July, 1629, proposed the transfer of charter and officers to America, and, by vacating the chair in October, made way for the election of Winthrop as governor. Thomas Goffe, another London merchant, who had been one of the adventurers in the New Plymouth enterprise, was named deputy-governor in the charter. These seem never to have come over to New England. Thomas Mayhew, proprietor of Martha's Vineyard, then its governor, Indian missionary, and patriarch, came over in 1634.

CHAP. VIII.

Of the wonderfull Preparation the Lord Christ by his Providence, wrought for his peoples abode in this Western world.

Now let all men know the admirable Acts of Christ for his Churches and chosen, are universally over the whole Earth at one and the same time, but sorry man cannot so discourse of them; And therefore let us leave our English Nation in way of preparation for this Voyage intended, and tell of the marvelous doings of Christ preparing for his peoples arrivall in the Western World, whereas the Indians report they beheld to their great wonderment that perspicuous bright blazing Comet (which was so famously noted in Europe); [1] anon after Sun set it appeared as they say in the South-west, about three houres, continuing in their Horizon for the space of thirty sleepes (for so they reckon their dayes) after which uncouth sight they expected some strange things to follow, and the rather, because not long before the whole Nation of the Mattachusets were so affrighted with a Ship that arrived in their Bay, having never seene any before,[2] thus they report some persons among them discerning a great thing to move toward them upon the Waters, wondering what Creature it should be, they run with their light cannowes, (which are a kinde of Boates made of Birch Rindes, and sowed together with the rootes of white Cedar-Trees) from place to place, stiring up all their Countreymen to come forth, and behold this monstrous thing; at this sudden news the shores for many miles were filled with this naked Nation, gazing at this wonder, till some of the stoutest among them manned out these Cannowes. Being armed with Bow and Arrowes, they approached within shot of the Ship, being becalmed, they let fly their long shafts at her, which being headed with bone some stuck fast, and others dropped into the water, they wondering it did not cry, but kept quietly on toward them, till all of a sudden the Master caused a piece of Ordnance to be fired, which stroke

---

[1] The celebrated comet of November, 1618, visible in daylight, and observed by Kepler and Gassendi.

[2] Captain John Smith seems to have sailed into Massachusetts Bay in 1614, and his ship may be the one here referred to.

such feare into the poore Indians, that they hasted to shore, having their wonders exceedingly increased; but being gotten among their great multitude, they waited to see the sequell with much amazement, till the Seamen firling up their sailes came to an Anchor, manned out their long bote, and went on shore, at whose approach, the Indians fled, although now they saw they were men, who made signes to stay their flight, that they may have Trade with them, and to that end they brought certaine Copper-Kettles; the Indians by degrees made their approach nearer and nearer till they came to them, when beholding their Vessells, which they had set forth before them, the Indian knocking them were much delighted with the sound, and much more astonished to see they would not breake, being so thin, for attaining those Vessells they brought them much Bever, fraughting them richly away according to their desires. This was the first working providence of Christ to stir up our English Nation, to plant these parts in hope of a rich Trade for Bever-skins, and this made some of our Countrymen make their abode in these parts, whom this Army of Christ at their comming over found as fit helps to further their designe in planting the Churches of Christ; Who by a more admirable act of his Providence not long after prepared for his peoples arrivall as followeth.

The Summer after the blazing Starre (whose motion in the Heavens was from East to West, poynting out to the sons of men the progresse of the glorious Gospell of Christ, the glorious King of his Churches) even about the yeare 1618. a little before the removeall of that Church of Christ from Holland to Plimoth in New England, as the ancient Indians report, there befell a great mortality among them, the greatest that ever the memory of Father to Sonne tooke notice of, chiefly desolating those places, where the English afterward planted.[1] The Country of Pockanoky, Agissawamg, it [2] was almost wholly

---

[1] The pestilence of 1616–1617 (*not* 1619) is best described in the first chapter of Mr. Charles Francis Adams's *Three Episodes of Massachusetts History.* Its character cannot now be determined. Its chief severity fell on the Massachusetts, whom it perhaps reduced from three thousand fighting men to fifty. Thus the English settlement of the Bay had little to fear from savage foes.

[2] It is evident that the printer has made some mistake here, but what the reading should be is uncertain. The country of Pokanoket is that lying westward

deserted, insomuch that the Neighbour Indians did abandon those places for feare of death, fleeing more West and by South, observing the East and by Northern parts were most smitten with this contagion. The Abarginny-men consisting of Mattachusets, Wippanaps and Tarratines [1] were greatly weakened, and more especially the three Kingdomes or Saggamore ships of the Mattachusets, who were before this mortality most populous, having under them seven Dukedomes or petty Saggamores, and the Nianticks and Narrowganssits, who before this came were but of little note, yet were they now not much increased by such as fled thither for feare of death. The Pecods (who retained the Name of a war-like people, till afterwards conquered by the English) were also smitten at this time. Their Disease being a sore Consumption, sweeping away whole Families, but chiefly yong Men and Children, the very seeds of increase. Their Powwowes, which are their Doctors, working partly by Charmes, and partly by Medicine, were much amazed to see their Wigwams lie full of dead Corpes, and that now neither Squantam nor Abbamocho [2] could helpe, which are their good and bad God and also their Powwows themselves were oft smitten with deaths stroke. Howling and much lamentation was heard among the living, who being possest with great feare, oftimes left their dead unburied, their manner being such, that they remove their habitations at death of any. This great mortality being an unwonted thing, feare[d] them the more, because naturally the Country is very healthy. But by this meanes Christ (whose great and glorious workes the Earth throughout are altogether for the benefit of his Churches and chosen) not onely made roome for his people to plant; but also tamed the hard and cruell hearts of these barbarous Indians, insomuch

from Plymouth, the region ruled over by Massasoit and Philip. Agissawam may be the place listed by William Wood (*New Englands Prospect*, 1634, *ad fin.*) under the name Igoshaum, since he calls Agawam Igowam. Unfortunately he does not give Igoshaum on his map; in the list it stands between "Igowam" (Ipswich) and "Chobocco" (Essex).

[1] "Aberginian" is used by Wood, and apparently by Johnson, to denote the Indians from the Massachusetts north-eastward, the Tarratines being seated in eastern Maine. The Niantics and Narragansetts were situated in Rhode Island, the Pequots in south-eastern Connecticut.

[2] Or Hobomok. A powwow was a medicine-man.

that halfe a handfull of his people landing not long after in
Plimoth-Plantation, found little resistance, of whom the
Author purposes not to speake particularly, being prevented
by the honoured Mr. Winslow, who was an eye-witnesse of the
worke:[1] onely thus much by the way, they were sent to keepe
possession for their Brethren and fellow Souldiers, who arrived
eight yeares after them, as in processe of this story will Godwilling appeare: and verily herein they quit themselves like
men, or rather Christ for and by them, maintaining the place
notwithstanding the multitude of difficulties they met withall
at their first landing, being in doubtfull suspence what intertainment these Barbarians would give them, having with
prayer supplicated the Lord in the Name of Christ their King
and guide in this their undertaking, they manned out a Boate
to discover what store of the Inhabitants were there. Now
these men, whose courage exceeded the number, being guided
by the provident hand of the most high, landed in some severall places; and by making fires gave signes of their approach.
Now the Indians, whose dwellings are most neer the water-side,
appeared with their Bowes bent and Arrowes one [on] the
string, let fly their long shafts among this little company,[2]
whom they might soon have inclosed, but the Lord otherwise
disposed of it, for one Captaine Miles Standish having his
fowling-peece in a reddinesse, presented full at them, his shot
being directed by the provident Hand of the most high God,
strook the stoutest *Sachem* among them one [on] the right
Arme, it being bent over his shoulder to reach an Arrow forth
his Quiver, as their manner is to draw them forth in fight.
At this stroke they all fled with great swiftnesse through the
Woods and Thickets, then the English, who more thirsted
after their conversion than destruction, returned to their
Bote without receiving any damage, and soon after arrived
where they left their Brethren, to whom they declared the
good hand of God toward them, with thankfull acknowledgement of this great worke of his in preserving them; Yet
did they all remaine full of incumbred thoughts, the Indians,

[1] The allusion is to Edward Winslow's *Good News from New England*
(London, 1624). "Prevented" in the sense of "anticipated."

[2] See Bradford, *History of Plymouth Plantation*, pp. 101, 102, of the edition
in this series.

of whose multitudes they had now some intelligence, together with experience of spirits, and also knew well without commerce with them they were not like long to subsist.

But hee, whose worke they went about, wrought so rare a Providence for them, which cannot but be admired of all that heare it. Thus it fell as they were discoursing in the Bote they had built for shelter, all of a sudden, an Indian came in among them, at whose speech they were all agast, he speaking in the English Language, *Much welcome Englishmen*, their wonder was the greater, because upon those Costes they supposed no English had so much as set foote, and verily Christ had prepared him on purpose to give his people intertainment, the Indian having lived in England two year or thereabout, after which he returned home, and at this time had wandred into those parts in company of other Indians.[1] All this, and the condition of the neere adjoyning Indians, hee soon discovered unto them, at which they were transported beyond themselves very much, what with joy and the mixture of their former feare and affection intervening with the other, surprised all their senses of a sudden, that long it was ere each party could take its proper place, yea, and beyond all this Christ Jesus, by the power of his blessed Spirit, did now work upon all their faculties both of Soule and Body, [that] the great impression of his present Providence might not soon be washed off with the following incumbred cares of a Desart Wildernesse; but to contract, they made use of the present opportunity, and by the instrumentall meanes of this Indian, became acquainted and reconciled with most of the Neighbouring Indians. And afterward planted a Church of Christ there, and set up civill Government, calling the Name of the place Plimoth: under this jurisdiction there are ten Churches at this very day,[2] this being the first place any English resorted unto for the advancement of the Kingly Government of Christ in this Westerne World.

[1] Johnson fuses into one the stories of Samoset and Squanto. Bradford, pp. 110–112.

[2] Plymouth, Scituate, Duxbury, Barnstable, Marshfield, Yarmouth, Sandwich, Taunton, Eastham, and Rehoboth.

CHAP. IX.

Of the first preparation of the Marchant Adventurers, in the Mattachusets.

Now it will be time to returne againe to England, to speake further of the people that wee left in way of preparation; who in the yeare 1628. sent forth some store of servants to provide against the wants of a Desart Wildernesse, amongst whom came over a mixt multitude, insomuch that very little appeared of the following worke, onely the much honoured Mr. John Indicat came over with them to governe, a fit instrument to begin this Wildernesse-worke, of courage bold undanted, yet sociable, and of a chearfull spirit, loving and austere, applying himselfe to either as occasion served. And now let no man be offended at the Authors rude Verse, penned of purpose to keepe in memory the Names of such worthies as Christ made strong for himselfe, in this unwonted worke of his.

John Endicat twice Governour of the English, inhabiting the Mattachusets Bay in N. England.[1]

Strong valiant John, wilt thou march on, and take up station first;
   Christ cal'd hath thee, his Souldier be, and faile not of thy trust;
Wilderness wants Christ's grace supplants, then plant his Churches
     pure.
   With Tongues gifted, and graces led, help thou to his procure;
Undanted thou wilt not allow Malignant [2] men to wast
   Christs Vineyard heere, whose grace should cheer his well-beloved's
     tast.

[1] John Endicott, one of the six patentees of 1628, was sent out in that year as local manager, and governed the colony at Naumkeag till Winthrop's arrival in 1630. He was five times (five years) deputy-governor of Massachusetts Bay, and governor fifteen times, 1644–1645, 1649–1650 (the two terms alluded to by our author above), 1651–1654, 1655–1665. The word "General" in the verses below refers to his election as sergeant-major general, the highest military office in the colony, to which he was chosen in 1645. He was a narrow, rigid, and choleric Puritan, but sturdy, upright, and useful.

[2] "Malignant" was among Puritan writers a favorite term by which to designate royalists and other opponents. The allusion in the next line is to Canticles vii. 12, then commonly interpreted as relating to Christ and the Church.

Then honoured be, thy Christ hath thee their Generall promoted:
To shew their love, in place above, his people have thee voted.
Yet must thou fall to grave with all the Nobles of the Earth,
Thou rotting worme, to dust must turn, and worse but for new birth.

The place picked out by this People to settle themselves
in, was in the bosome of the out-stretched arme of Cape
Anne, now called Gloster, but at the place of their abode
they began to build a Town, which is called Salem. After
some little space of time, having made tryall of the Sordid
spirits of the Neighbouring Indians, the most bold among
them began to gather to divers places, which they began to
take up for their owne. Those that were sent over servants,
having itching desires after novelties, found a reddier way to
make an end of their Masters provision, then they could finde
meanes to get more; They that came over their own men
had but little left to feed on, and most began to repent when
their strong Beere and full cups ran as small as water in a
large Land, but little Corne, and the poore Indians so far
from relieving them, that they were forced to lengthen out
their owne food with Acorns, and that which added to their
present distracted thoughts, the Ditch betweene England
and their now place of abode was so wide, that they could
not leap over with a lope-staffe,[1] yet some delighting their
Eye with the rarity of things present, and feeding their fan-
cies with new discoveries at the Springs approach, they made
shift to rub out the Winters cold by the Fire-side, having
fuell enough growing at their very doores, turning down
many a drop of the Bottell, and burning Tobacco with all the
ease they could, discoursing betweene one while and another,
of the great progresse they would make after the Summers-
Sun had changed the Earths white furr'd Gowne into a greene
Mantell. Now the vernall of thirty nine [twenty-nine] being
come, they addrest themselves to coste it as far as they durst
for feare of loosing themselves, or falling into the hands of
unknown Indians, being kept in awe by a report of a cruell
people, not far of[f,] called the Tarratines.[2] All this while

[1] Leaping-pole. It is possible that Johnson is hardly just to Endicott's
men. We know from Bradford that they had much illness during the winter of
1628–1629.

[2] Of the region east of the Penobscot.

little like-lihood there was building the Temple for Gods worship, there being only two that began to hew stones in the Mountaines, the one named Mr. Bright, and the other Mr. Blaxton,[1] and one of them began to build, but when they saw all sorts of stones would not fit in the building, as they supposed, the one betooke him to the Seas againe, and the other to till the Land, retaining no simbole of his former profession, but a Canonicall Coate.

Chap. X.

Of the first Church of Christ, gathered at Salem in the Matta-chusets Government.

This yeare 1629. came over three godly Ministers of Christ Jesus, intending to shew his power in his peoples lowest condition as his manner is, thereby to strengthen their Faith in following difficulties, and now although the number of the faithfull people of Christ were but few, yet their longing desires to gather into a Church was very great;[2] And therefore addressed themselves to finde out the blessed Rules of Christ for preserving herein, who through the assistance of his Blessed Spirit, found that the Word of God, penned by

[1] Rev. Francis Bright, an Oxford man, "trained upp under Mr. Davenport," came out to Salem in 1629 as a minister engaged by the Company, along with Higginson and Skelton, but went back to England in 1630. Rev. William Blaxton or Blackstone, B. A. in 1617 of Emmanuel College, Cambridge (and therefore presumably a Puritan), M. A. in 1621, had come out to Massachusetts Bay in 1623 with Robert Gorges, and settled about 1625 on the peninsula now occupied by Boston, its first, and for five years its sole, inhabitant. A bookish recluse, occupied with his garden and orchard, he yet welcomed and even invited Winthrop and his company to his peninsula. But he liked, he said, to be under the "lord-brethren" as little as to be under the "lord-bishops," and in 1634 he retired to a place he called Study Hill, in what is now Rhode Island, where he lived quietly till 1675.

[2] The founding of the Salem church is a chief point of departure in the ecclesiastical history of New England. It established Congregationalism as the polity of Massachusetts Bay, the essential features being (1) the local church, (2) composed of converted believers, (3) united by a covenant, (4) choosing and (5) itself ordaining its ministers, namely, (6) pastor, teacher, and ruling elder. The fullest description of the event is in Bradford's *History of Plymouth Plantation*, pp. 260–262.

the Apostles in many Epistles, written to particular Churches, consisting of such as are beloved Saints, by calling appearing so in the judgement of Charity, being tryed by the rule of the word, not scandalous in their Lives, for the society of such they sought, and in these beginnings found very few, seven being the lest [least] number a Church can be gathered, or conceived by just consequence from the Word of God.   Having fasted and prayed with humble acknowledgement of their own unworthinesse to be called of Christ to so worthy a worke, they joyned together in a holy Covenant with the Lord, and one with another, promising by the Lords Assistance to walke together in Exhorting, Admonishing, and Rebuking one another, and to cleave to the Lord with a full purpose of heart, according to the blessed Rules of his Word made known unto them, and further they seeing by light of Scripture the Lord Christ ascended up on high to give gifts unto men, not onely extraordinary as Apostles, etc. before the Canon of the Scripture was perfected, but also ordinary as Pastors and Teachers, and that such are to be fitted with gifts according, for so mighty a worke, as is the Feeding and Ruling the Flock of Christ, Wherefore they Elected [1] and Ordained one Mr. Higginson to be Teacher of this first Church of Christ, set up in those parts, a man indued with grace, apt to teach, and mighty in the Scriptures, Learned in the Tongues, able to convince gain-sayers, aptly applying the word to his hearers, who departed this life not long after, of whom it may be said.

The Reverend Mr. Higgingson, first Pastor of the Church of Christ at Salem in New England.

What Golden gaine made Higginson remove,
From fertill Soyle to Wildernesse of Rocks;
'Twas Christs rich Pearle stir'd up thee toile to love,
For him to feed in Wildernesse his flocks.

---

[1] July 20, 1629. The elections were conducted by written ballot, the first known instance of its use in America. Rev. Francis Higginson, M.A. of Cambridge 1613, had been sent out this spring by the Company. His interesting description of the country, *New England's Plantation*, was printed in London in 1630. Just a year after the date of his ordination, namely, on August 6, 1630, he died.

First Teacher, he here, Sheepe and Lambs together,
  First crownd shall be hee in the Heavens of all
Christs Pastors here, but yet Christ['s] folke had rather
  Him here retaine; blest he whom Christ hath call'd.

They also called to the Office of an Exhorting Elder [1]
Mr. Scelton, a man of a gratious Speech, full of Faith and
furnished by the Lord with gifts from above, to begin this
great worke of his, that makes the whole Earth to ring againe
at this present day.

*The Reverend Mr. Scelton, first Pastor of the Church of Christ, at
Salem in New England, 1630.*

Scelton for Christ did leave his Native soile,
  Christ['s] Grace first wrought for him, or he had never
A Pastor been in Wildernesse to toile,
  Where Christ his Flock doth into Churches gather;
For five yeares space to end thy war-faire thou
  Must meete with wantes, what wants can be to him
Whose Shepheard's Christ? Earths fullnesse hath for you,
  And Heavens rich Crowne for thee, with's conquest win.

This Church of Christ, being thus begun, the Lord with the
Water-spouts of his tender Mercy caused to increase and
fructify. And now let every Eare listen, and every heart
admire, and inlarge it selfe to the astonishment of the whole
man at this wonderous worke of the great Jehovah, that in
thrice seven yeares [2] (after the beginning of this Worke)
wrought such fearfull Desolations, and wonderfull Alterations among our English Nation, and also in this dismall Desart, wasting the naturall Inhabitant with deaths
stroke, and that as is former touched, the Mattachusets,
who were a populous Nation, consisting of 30000 able
men, now brought to lesse then 300. and in their roome
and place of abode this poore Church of Christ consisting
at their beginning, but of seven persons, increased to forty

---

[1] Or pastor. Samuel Skelton was also a Cambridge M.A. He died in
1634, hence the "five yeares space" in the verses below. In their caption read
1629 for 1630.

[2] Reckoning from 1629 to 1650.

three [1] Churches in joynt Communion one with the other, professing One God, One Christ, and one Gospell, and in those Churches about 7750. Soules in one profession of the Rules of Christ, and that which makes the worke more admirable in the Eyes of all beholders, mens habitations are cut out of the Woods and Bushes, neither can this place be entered by our English Nation, but by passing through a dreadfull and terrible Ocean of nine hundred Leagues in length.

Chap. XI.

Of the Glorious beginnings of a thorough Reformation in the Churches of Christ.

Further know these are but the beginnings of Christs glorious Reformation, and Restauration of his Churches to a more glorious splendor than ever. Hee hath therefore caused their [the] dazeling brightnesse of his presence to be contracted in the burning-Glasse of these his peoples zeale, from whence it begins to be left upon many parts of the World with such hot reflection of that burning light, which hath fired many places already, the which shall never be quenched till it hath burnt up Babilon Root and Branch. And now let the Reader looke one the 102. Psalme, the Prophet Isaia 66. Chapter; take this Sharpe Sword of Christs Word, and all other Scriptures of like nature, and follow on yee valiant of the Lord; And behold the worthies of Christ, as they are boldly leading forth his Troopes into these Westerne Fields, marke them well Man by Man as they march, terrible as an Army with Banners, croud in all yee that long to see this glorious sight; see, ther's their glorious King Christ one [on] that white Horse, whose hoofes like flint cast not only sparkes, but flames of fire in his pathes. Behold his Crown beset with Carbunkles, wherein the names of his whole Army are written. Can there be ever night in his Presence, whose eyes are ten thousand times higher [brighter] than the Sun? Be-

---

[1] Just how the number forty-three is reached is uncertain. Johnson counts ten in Plymouth Colony, p. 43, *supra;* he mentions the church of Martha's Vineyard, p. 264, *post,* and his chapter-headings plainly count thirty in Massachusetts proper; but **these would** make but forty-one.

hold his swiftnes, all you that have said, where is the promise of his comming? Listen a while, hear what his herauld proclaimes, Babylon is fallen, is fallen, both her Doctrine and Lordly rabble of Popes, Cardinalls, Lordly-Bishops, Friers, Monks, Nuns, Seminary-Priests, Jesuits, Ermites, Pilgrims, Deans, Prebends, Arch-Deacons, Commissaries, Officialls, Proctors, Somners, Singing-men, Choristers, Organist, Bellows-blowers, Vergers, Porters, Sextons, Beads-men, and Bel-ringers and all others who never had name in the Word of God; [1] together with all her false Doctrines, although they may seeme otherwise never so contradictory, as Arians, who deny the God-head of Christ, and Gortenists who deny the Humanity of Christ: Papists, who thinke to merit Heaven by the Workes of the Law, Antinomians, who deny the Law of God altogether as a rule to walke by in the obedience of Faith, and deny good works to be the Fruit of Faith, Arminians, who attribute Gods Election or Reprobation to the will of Man, and Familists, who forsake the revealed Will of God, and make men depend upon strong Revelations, for the knowledge of Gods Electing Love towards them, Conformitants or Formalists, who bring in a forme of worship of their owne, and joyne it with the worship God hath appointed in his Word, Seekers, that deny all manner of worship or Ordinances of Christ Jesus, affirming them to be quite lost, and not to be attained till new Apostles come.

Chap. XII.

Of the voluntary banishment, chosen by this People of Christ, and their last farewell taken of their Country and Friends.

And now behold the severall Regiments of these Souldiers of Christ, as they are shipped for his service in the Westerne World, Part thereof being come to the Towne and Port of Southamptan in England, where they were to be shipped, that they might prosecute this designe to the full, one Ship

---

[1] It will be remembered that Johnson was a Canterbury man, familiar with cathedral usages and archiepiscopal courts.

called the *Eagle*,[1] they wholy purchase, and many more they
hire, filling them with the seede of man and beast to sow this
yet untilled Wildernesse withall, making sale of such Land
as they possesse, to the great admiration of their Friends and
Acquaintance, who thus expostulate with them, "What, will
not the large income of your yearly revenue content you,
which in all reason cannot chuse but be more advantagious
both to you and yours, then all that Rocky Wildernesse,
whither you are going, to run the hazard of your life?   Have
you not here your Tables filled with great variety of Foode,
your Coffers filled with Coyne, your Houses beautifully built
and filled with all rich Furniture? (or otherwise) have you not
such a gainfull Trade as none the like in the Towne where you
live?   Are you not inriched daily?   Are not your Children
very well provided for as they come to years? (nay) may you
not here as pithily practise the two chiefe Duties of a Christian
(if Christ give strength), namely Mortification and Sanctification, as in any place of the World?   What helps can you have
there that you must not carry from hence?"   With bold
resolvednesse these stout Souldiers of Christ reply; as Death,
the King of terror, with all his dreadfull attendance, inhumane
and barbarous tortures, doubled and trebled by all the in-
fernal furies, have appeared but light and momentany to the
Souldiers of Christ Jesus, so also the Pleasure, Profits and
Honours of this World set forth in their most glorious splendor and magnitude by the alluring Lady of Delight, proffer-
ing pleasant embraces, cannot intice with her Syren Songs,
such Souldiers of Christ, whose aymes are elevated by him,
many Millions above that brave Warrier Ulysses.

Now seeing all can be said will but barely set forth the im-
moveable Resolutions that Christ continued in these men;
Passe on and attend with teares, if thou hast any, the following discourse, while these Men, Women and Children are taking
their last farwell of their Native Country, Kindred, Friends
and Acquaintance, while the Ships attend them; Many make
choise of some solitary place to eccho out their bowell-breaking
affections in bidding their Friends farwell.   "Deare friends"

---

[1] Winthrop's "admiral" or flag-ship, a ship of three hundred and fifty tons.
The name was changed to *Arbella*; see p. 56, *post*. Johnson probably was a
passenger in this ship.

(sayes one) "as neare as my owne soule doth thy love lodge in my brest, with thought of the heart-burning Ravishments, that thy Heavenly speeches have wrought: my melting soule is poured out at present with these words." Both of them had their farther speach strangled from the depth of their inward dolor, with breast-breaking sobs, till leaning their heads each on others shoulders, they let fall the salt-dropping dews of vehement affection, striving to exceede one another, much like the departure of David and Jonathan: having a little eased their hearts with the still streames of Teares, they recovered speech againe. "Ah! my much honoured friend, hath Christ given thee so great a charge as to be Leader of his People into that far remote, and vast Wildernesse, I [ay], oh, and alas, thou must die there and never shall I see thy Face in the flesh againe. Wert thou called to so great a taske as to passe the pretious Ocean, and hazard thy person in Battell against thousands of Malignant Enemies there, there were hopes of thy return with triumph; but now after two, three, or foure moneths spent with daily expectation of swallowing Waves and cruell Pirates, you are to be Landed among barbarous Indians, famous for nothing but cruelty, where you are like to spend your days in a famishing condition for a long space." Scarce had he uttered this, but presently hee lockes his friend fast in his armes; holding each other thus for some space of time, they weepe againe. But as Paul to his beloved flock, the other replies, "What doe you weeping and breaking my heart? [1] I am now prest for the service of our Lord Christ, to re-build the most glorious Edifice of Mount Sion in a Wildernesse, and as John Baptist, I must cry, Prepare yee the way of the Lord, make his paths strait, for behold hee is comming againe, hee is comming to destroy Antichrist, and give the whore double to drinke the very dregs of his wrath. Then my deare friend unfold thy hands, for thou and I have much worke to doe, I [ay] and all Christian Souldiers the World throughout."

Then hand in hand they leade each other to the Sandy-banks of the brinish Ocean, when clenching their hands fast, they unloose not til inforced to wipe their watery-eyes, whose

[1] Acts xxi. 13. Johnson quotes sometimes from the Geneva Bible, sometimes, apparently, from the Authorized Version; here from the former.

constant streames forced a watery-path upon their Cheekes, which to hide from the eyes of others they shun society for a time, but being called by occasion, whose bauld back-part none can lay hold one [on]; They thrust in among the throng now ready to take Ship, where they beheld the like affections with their own among divers Relations. Husbands and Wives with mutuall consent are now purposed to part for a time 900 Leagues asunder, since some providence at present will not suffer them to goe together; they resolve their tender affections shall not hinder this worke of Christ. The new Married and betrothed man, exempt by the Law of God from war, now will not claime their priviledge, but being constrained by the Love of Christ, lock up their naturall affections for a time, till the Lord shall be pleased to give them a meeting in this Westerne World, sweetly mixing it with spirituall love in the meane time. Many Fathers now take their yong Samuells, and give them to this service of Christ all their Lives. Brethren, Sisters, Unkles, Nephewes, Neeces, together with all Kindred of bloud that binds the bowells of affection in a true Lovers knot, can now take their last farewell, each of other, although naturall affection will still claime her right, and manifest her selfe to bee in the body by looking out at the Windowes in a mournefull manner. Among this company, thus disposed, doth many Reverend and godly Pastors of Christ present themselves, some in a Seamans Habit, and their scattered sheepe comming as a poore Convoy loftily take their leave of them as followeth, "What dolefull dayes are these, when the best choice our Orthodox Ministers can make is to take up a perpetuall banishment from their native soile, together with their Wives and Children; wee their poore sheepe they may not feede, but by stoledred[1] should they abide here. Lord Christ, here they are at thy command, they go; this is the doore thou hast opened upon our earnest request, and we hope it shall never be shut: for Englands sake they are going from England to pray without ceasing for England. O England! thou shalt finde New England prayers prevailing with their God for thee, but now woe alas, what great hardship must these our in-

---

[1] Stealth.

deared Pastors indure for a long season." With these words
they lift up their voyces and wept, adding many drops of
salt liquor to the ebbing Ocean; Then shaking hands they
bid adue with much cordiall affection to all their Brethren,
and Sisters in Christ, yet now the Scorne and Derision of
those times, and for this their great enterprise counted as
so many crackt-braines; but Christ will make all the earth
know the wisdome he hath indued them with, shall over-
top all the humane policy in the World, as the sequell
wee hope will shew; Thus much shall suffice in generall
to speake of their peoples farewell they tooke from time
to time of their Country and Friends.

Chap. XIII.

Of the charges expended by this poore People, to injoy Christ in
his purity of his Ordinances.

And now they enter the Ships, should they have cast up
what it would have cost to people New England before hand,
the most strongest of Faith among them would certainly
have staggered much, and very hardly have set saile. But
behold and wonder at the admirable Acts of Christ, here it is
cast up to thy hand, the passage of the persons that peopled
New England cost ninety five thousand pounds; [1] the Swine,
Goates, Sheepe, Neate and Horse, cost to transport twelve
thousand pound besides the price they cost; getting food for
all persons for the time till they could bring the Woods to
tillage amounted unto forty five thousand pounds; Nayles,
Glasse and other Iron-worke for their meeting-houses, and
other dwelling houses, before they could raise any meanes in
the Country to purchase them, Eighteene thousand pounds;
Armes, Powder, Bullet and Match, together with their great
Artillery, twenty two thousand pounds: the whole sum
amounts unto one hundred ninety two thousand pound,

---

[1] At four and a half pounds sterling per passenger, which is a fair estimate
of ocean passage-money at this time, this corresponds with the estimate, given at
the end of the next chapter, of the total immigration into New England down to
the outbreak of the Civil War in England in 1642. After that date emigration
from England nearly ceased.

beside that which the Adventurers laid out in England, which was a small pittance compared with this, and indeed most of those that cast into this Banke were the chiefe Adventurers.   Neither let any man thinke the sum above expressed did defray the whole charge of this Army, which amounts to above as much more, onely this sum lies still in banke, and the other they have had the income againe; This therefore is chiefly presented to satisfie such as thinke New England men have beene bad husbands in mannaging their Estates.   Assuredly here it lies in banke, put out to the greatest advantage that ever any hath beene for many hundred of yeares before, and verily although in casting it up some hundreds may be miscounted (for the Author would not willingly exceede in any respect) but to be sure Christ stands by and beholds every mite that (in the obedience of Faith) is cast into this Treasury: but what doe wee answering men? the money is all Christs, and certainly hee will take it well that his have so disposed of it to his advantage; by this meanes hee hath had a great income in England of late, Prayers, Teares and Praise, and some Reformation; Scotland and Ireland have met with much of the profit of this Banke, Virginia, Bermodas and Barbados have had a taste,[1] and France may suddenly meete with the like.   Therefore repent you not, you that have cast in your Coyne, but tremble all you that with a penurious hand have not onely cast in such as are taking out, to hord it up in your Napkins, remember Ananias and Saphirah, how darest thou doe it in these dayes, when the Lord hath need of it?   Gentle Reader make use of this memorable Providence of Christ for his New England Churches, where had this poore people this great sum of money? the mighty Princes of the Earth never opened their Coffers for them, and the generality of these men were meane and poore in the things of this life, but sure it is the work is done, let God have the glory, who hath now given them food to the full, and some to spare for other Churches.

---

[1] See bk. iii., ch. xi., *post.*

Chap. XIV.

*Of the wonderfull preservation of Christ, in carrying his People
    Men, Women, Children, through the largest Ocean in the
    World.*

And now you have had a short survay of the charges of
their New England Vayages, see their progresse. Being
safe aboard, weighing Anker and hoysting saile they betooke
them to the protection of the Lord on the wide Ocean. No
sooner were they dispersed by reason of the widenesse of
the Sea, but the *Arrabella* (for so they called the *Eagle*, which
the company purchased, in honour of the Lady Arrabella,
Wife to that godly Esquire, Izack Johnson)[1] espied foure
Ships, as they supposed, in pursuit of them, their suspition
being the more augmented by reason of a report (when they
lay in harbor) of foure Dunkerk-men of war,[2] who were said
to lie waiting for their comming forth. At this fight they
make preparation, according to their present condition,
comforting one another in the sweete mercies of Christ: the
weaker sex betooke them to the Ships hold, but the men one
[on] Decks waite in a readinesse for the enemies approach.
At whose courage many of the Seamen wonder, not knowing
under whose command these their passengers were, even he
who makes all his Souldiers bold as Lions. Yet was he not
minded to make triall of his peoples valiantcy in fight at this
time, for the ships comming up with them proved to be their
own Countrymen and friends, at which they greatly rejoyced,
seeing the good hand of their God was upon them, and are
further strengthened in Faith to rely one [on] Christ, for the
future time, against all Leakes, Stormes, Rockes, Sands, and

---

[1] Isaac Johnson, one of the "assistants," and reputed the richest of the
immigrants, was married to Lady Arbella or Arabella Fiennes, sister of the
Earl of Lincoln. She died within three months after her arrival in New England,
and her husband less than a month after her. See ch. xvii., *post*.

[2] Till November, 1630, England was still nominally at war with Spain.
Dunkirk was a Spanish possession. Its position with respect to the Straits of
Dover made it an advantageous port from which men-of-war and privateers
could prey upon English commerce in the Channel, and they did so in time of
peace as well as in time of war.

all other wants a long Sea-voyage procures, sustaining them
with all meeknesse and patience, yet sensible of the Lords
frownes, humbling their soules before him, and also rejoycing
in his deliverances in taking the cup of Salvation, and pay-
ing the tribute of thankfulnesse to the most high, whose provident hand was diversly directed toward them, purposely to
point out the great hardships they must undergoe in this
their Christian warfare, and withall to tell them, although
their difficulties were many and mournfull, yet their victories
should be much more glorious and joyfull, eminently eyed of
the whole World. But now keeping their course so neere as
the winds will suffer them, the billowes begin to grow lofty
and rageing, and suddenly bringing them into the vale of
death, covering them with the formidable flouds, and dash-
ing their bodies from side to side, hurling their unfixed goods
from place to place. At these unwonted workes many of
these people, amazed, finde such opposition in nature, that her
principles grow feeble, and cannot digest her food, loathing
all manner of meat, so that the vitall parts are hindered from
co-operating with the Soule in spirituall duties, insomuch
that both Men, Women and Children are in a helplesse condition for present, and now is the time if ever of recounting
this service they have, and are about to undertake for Christ;
but he, who is very sensible of his peoples infirmities, rebukes
the winds and Seas for their sakes, and then the reverend and
godly among them begin to exhort them in the name of the
Lord, and from the Lord, being fitted with such words as
much incourrages the worke they are going about. Many of
their horses and other Cattell are cast over-board by the way,
to the great disheartning of some, but Christ knew well how
far his peoples hearts would be taken off the maine worke
with these things. And therefore although he be very tender in providing outward necessaries for his, yet rather than
this great worke (he intends) should be hindered, their Tables
shall be spred but thinly in this Wildernesse for a time.
After the Lord had exercised them thus severall ways, he sent
Diseases to visit their Ships, that the desart Land they were
now drawing near unto might not be deserted by them at
first enterance, which sure it would have been by many, had
not the Lord prevented by a troublesom passage. At fortv

dayes end, or thereabout, they cast to sound the Seas depth, and find them sixty fadom, by which they deem the bankes of New found Land are near, where they being provided with Cod-line and Hooke hale up some store of fish to their no small refreshing, and within some space of time after they approach the Cost of New England, where they are againe provided with Mackarell, and that which was their greater rejoycing, they discover Land; at sight thereof they blessed the Lord.

But before the Author proceed any further in this Discourse, take here a short survay of all the Voyages by Sea, in the transportation of these Armies of the great Jehova, for fifteene years space to the year 1643, about which time England began to indeavour after Reformation, and the Souldiers of Christ were set at liberty to bide his battells at home, for whose assistance some of the chiefe worthies of Christ returned back. The number of Ships that transported passengers in this space of time, as is supposed, is 298.[1] Men, Women and Children passing over this wide Ocean, as near as at present can be gathered, is also supposed to be 21200 or thereabout.

CHAP. XV.

An Exhortation to all People, Nations and Languages, to indeavour the advancing of the Kingdome of Christ in the purity of his Ordinances, seeing he hath done such admirable Acts for these poore shrubs.

And now all you whose affections are taken with wonderfull matters (Attend) and you that thinke Christ hath forgotten his poore despised people (Behold) and all you that hopefully long for Christs appearing to confound Antichrist (Consider) and rejoyce all yee his Churches the World through-

---

[1] At the beginning of ch. xvi. the number is stated as one hundred and ninety-eight, which is more likely what Johnson wrote or meant to write. Somewhat more than a hundred such ships are enumerated in the pages of Winthrop for the period 1630–1643. In the sixty cases in which he gives the number of passengers brought, it averages a little over one hundred, as would also be true of one hundred and ninety-eight ships bringing twenty-one thousand two hundred passengers.

out, for the Lambe is preparing his Bride, and oh! yee the
antient Beloved of Christ, whom he of old led by the hand
from Egypt to Canaan, through that great and terrible Wildernesse, looke here, behold him whom you have peirced,
preparing to peirce your hearts with his *Wonder-working
Providence*, and to provoke you by this little handfull of his
people to looke on him, and mourne. Yet let no man think
these few weake Wormes would restraine the wonderfull
Workes of Christ, as onely to themselves, but the quite contrary, these [are] but the Porch of his glorious building in
hand, and if hee have shewed such admirable acts of his
providence toward these, what will he doe when the whole
Nation of English shall set upon like Reformation according to the direct Rule of his Word? Assured confidence
there is also for all Nations, from the undoubted promise
of Christ himselfe.

The Winter is past, the Raine is changed and gone, come
out of the holes of the secret places, feare not because your
number is but small, gather into Churches, and let Christ be
your King; yee Presbytery, Lord it not over them or any
Churches, but feed every one, that one flock over which
Christ hath made you overseers, and yee people of Christ
give your Presbytery double honours, that they with you
may keepe the watch of the Lord over his Churches. Yee
Dutch come out of your hods-podge, the great mingle-mangle
of Religion among you hath caused the Churches of Christ to
increase so little with you, standing at a stay like Corne
among Weeds, Oh, yee French! feare not the great swarmes
of Locusts, nor the croking Frogs in your Land, Christ is
reaching out the hand to you, look what hee hath done for
these English, and sure hee is no Respecter of Persons, etc.:
yee Germanes that have had such a bloudy bickering, Christ
is now comming to your aide, then cast off your loose, and
carelesse kinde of Reformation; gather into Churches, and
keepe them pure, that Christ may delight to dwell among you:
oh Italy! The Seat and Center of the Beast, Christ will now
pick out a People from among you for himselfe, see here what
wonders hee workes in little time. Oh! yee Spaniards and
Portugalls, Christ will shew you the abominations of that
beastly Whore, who hath made your Nations drunke with the

Wine of her Fornication.[1] Dread not that cruell murtherous
Inquisition, for Christ is now making Inquisition for them,
and behold, here how hee hath rewarded them, who dealt
cruelly with these his people.

Finally, oh all yee Nations of the World, behold great is
the worke the glorious King of Heaven and Earth hath in
hand; beware of neglecting the call of Christ: and you the
Seed of Israel both lesse and more, the ratling of your dead
bones together is at hand, Sinewes, Flesh and Life: at the
Word of Christ it comes. Counsellers and Judges you shall
have as at the begining to fight for you, as Gidion, Bareck,
Jeptha, Samson etc. then sure your deliverance shall be
sudden and wonderfull. If Christ have done such great
things for these low Shrubs, what will his most Admirable,
Excellent and wonderfull Worke for you be, but as the Resurrection from the dead, when all the miraculous acts of his
wonderfull power shewed upon Pharoah for your fore-Fathers
deliverance shall be swallowed up with those far greater
workes that Christ shall shew for your deliverance upon the
whole World, by Fiers and Bloud destroying both Pope and
Turke, when you shall see great smoake and flames ascending
up on high, of that great Whore, *Revel.* 14 and 11. verse, and
the 17. and 16. verse, and the 18. the 8. and 18. vers. Then
oh! you People of Israel gather together as one Man, and grow
together as one Tree. Ezek. 37. and 23. For Christ the great
King of all the Earth is now going forth in his great Wrath
and terrible Indignation to avenge the bloud of his Saints,
Ezek. 38 and 19. vers. and now for the great and bloudy
Battell of Gog and Magog,[2] Rivers of bloud, and up to the
Horse-bridles, even the bloud of those [who] have drunke
bloud so long. Oh! dreadfull day, when the patience and
long-suffering of Christ, that hath lasted so many hundreds
of yeares, shall end. What wonderous workes are now suddenly to be wrought for the accomplishment of these things!
Then judge all you (whom the Lord Christ hath given a discerning spirit) whether these poore New England People, be
not the forerunners of Christs Army, and the marvelous provi-

---

[1] Revelation xiv. 8, Babylon being currently identified with the Church of
Rome.

[2] Revelation xx. 8.

dences which you shall now heare, be not the very Finger of
God, and whether the Lord hath not sent this people to
Preach in this Wildernesse, and to proclaime to all Nations,
the neere approach of the most wonderfull workes that ever
the Sonnes of men saw.   Will not you believe that a Nation
can be borne in a day?   here is a worke come very neare it;
but if you will believe you shall see far greater things than
these, and that in very little time, and in the meane time
looke on the following Discourse.

CHAP. XVI.

*Of the admirable Acts of Christs Providence, in delivering
this his people in their Voyages by Sea, from many foule
dangers.*

You have heard of about 198. Ships passing the perillous
Ocean, of all which I heare of but one that ever miscarried; [1]
yet shall you here see some of the great dangers they were in.
The Ship this Author came in, a foggy morning, anon by
breake of day was ready to be steamed by a Pirate, but being
unready for fight they passed by; others by a fog, have been
delivered from farther chase of them, so that of this great
number never did any Pirate make one shot at them, according to best intelligence.   Their deliverance from leakes also
hath been no lesse wonderfull, some so neare sinking, that the
loving affection betweene Husband and Wife, hath caused
them to fould each other in their Armes, with Resolution to
die together, and make the Sea their Grave, yet not ceasing
to call on the Lord, their present helpe in time of need, who
is minded to manifest his great care for this his people to all
that shall come to hear thereof, And therefore directs to
meanes for freeing their ships, being now ready to founder
in the depthlesse Ocean.   And further, as if these deliverances
were too little to expresse the tender care Christ hath of his,
to free them from all dangers, those that occupy their businesse in the deepe, and see the Wonders of God upon the
waters, are taken with great astonishment to behold the
extraordinary hand of the most High, in transportation of

[1] The *Gabriel*, lost at Pemaquid, Maine, in 1635.

this people, in that their ships all of a sudden are brought so neer the ground, and yet strike not, their Pilots missing ofttimes of their skill on those unwandered Coasts, but their Jehovah hee misses not to be an exact Pilot in the most thickest fogge and darkest nights, for thus it befell.

The night newly breaking off her darknesse, and the daylight being clouded with a grosse vapor, as if nights Curtaines remained halfe shut, the Sea-men and Passengers standing on the Decks, suddenly fixed their eyes one [on] a great Boat (as they deemed) and anon after they spied another, and after that another; but musing on the matter, they perceived themselves to be in great danger of many great Rocks. With much terror and affrightment, they turned the Ship about, expecting every moment to be dasht in pieces against the Rocks. But he whose providence brought them in, Piloted them out againe, without any danger, to their great Rejoycing. And assuredly (so extraordinarily eminent and admirable to the eyes of many beholders, was the wonderfull workes in magnifying the Rich grace toward this his people in prefering them) that many Masters of Ships left their Sea-imployment for a time, and chose rather to suffer the wants of a Wildernesse with the people of God, than to increase their estates in a full-fed Land, and verily so taken they were, that they fell down at Christs Feet, and were placed by him as living stones, Elect and Pretious in his Churches; also many other Seamen were brought to seeke after Christ in his Ordinances, by which it appeares some great worke, by some far surpassing all this, hath Christ ere long to doe, that hee thus fitteth Instruments. Then all you that occupy shipping prepare for his service, who will assuredly prove the best owner that ever you went to Sea for.

Furthermore, the condition of those persons [that] passed the Seas, in this long and restlesse Voyage (if rightly considered) will more magnifie the grace of Christ in this great Worke. First, such were many of them that never before had made any path through the Waters, no not by boat, neither so much as seene a Ship, others so tenderly brought up that they had little hope of their Lives continuance under such hardships, as so long a Voyage must needs inforce them to indure, others there were, whose age did rather call for a quiet Couch to rest

them on, than a pinching Cabbin in a Reeling Ship, others
whose weake natures were so borne downe with Disease,
that they could hardly craule up the Ships-side, yet ventured
their weake Vessells to this Westurne World.   Here also might
you see weakly Women, whose hearts have trembled to set
foote in Boate, but now imboldened to venter through these
tempestuous Seas with their young Babes, whom they nurture up with their Breasts, while their bodies are tossed on
the tumbling Waves; also others whose Wombes could not
containe their fruit, being ready for the Worlds-light, travailed and brought forth upon this depthlesse Ocean in this
long Voyage, lively and strong Children yet living, and like
to prove succeeding Instruments in the Hands of Christ, for
furthering this worke; among other Sea-borne Cotten, now
a young student in a Colledge in Cambridge, being Son to that
Famous and Renowned Teacher of Christ, M. John Cotten; [1]
by all this and much more that might be said, for almost
every one you discourse withall will tell you of some Remarkable Providence of God shewed toward them in this their
Voyage, by which you may see the Worke of Christ, is not to
bee laid aside because of difficulties.

Chap. XVII.

Of the first leading of these People of Christ, when the Civill
Government was Established.

But to goe on with the Story, the 12 of July [2] or thereabout, 1630, these Souldiers of Christ first set foote one this
Westerne end of the World; where arriveing in safety, both
Men, Women and Children, on the North side of Charles River,
they landed neare a small Island, called Noddells Island, [3]

---

[1] Rev. John Cotton (1584–1652), rector of St. Botolph's Church, Boston,
Lincolnshire, "perhaps the most influential of the non-conforming ministers in
Old or New England," came out in the *Griffin* in 1633, and speedily became teacher
of the Boston church.   His son Seaborn, born on the voyage, was graduated at
Harvard College in 1651, and was afterward minister at Hampton, N. H.

[2] The *Arbella* arrived in Salem harbor June 12, not July 12.

[3] Noddle's Island is now East Boston.   Maverick lived there from 1635 on,
and was living there when Johnson wrote, but the place where he entertained
Winthrop and his friends with characteristic hospitality was situated at Winni-

where one Mr. Samuel Mavereck then living, a man of a very loving and curteous behaviour, very ready to entertaine strangers, yet an enemy to the Reformation in hand, being strong for the Lordly Prelaticall power, one [on] this Island he had built a small Fort with the helpe of one Mr. David Tompson,[1] placing therein foure Murtherers to protect him from the Indians. About one mile distant upon the River ran a small creeke, taking its Name from Major Gen. Edward Gibbons,[2] who dwelt there for some yeares after; One [on] the South side of the River one [on] a point of Land called Blaxtons point, planted Mr. William Blaxton, of whom we have former spoken: to the South-East of him, neare an Island called Tompsons Island lived some few Planters more. These persons were the first Planters of those parts, having some small Trading with the Indians for Beaver-Skins, which moved them to make their aboade in those parts, whom these first Troopes of Christs Army, found as fit helpes to further their worke. At their arrivall those small number of Christians gathered at Salem, greatly rejoycing, and the more, because they saw so many that came chiefly for promoting the great Work of Christ in hand. The Lady Arrabella and some other godly Women aboad at Salem, but their Hus-

simmet, now Chelsea. In his account of Winnisimmet in his *Briefe Discription of New England* (1660) he refers to a "house yet standing there which is the Antientest house in the Massachusetts Government, a house which in the yeare 1625 I fortified with a Pillizado and fflankers and guns both belowe and above in them." Samuel Maverick was a gentleman connected with the Gorges interest, who came to New England in 1624, married the widow of David Thompson, and had a large property. The relations of this "old planter" with the Massachusetts authorities were as a rule not friendly. In 1646 he was fined and imprisoned for a protest against their exclusive policy, and in 1664 he was one of the four royal commissioners sent out to subdue them.

[1] David Thompson was another "old planter," a Scottish gentleman, and perhaps an agent of Gorges. He first dwelt in a great house and fort he had built in 1623 near the present site of Portsmouth, N. H., where he had a large grant of land from the Council for New England. In 1625 or 1626 he removed to the island in Boston harbor still called Thompson's Island; but he died before the great migration, probably in 1628.

[2] Edward Gibbons had been a member of Morton's roistering crew at Merry Mount, but had been converted by witnessing the solemn ceremony of the gathering of the Salem church in 1629. Later, removing from Charlestown to Boston, he became a prominent merchant there, and was elected major-general or chief commander of the colony's militia in 1649.

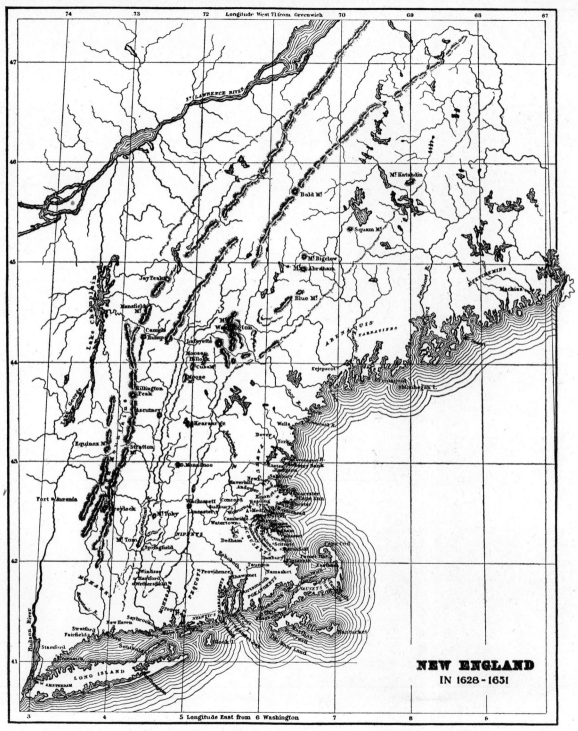

MAP OF NEW ENGLAND IN 1628–1651

From Palfrey's "History of New England"

bands continued at Charles Town, both for the settling the civill Government, and gathering another Church of Christ. The first Court was holden aboard the *Arrabella* the 23. of August. When the much honoured John Wintrope Esq. was chosen Governour for the remainder of that yeare, 1630.[1] Also the worthy Thomus Dudly Esq. was chosen Deputy Governour, and Mr. Simon Brodestreet Secretary, the people after their long Voyage were many of them troubled with the Scurvy, and some of them died. The first station they tooke up was at Charles Towne, where they pitched some Tents of Cloath, other built them small Huts, in which they lodged their Wifes and Children. The first beginning of this worke seemed very dolorous; First for the death of that worthy personage Izaac Johnson Esq. whom the Lord had indued with many pretious gifts, insomuch that he was had in high esteeme among all the people of God, and as a chiefe Pillar to support this new erected building. He very much rejoyced at his death, that the Lord had been pleased to keepe his eyes open so long, as to see one Church of Christ gathered before his death, at whose departure there was not onely many weeping eyes, but some fainting hearts, fearing the fall of the present worke. For future Remembrance of him mind this Meeter.

Izaac Johnson Esquire, beloved of Christ and his people, and one of the Magistrates of New England.

What mov'd thee on the Seas upon such toyle with Lady-taking;
   Christs drawing love all strength's above, when way for his hee's
   making.
Christ will have thee example be, honoured with's graces, yeilding
   His Churches aid, foundation laid, now new one Christ a building.

[1] An error. No election took place till spring, the time fixed by the charter; and this August meeting was but a court of assistants, not a general court, competent to elect. Winthrop was governor 1629–1634, 1637–1640, 1642–1644, 1646–1649. See his *Journal* in this series, the chief record of early Massachusetts, as he was its chief figure. Dudley, a narrower and sterner Puritan, was deputy-governor during most of the years named, and four times governor. Bradstreet, a younger man but one of great ability, was governor during the last seven years under the first charter, 1679 to 1686, and from 1689 to 1692, after having been an "assistant" (member of the council) throughout the whole period from 1630 to 1679.

Thy Faith, Hope, Love, Joy, Meeknesse prove improved for thy Lord,
  As he to thee, to people be, in Government accord.
Oh! people why doth Christ deny this worthies life to lengthen?
  Christ onely trust, Johnsons turnd dust, and yet hee's crownd and
        strengthend.

The griefe of this people was further increased by the sore
sicknesse which befell among them, so that almost in every
Family Lamentation, Mourning, and woe was heard, and no
fresh food to be had to cherish them. It would assuredly
have moved the most lockt up affections to Teares no doubt,
had they past from one Hut to another, and beheld the pite-
ous case these people were in, and that which added to their
present distresse was the want of fresh water, for although
the place did afford plenty, yet for present they could finde
but one Spring, and that not to be come at but when the tide
was downe, which caused many to passe over to the South-
side of the River,[1] where they afterward erected some other
Townes, yet most admirable it was to see with what Christian courage many of these Souldiers of Christ carried it amidst
all these calamities, and in October, the Governour Deputy
and Assistants held their second Court on the South-side of
the River;[2] Where they then began to build, holding correspondency with Charles Towne, as one and the same.

At this Court many of the first Planters came, and were
made free, yet afterward none were admitted to this fellowship, or freedome, but such as were first joyned in fellowship
with some one of the Churches of Christ, their chiefest aime
being bent to promote his worke altogether. The number
of Freemen this yeare was 110. or thereabout.[3]

[1] Charles.

[2] Again an error. The *Records* show two more meetings of the Court of
Assistants at Charlestown, September 7 and 28, 1630, and then the General Court
at Boston, October 19. Boston was given a separate name September 7.

[3] No freemen were admitted in 1630. In October one hundred and nine
men (including Johnson) applied for admission; one hundred and sixteen (also
including our author) were admitted in May, 1631, at which time the law making
membership in one of the local churches a requirement for admission as a freeman was adopted. That law was maintained till 1664.

Chap. XVIII.

Of the second Church of Christ, gathered at Charles Towne in the Mattacusets Bay, 1631.

And now the new-come Souldiers of Christ strengthen themselves in him, and gather a Church at Charles Towne, whose extent at present did reach to both sides of the River, and in very little time after was divided into two Churches.[1] The Reverend and judicious Mr. John Wilson was called to be Pastor thereof,[2] a Man full of Faith, Courage and Zeale for the truth of Christ, persecuted and hunted after by the usurping Prelates (and forced for present to part from his indeared Wife) yet honoured by Christ, and made a powerfull instrument in his hands for the cutting downe of Error, and Schisme, as in the sequell of this History will appeare, in whose weaknesse Christs power hath appeared.

The Grave and Reverend Mr. John Wilson, now Pastor of the Church of Christ at Boston, in New England.

John Wilson will to Christs will submit,
    In Wildernesse, where thou hast Trialls found,
Christ in new making did compose thee fit,
    And made thy Love, zeale, for his truth abound.
Then it's not Wilson, but Christ by him hath
    Error cut down when it o'retopping stood,
Thou then 'Gainst it didst shew an holy wrath,
    Saving mens soules from this o're-flowing floud.
They thee deprave, thy Ministrey dispise,
    By thy thick utterance seeke to call Men back

---

[1] The separate church in Charlestown was formed in November, 1632, the First Church of Boston being held to date from July 30, 1630, and to be the original church, transferred from Charlestown to the south bank of the Charles. But in reality the Dorchester church antedated it by a month.

[2] John Wilson (1588–1667), son of a prebendary of Windsor, and himself a minister of the Church of England, came out with Winthrop, and became first teacher, then pastor, of the Boston church. A pillar of orthodoxy in the Antinomian troubles, he was usually overshadowed by his more talen, d colleague, John Cotton, teacher of the same church.

From hearing thee, but Christ for thee did rise
　And turnd the wheel-right over them to crack.[1]
Yea, caused thee with length of dayes to stand
　Steadfast in's house, in old Age fruit to bring;
I [ay] and thy seed raise up by his command,
　His Flock to feed; rejoyce my Muse and sing
That Christ doth dust regard so plentiously,
　Rich gifts to give, and heart to give him his;
Estate and person thou spends liberally;
　Christ thee and thine will Crown with lasting Blisse.

This, as the other Churches of Christ, began with a small number in a desolate and barren Wildernesse, which the Lord in his wonderfull mercy hath turned to fruitfull Fields. Wherefore behold the present condition of these Churches compared with their beginnings; as they sowed in teares, so also have they Reaped in joy, and shall still so go on if plenty and liberty marre not their prosperity. This Towne of Charles is situated one the North-side of Charles River, from whence it tooke its Name, the River being about five or six fathom deepe; Over against the Town many small Islands lieing to the Seaward of it, and Hills one either side. By which meanes it proves a very good harbor for Ships, which hath caused many Sea-men and Merchants to sit downe there. The forme of this Towne in the frontice piece thereof, is like the Head, Neck and Shoulders of a Man, onely the pleasant and Navigable River of Mistick runs through the right shoulder thereof, and by its neare approach to Charles River in one place makes a very narrow neck, by which meanes the chiefe part of the Towne, whereon the most building stands, becomes a Peninsula: it hath a large Market-place neer the water side built round with Houses, comly and faire, forth of which there issues two streetes orderly built with some very faire Houses, beautified with pleasant Gardens and Orchards, the whole Towne consists in its extent of about 150. dwelling Houses. Their meeting house for Sabbath assembly stands in the Market-place, very comly built and large, the Officers of this Church are at this day one Pastor, and one Teacher, one Ruling Elder, and three Deacons, the number of Soules

---

[1] A pun on the name of Rev. John Wheelwright, Mrs. Hutchinson's brother-in-law and chief upholder in the Antinomian controversy.

are about 160. Wonderfull it is to see that in so short a time such great alterations Christ should worke for these poore people of his: their Corne Land in Tillage in this Towne is about 1200. Acres, their great Cattell are about 400. head, Sheepe neare upon 400. as for their horse you shall hear of them, Godwilling, when we come to speak of their Military Discipline.[1]

CHAP. XIX.

Of the Third Church of Christ gathered at Dorchester, 1631.[2]

The third Church of Christ gathered under this Government was at Dorchester, a frontire Town scituated very pleasantly both for facing the Sea, and also its large extent into the main Land, well watered with two small Rivers; neere about this Towne inhabited some few ancient Traders, who were not of this select band, but came for other ends, as Morton of Merrymount,[3] who would faine have resisted this worke, but the provident hand of Christ prevented. The forme of this Towne is almost like a Serpent turning her head to the North-ward, over against Tompsons Island, and the Castle; her body and wings being chiefly built on, are filled somewhat thick of Houses, onely that one of her Wings is clipt, her Tayle being of such a large extent that shee can hardly draw it after her; Her Houses for dwelling are about one hundred and forty, Orchards and Gardens full of Fruit-

[1] This interesting description of Charlestown, where Johnson lived about six years (see the Introduction), is to be understood as referring, not to the year 1631, mentioned in the heading of the chapter, but to the date of the composition of the book, about 1650. The same is true of the descriptions of other towns.

[2] The date, as in the heading of the preceding chapter, is incorrect. The Dorchester people, who came in a separate ship, arriving earlier than Winthrop's fleet, had organized a church in Plymouth, England, just before sailing, and had chosen Rev. John Maverick as teacher, and Rev. John Warham as pastor. This church may be regarded as the second rather than the third of the Massachusetts churches; and Dorchester was in the first years of the colony the largest and most flourishing of the towns.

[3] Thomas Morton, a "pettifogger of Furnivall's Inn" and partner of Captain Wollaston, had persuaded some of the latter's men to join him in maintaining at "Merry Mount" a jovial but disorderly settlement, which the neighboring settlers, under Captain Miles Standish, suppressed in 1628. See Bradford, pp. 236–243.

trees, plenty of Corne-Lande, although much of it hath been long in tillage, yet hath it ordinarily good crops, the number of Trees are neare upon 1500. Cowes, and other Cattell of that kinde about 450. Thus hath the Lord been pleased to increase his poore dispersed people, whose number in this Flock are neare about 150. Their first Pastor called to feede them was the Reverend, and godly Mr. Maveruck.[1]

Maveruck thou must put period to thy dayes,
    In Wildernesse thy kindred thee provoke
To come, but Christ doth thee for high ends Raise,
    Amongst his worthies to strike many a stroke.
Thy godly Life, and Doctrine speake, though thou
    In dust art laid, yet Christ by thee did feede
His scattered Lambes, they gathered are by you;
    Christ calls thee home, but flock he leaves to feede.

Chap. XX.

Of the Fourth Church of Christ gathered at Boston, 1631.[2]

After some little space of time the Church of Christ at Charles Town, having their Sabbath assemblies oftenest on the South side of the River, agreed to leave the people on that side to themselves, and to provide another Pastor for Charles Towne, which accordingly they did. So that the fourth Church of Christ issued out of Charles Towne, and was seated at Boston, being the Center Towne and Metropolis of this Wildernesse worke (but you must not imagine it to be a Metropolitan Church). Invironed it is with the Brinish flouds, saving one small Istmos, which gives free accesse to the Neighbour Townes by Land on the South side; on the North west, and North East, two constant Faires [Ferries] are kept for daily traffique thereunto. The forme of this Towne is like a heart, naturally scituated for Fortifications, having two Hills on the frontice part thereof next the Sea, the one well

---

[1] Rev. John Maverick died in 1636. A marginal note here reads: "Mr. Wareham and other of their Teaching Elders, you shall reade of when the Canecktoco [Connecticut] is planted." See ch. xxxiii., *post.*

[2] Again an error. The Boston and Watertown churches (1630) were the third and fourth, those of Roxbury and Lynn (1632) the fifth and sixth, and the new church of Charlestown (November, 1632, see p. 67, note 1) the seventh.

fortified on the superfices thereof, with store of great Artillery well mounted, the other hath a very strong battery built of whole Timber, and filled with Earth. At the descent of the Hill in the extreme poynt thereof, betwixt these two strong armes lies a large Cave [Cove] or Bay, on which the chiefest part of this Town is built, over-topped with a third Hill; all three like over-topping Towers keepe a constant watch to fore-see the approach of forrein dangers, being furnished with a Beacon and lowd babling Guns, to give notice by their redoubled eccho to all their Sister-townes. The chiefe Edifice of this City-like Towne is crowded on the Sea-bankes, and wharfed out with great industry and cost, the buildings beautifull and large, some fairely set forth with Brick, Tile, Stone and Slate, and orderly placed with comly streets, whose continuall inlargement presages some sumptuous City. The wonder of this moderne Age, that a few yeares should bring forth such great matters by so meane a handfull, and they so far from being inriched by the spoiles of other Nations, that the states of many of them have beene spoiled by the Lordly Prelacy, whose Lands must assuredly make Restitutions. But now behold the admirable Acts of Christ; at this his peoples landing, the hideous Thickets in this place were such, that Wolfes and Beares nurst up their young from the eyes of all beholders, in those very places where the streets are full of Girles and Boys sporting up and downe, with a continued concourse of people. Good store of Shipping is here yearly built, and some very faire ones: both Tar and Mastes the Countrey affords from its own soile; also store of Victuall both for their owne and Forreiners-ships, who resort hither for that end: this Town is the very Mart of the Land, French, Portugalls and Dutch come hither for Traffique.

Chap. XXI.

Of the Fift Church of Christ, gathered at Roxbury, 1631.[1]

The fift Church of Christ was gathered at Roxbury scituated between Boston and Dorchester, being well watered with coole and pleasant Springs issuing forth the Rocky-hills,

---

[1] See the last preceding note.

and with small Freshets, watering the Vallies of this fertill
Towne, whose forme is somewhat like a wedge double pointed,
entring betweene the two foure-named Townes, filled with a
very laborious people, whose labours the Lord hath so blest,
that in the roome of dismall Swampes and tearing Bushes,
they have very goodly Fruit-trees, fruitfull Fields and Gardens,
their Heard of Cowes, Oxen and other young Cattell of that
kind about 350. and dwelling-houses neere upon 120. Their
streetes are large, and some fayre Houses, yet have they built
their House for Church-assembly, destitute and unbeautified
with other buildings. The Church of Christ here is increased
to about 120. persons, their first Teaching Elder called to
Office is Mr. Eliot[1] a yong man at his comming thither, of a
cheerfull spirit, walking unblameable, of a godly conversation, apt to teach, as by his indefatigable paines both with
his own flock, and the poore Indians doth appeare, whose
Language he learned purposely to helpe them to the knowledge of God in Christ, frequently Preaching in their Wigwams, and Catechizing their Children.

Mr. Eliot Pastor of the Church of Christ at Roxbury, in New England,
much honoured for his labours in the Lord.

Great is thy worke in Wildernesse, Oh man,
    Young Eliot neere twenty yeares thou hast
In Westerne world with miccle toile thy span
    Spent well-neere out, and now thy gray hayrs gracest [graced]
Are by thy Land-Lord Christ, who makes use of thee
    To feede his flock, and heathen people teach
In their own Language, God and Christ to see;
    A Saviour their blind hearts could not reach.
Poore naked Children come to learne Gods Mind
    Before thy face with reverend regard;
Blesse God for thee may these poore heathen blind,
    That from thy mouth Christs Gospell sweete have heard.
Eliot, thy name is through the wild woods spread,
    In Indians mouths frequent's thy fame, for why?

    John Eliot (1604–1690), the celebrated "apostle to the Indians," began
his missionary work with them in 1646, gathered a body of his "praying Indians"
into a church at Natick in 1660, and translated the Bible into their language
(first ed., O. T., 1663; N. T., 1661).

In sundry shapes the Devills made them dread;
　And now the Lord makes them their Wigwams fly.
Rejoyce in this, nay rather joy that thou
　Amongst Christs Souldiers hast thy name sure set,
Although small gaine on Earth accrew to you,
　Yet Christ to Crowne will thee to Heaven soone fet.

Chap. XXII.

Of the Sixth Church of Christ, gathered at Linn. 1631.

The Sixth Church of Christ was gathered at Linn, betweene
Salem and Charles Towne, her scituation is neere to a River,
whose strong freshet at breaking up of Winter filleth all her
Bankes, and with a furious Torrent ventes it selfe into the
Sea; This Towne is furnished with Mineralls of divers kinds,
especially Iron and Lead. The forme of it is almost square,
onely it takes two large a run into the Land-ward (as most
Townes do). It is filled with about one hundred Houses for
dwelling; Here is also an Iron Mill in constant use, but as for
Lead they have tried but little yet. Their meeting-house
being on a levell Land undefended from the cold Northwest-
wind; And therefore made with steps descending into the
Earth. Their streetes are straite and comly, yet but thin
of Houses, the people mostly inclining to Husbandry, have
built many Farmes Remote there, Cattell exceedingly multi-
plied, Goates which were in great esteeme at their first comming, are now almost quite banished, and now Horse, Kine
and Sheep are most in request with them. The first feeder
of this flock of Christ was Mr. Stephen Batchelor,[1] gray and
aged, of whom as followeth:

Through Ocean large Christ brought thee for to feede,
　His wandering flock with's word thou hast oft taught,
Then teach thy selfe with others thou hast need·
　Thy flowing fame unto low ebbe is brought.

---

[1] Batchellor was an ejected Puritan minister, who had associated himself
with the Company of Husbandmen, or Company of the Plough, a group which
had from the Council for New England a large grant in southwestern Maine.
When he arrived in New England in 1632 and found that their colony had failed,

Faith and Obedience Christ full near hath joyn'd,
    Then trust on Christ, and thou againe mayst be
Brought on thy race though now far cast behinde;
    Run to the end, and crowned thou shalt be.

Chap. XXIII.

Of the seventh Church of Christ gathered at Water-Towne, 1631.

The Seaventh Church of Christ gathered out of this wandering Race of Jaccobites [1] was at Water-Towne, scituate upon one of the Branches of Charles River, a fruitfull plat, and of large extent, watered with many pleasant Springs, and small Rivulets, running like veines throughout her Body, which hath caused her inhabitants to scatter in such manner, that their Sabbath-Assemblies prove very thin if the season favour not, and hath made this great Towne (consisting of 160. Families) to shew nothing delightfull to the eye in any place; this Towne began by occasion of Sir Richard Saltingstall,[2] who at his arrivall, having some store of Cattell and servants, they wintered in those parts: this Town aboundes in severall sorts of Fish at their seasons, Basse, Shad, Alewifes, Frost-fish, and Smelts: their herd of Kine, and Cattell of that kinde are about 450. with some store of Sheepe and Goates. Their Land in tillage is neere upon 1800. Acres. This Church is increased to neer about 250. soules in Church-fellowship.

he and his group settled at Lynn. There he was minister till 1635 only. Thence he went on, to Ipswich, to Newbury, to Hampton, N. H., where after a brief pastorate he was deposed and excommunicated for immoral conduct, and finally to Portsmouth, where he was living in most unhappy circumstances when Johnson penned these admonitory verses. The date above should be 1632, that above the next chapter 1630.

[1] Johnson often uses this term for the chosen people of New England. The explanation is only to be found by referring to what he had written in the town records of Woburn concerning those making the preliminary exploration of that township in 1640: "Lik Jacobits laying them downe to rest where night drue on." The allusion is to Genesis xxviii. 11; the phrase, thus coined, became a favorite one with the author.

[2] Sir Richard Saltonstall, nephew of a lord mayor of London, was one of the original grantees of the Massachusetts patent, and now an assistant. He returned to England the next year, but was always a stout friend of the colony. For his son Richard, who remained in New England, see p. 102, *post*.

Their first Pastor was Mr. Phillips,[1] a man mighty in the Scriptures, and very diligent to search out the minde of Christ therein contained, of whom as followeth:

> The pennury of Wildernesse shall not
>   Daunt Phillips, and diswade his undertaking
> This Voyage long: for Christ hath made him hot
>   With zeal for's truth, thy native soile forsaken
> To follow Christ his bannisht flock to feede,
>   With restlesse toile thus honour'd Christ hath thee,
> Then it maintaine though thou thy people neede;
>   Christ would thou shouldst of them aye honoured be.
> Till death thou hast been souldier in this War;
>   Darke types the shaddowes of good things now come
> By thee have been unfoulded very far;
>   Cleer'd baptimes light from error broch'd by some,
> As by thy worke in Print appeares this day.
>   Though thou thy days hast ended on this Earth,
> Yet still thou livest in Name and Fame alway;
>   Christ thee poore dust doth crowne with lasting Mirth.

CHAP. XXIV.

Of the great cheerfulnesse of their Souldiers of Christ, in and under the penuries of a Wildernesse.

These were the beginnings of these resolute Souldiers of Christ Jesus in the yeare, 1631, Even to lay the Foundation of their severall Churches of Christ, built onely on him as their chiefe Corner Stone.   But as his chosen Israel met with many difficulties after their returne from Captivity, in building the Temple and City, which they valiantly waded through, So these weake wormes (Oh Christ to thy praise be it spoken) were most wonderfully holpen in such distresses, as to appearance of man seemed to be both hopelesse, and helplesse, threatning destruction to the whole building, and far from accomplishing such great things as you have in part seene

---

[1] George Phillips, M.A. Cambridge 1617, pastor of the Watertown church from 1630 to his death in 1644, had a leading part in committing the colony to the Separatist or Congregational polity.   The work alluded to in the verses below is apparently *A Reply to a Confutation of some Grounds for Infant's Baptism* (London, 1645).

already, and shall in the following discourse (God willing) see
more abundantly, adding a strong testimony to the work,
that as it was begun by Christ, so hath it beene carried on by
him, and shall to the admiration of the whole World be perfected in his time, and unlesse men will be wilfully blinde,
they must needs see and confesse the same, and that the influence thereof hath already run from one end of the Earth
unto the other.

This yeare 1631. John Winthrop Esq. was chosen Governour, pickt out for the worke, by the provident hand of the
most high, and inabled with gifts accordingly; then all the
folke of Christ, who have seene his face and beene partaker
of the same, remember him in this following Meeter.

*John Winthrope Esq. Eleven times Governour of the English Nation,
inhabiting the Mattacusets Bay in New England.*

Why leavest thou, John, thy station, in Suffolk, thy own soile,[1]
   Christ will have thee a pillar be, for's people thou must toyle;
He chang'd thy heart, then take his part, 'gainst prelates proud
     invading
   His Kingly throne set up alone, in wildernesse their shading.
His little flocks from Prelates knocks, twice ten years rul'd thou hast,
   With civill sword at Christs word, and eleven times been trast
     [traced ?]
By Name and Note, with peoples vote, their Governour to be;
   Thy means hast spent, 'twas therefore lent, to raise this work by thee.
Well arm'd and strong with sword among Christ['s] armies marcheth
     he,
   Doth valiant praise, and weak one raise, with kind benignity.
To lead the Van 'gainst Babylon, doth worthy Winthrop call;
   Thy Progeny shall Battell try, when Prelacy shall fall.
With fluent Tongue thy Pen doth run, in learned Latine phrase,
   To Sweads, French, Dutch, thy Neighbours, which thy lady rhet-
     orick praise.
Thy bounty feeds Christs servants needs, in wilderness of wants
   To Indians thou Christs Gospell now 'mongst heathen people plants.
Yet thou poore dust, now dead and must to rottennesse be brought,
   Till Christ restore thee glorious, more then can of dust be
     thought.

       [1] Winthrop was lord of the manor of Groton, in Suffolk.

The much honoured Thomas Dudly Esquire was chosen Deputy Governour, and the number of Free-men added was about 83.[1] Those honoured persons who were now in place of Government, having the propagation of the Churches of Christ in their eye, laboured by all meanes to make roome for Inhabitants, knowing well that where the dead carkass is, thither will the Eagles resort. But herein they were much opposed by certaine persons, whose greedy desire for land much hindered the worke for a time, as indeed all such persons do at this very day, and let such take notice how these were cured of this distemper, some were taken away by death, and then to be sure they had Land enough, others fearing poverty, and famishment, supposing the present scarcity would never be turned into plenty, removed themselves away, and so never beheld the great good the Lord hath done for his people, but the valiant of the Lord waited with patience, and in the misse of beere supplied themselves with water, even the most honoured as well as others, contentedly rejoycing in a Cup of cold water, blessing the Lord that had given them the taste of that living water, and that they had not the water that slackes the thirst of their naturall bodies, given them by measure, but might drinke to the full; as also in the absence of Bread they feasted themselves with fish. The Women once a day, as the tide gave way, resorted to the Mussells, and Clambankes, which are a Fish as big as Horsemussells, where they daily gathered their Families food with much heavenly discourse of the provisions Christ had formerly made for many thousands of his followers in the wildernesse. Quoth one, "My Husband hath travailed as far as Plimoth" (which is neere 40 miles,) "and hath with great toile brought a little Corne home with him, and before that is spent the Lord will assuredly provide": quoth the other, "Our last peck of Meale is now in the Oven at home a baking, and many of our godly Neighbours have quite spent all, and wee owe one Loafe of that little wee have"; Then spake a third, "My husband hath ventured himselfe among the Indians for Corne, and can get none, as also our honoured Governour hath distributed his so far, that a day or two more will put

---

[1] The correct number is 126.

an end to his store, and all the rest, and yet methinks our
Children are as cheerefull, fat, and lusty with feeding upon
those Mussells, Clambanks and other Fish as they were in
England, with their fill of Bread, which makes mee cheerfull
in the Lords providing for us, being further confirmed by the
exhortation of our Pastor to trust the Lord with providing
for us; whose is the Earth and the fulnesse thereof." And
as they were incouraging one another in Christs carefull providing for them, they lift up their eyes and saw two Ships comming in, and presently this newes came to their Eares, that
they were come from Jacland [1] full of Victualls, now their
poore hearts were not so much refreshed in regard of the food
they saw they were like to have, as their soules rejoyced in
that Christ would now manifest himselfe to be the Commissary
Generall of this his Army, and that hee should honour them
so far as to be poore Sutlers for his Camp. They soone up
with their Mussells, and hie them home to stay their hungry
stomacks. After this manner did Christ many times graciously provide for this his people, even at the last cast.

Chap. XXV.

*Of the Lords gracious protection of his people, from the barbarous
cruelties of the Heathen.*

About this time the Indians that were most conversant
among them, came quaking and complaining of a barbarous
and cruell people called the Tarratines,[2] who they said would
eat such Men as they caught alive, tying them to a Tree, and
gnawing their flesh by peece-meales off their Bones, as also
that they were a strong and numerous people, and now comming, which made them flee to the English, who were but very
few in number at this time, and could make but little resistance, being much dispersed, yet did they keepe a constant
watch, neglecting no meanes Christ had put into their hands
for their owne safety, in so much that they were exceedingly

[1] Probably a misprint for Ireland. From other sources we know of but *one*
ship laden with provisions coming in at this time, the *Lion*, from Bristol.

[2] See Winthrop, under August 8, 1631, vol. I., pp. 66, 67, of the edition in
this series.

weakned with continued labour, watching and hard diet, but the Lord graciously upheld them in all, for thus it befell neere the Towne of Linn, then called Saugust, in the very dead of the night (being upon their watch, because of the report that went of the Indians approach to those parts) one Lieutenant Walker, a man indued with faith, and of a couragious spirit, comming to relieve the Centinell, being come up with him, all of a sudden they heard the Sticks crack hard by them, and withall he felt something brush hard upon his shoulder, which was an Indian arrow shot through his Coat, and the wing of his buffe-Jacket. Upon this hee discharged his Culliver directly toward the place, where they heard the noise, which being deeply loden brake in pieces, then they returned to the Court of Guard, and raised such small forces as they had; comming to the light they perceived he had an other Arrow shot through his Coat betwixt his Legs. Seeing this great preservation they stood upon their Guard till Morning, expecting the Indians to come upon them every moment, but when daylight appeared, they soone sent word to other parts, who gathered together, and tooke counsell how to quit themselves of these Indians, whose approach they demed would be sudden. They agreed to discharge their great Guns. The redoubling eccho rattling in the Rocks caused the Indians to betake themselves to flight (being a terrible unwonted sound unto them) or rather he who put such trembling feare in the Assyrians Army, struck the like in these cruell Canniballs. In the Autumne following, the Indians, who had all this time held good correspondency with the English, began to quarrell with them about their bounds of Land, notwithstanding they purchased all they had of them, but the Lord put an end to this quarrell also, by smiting the Indians with a sore Disease, even the small Pox; of the which great numbers of them died, yet these servants of Christ minding their Masters businesse, were much moved in affection toward them to see them depart this life without the knowledge of God in Christ. And therefore were very frequent among them for all the noysomenesse of their Disease, entring their Wigwams, and exhorting them in the Name of the Lord. Among others one of the chiefe Saggamores of the Mattachusets, whom the English named Saggamore

John,[1] gave some good hopes, being alwayes very courteous to them, whom the godly, and much honour'd among the English, visiting a little before his death, they instructing him in the knowledge of God, Quoth hee, "by and by mee Mattamoy,[2] may be my two Sons live, you take them to teach much to know God."

Accordingly the honoured Mr. John Winthrop, and the Reverend Mr. John Wilson tooke them home, notwithstanding the infectiousnesse of the Disease their Father died of. The mortality among them was very great, and increased among them daily more and more, insomuch that the poore Creatures being very timorous of death, would faine have fled from it, but could not tell how, unlesse they could have gone from themselves; Relations were little regarded among them at this time, so that many, who were smitten with the Disease, died helplesse, unlesse they were neare, and known to the English: their Powwowes, Wizards, and Charmers, Athamochas[3] Factors, were possest with greatest feare of any. The Winters piercing cold stayed not the strength of this hot Disease, yet the English endeavouring to visit their sick Wigwams, helpe them all they could, but as they entred one of their matted Houses, they beheld a most sad spectacle, death having smitten them all save one poore Infant, which lay on the ground sucking the Breast of its dead Mother, seeking to draw living nourishment from her dead breast. Their dead they left oft-times unburied, wherefore the English were forced to dig holes, and drag their stinking corps into them. Thus did the Lord allay their quarrelsome spirits, and made roome for the following part of his Army. This yeare came over more supplies to forward the worke of Christ.

[1] Nanepashemet had been the principal chief of the Indians on the north side of the Bay. Sagamore John, his oldest son and successor, died in December, 1633.

[2] *Mattamoi* — to die (Wood, *New Englands Prospect*).

[3] Misprint for Abbamocho's, *i. e.*, the Devil's.

CHAP. XXVI.

Of the gratious provisions the Lord made for his people.

The yeare 1632. John Winthrope Esquire, was chosen Governour againe, and the antient Thomas Dudly Esquire, was Deputy Governour, a man of a sound judgement in matters of Religion and well read, bestowing much labour that way, of whom as followeth:

The honoured, aged, stable and sincere servant of Christ, zealous for his truth Thomas Dudly, Esq. foure times Governour of the English Nation, in the Mattacusets, and first Major Generall of the Millitary Forces.[1]

What Thomas, now believe dost thou that riches men may gaine,
  In this poore Plot Christ doth allot his people to sustaine?
Rich Truth thou'lt buy and sell not, why, no richer Jem can be,
  Truths Champion in campion,[2] Christ's grace hath placed thee.
With civill Sword, at Christs Word, early cut off wilt thou
  Those Wolvish sheep, amongst flocks do creep, and damned doctrine low [sow?].
To trembling age, thou valiant sage, one foot wilt not give ground,
  Christs Enemies from thy face flies, his truth thou savest sound.
Thy lengthened dayes, to Christs praise, continued are by him:
  To set, by thee, his people free from foes that raging bin.
Wearied with yeares, it plaine appeares, Dudly not long can last,
  It matters not, Christ Crown thee got, its now at hand, hold fast.[3]

This yeare was the first choise of Magistrates by free-men,[4] whose number was now increased, fifty three or thereabout. To declare the manner of their Government is by the Author deferred till the year 1637, where the Reader may behold Government both in Churches and Common-wealth, to be an institution of the Lord, and much availeable through his blessing for the accomplishment of his promises to his people.

[1] Dudley was elected governor in 1634, 1640, 1645, and 1650, and was chosen the first major-general of the colony's military forces in 1644.

[2] Campaign.   [3] Dudley died in July, 1653, aged 76.

[4] In October, 1630, the General Court had provided that thereafter the governor and deputy-governor should be elected by the assistants, while the freemen, or members of the Company, should elect only the assistants. Now (May, 1632) the earlier system was restored, whereby governor, deputy-governor, and assistants were all alike chosen by the freemen in General Court.

This year these fore-runners of the following Army of Christ, after the sight of many of the admirable Acts of his providence for them, begun to take up steddy resolution through the helpe of him to wade through the Ocean they were farther like to meete withall, and therefore began to plant the yet untilled Earth, having as yet no other meanes to teare up the bushy lands, but their hands and howes, their bodies being in very ill temper by reason of the Scurvy (a Disease in those dayes very frequent) to undergoe such extremity, but being prick'd on with hungers sharpe gode, they keepe doing according to their weake abilities, and yet produce but little food for a long season, but being perswaded that Christ will rather raine bread from Heaven, then his people should want, being fully perswaded, they were set on the worke at his command.   Wherefore they followed on with all hands, and the Lord (who hath the Cattell of thousand Hills, and the Corne of ten thousand Vallies, the whole Earth, and fulnesse of it) did now raise up fresh supplies to be added to these both of men and provision of food, men no lesse valiant in Faith then them, the former amongst whom was the Reverend Mr. Welds and Mr. James, who was welcomed by the people of Christ at Charles Towne, and by them called to the Office of a Pastor, where hee continued for some yeares, and from thence removed to New haven, upon some seed of prejudice sowne by the enemies of this worke.[1]   But good Reader doe thou behold, and remember him farther in the following Lines;

> Thy Native soile, Oh James, did thee approve,
>   Gods people there in Lincolneshire commend
> Thy courteous speech and worke of Christian love,
>   Till Christ through Seas did thee on Message send.
> With learned skill his mind for to unfold,
>   His people in New England thou must feed,
> But one sad breach did cut that band should hold;
>   Then part wilt thou least [lest] farther jars should breed.

[1] Thomas James became pastor of the Charlestown church at its organization in November, 1632; after difficulties with his church he removed to New Haven in 1638.   Thence in 1643 he went to Virginia with Knowles and Thompson (see bk. III., ch. XI.) to establish Congregationalism, was banished, and retired to England.   His son, Thomas James, alluded to in the last lines of the verses, was in 1650 ordained as pastor of the church at Easthampton, Long Island, and preached there till 1696.

Yet part thou wilt not with Christs Truth, thy crowne.
But my Muse waile that any souldier should
In fighting slip, why James thou fallest not downe,
Back thou retreats their valiant fighting, hold
Fast on thy Christ, who thine may raise with thee,
His bands increase, when leaders he provides,
Thy Son young student may such blessing be,
Thy losse repayre, and Christ thee crown besides.

Although the great straites this Wildernesse people were in for want of food, was heard of among the godly people in England, yet would they not decline the worke, but men of Estates sold their possessions, and bought plenty of foode for the Voyage, which some of them sent before hand, by which meanes they were provided for, as also the Lord put it into the hearts of such as were Masters, and Undertakers of Ships, to store their Vessells so well that they had to spare for this peoples need, and further Christ caused abundance of very good Fish to come to their Nets and Hookes, and as for such as were unprovided with these meanes, they caught them with their hands, and so with Fish, wild Onions and other Herbs were sweetly satisfied till other provisions came in. Here must labouring men a little be minded, how ill they recompenced those persons, whose estates helpe them to food before they could reape any from the Earth, that forgetting those courtesies they soon by excessive prises took for their worke, made many File-leaders fall back to the next Ranke, advancing themselves in the meane time. About this time the Church of Christ at Roxbury, being a diligent people, early prevented their Brethren in other Churches by calling the Reverend Mr. Welds [1] to be their Pastor, of whom you may see somewhat farther in the following lines:

To worke, oh Welds! in wildernesse betime
Christ thee commands, that thou his folke should's follow:
And feede his flock in Covenant band combine,
With them through him his glorious name to hallow;

[1] Thomas Welde, Eliot's colleague at Roxbury, was as famous for uncompromising orthodoxy as Eliot was for gentle piety and missionary zeal. He had a leading part in the persecution of the Antinomians. In 1641 he went back to England with Hugh Peters, as agent of the colony, and never returned.

Seven yeares thou stoutly didst wade through with toile
   These desart cares, back by advice againe
Thou didst returne unto thy native soile,
   There to advance Christs Kingdome now remaine.
In Pulpit, and with Pen thou hast the truth
   Maintained, and clear'd from scandalous reproach
Christs churches here, and shew'd their lasting Ruth,
   That dare 'gainst Christ their own inventions broach;
     Then sage, in age, continue such to be,
     Till Christ thee crowne, his gifts to thee are free.

This yeare of sad distresses was ended with a terrible cold Winter, with weekly Snowes, and fierce Frosts betweene while congealing Charles River, as well from the Towne to Sea-ward, as above, insomuch that men might frequently passe from one Island to another upon the Ice. Here Reader thou must be minded of an other admirable Act of Christ for this yeare, in changing the very nature of the seasons, moderating the Winters cold of late very much, which some impute to the cutting downe the woods, and breaking up the Land; But Christ have the praise of all his glorious Acts. About this time did the valiant in faith, and Reverend Pastor Mr. John Wilson returne to England, and surely the power of Christ hath notably appeared in this weake sorry man. You must needs see the Author will flatter no man, yet will he not be wanting to tell the noble Acts of Christ Jesus, in making men strong for himselfe; here is one borne up in the armes of his mercy, often through the perillous Seas night and dayes, yea, weeks and months, upon the great deepe, and now having with his owne eyes beheld the manifold troubles these poore were in, yet at this very time hies him back to his Native soile, where his indeared Wife did yet remaine, purposely to perswade her to cast her cares upon the Lord, as he himself had already done, and then assuredly the wants of a Wildernesse would never hurt her. At the departure of this holy Man of God, many of his peoples hearts waxed very sad, and having looked long for his returne, Their eyes now began to faile in missing of their expectation. They according to their common course in time of great straites, set and appointed a day wholy to be spent in seeking the pleasing Face of God in Christ, purposing the Lord assisting to afflict their soules, and give him the honour of his All-seeingness, by a downe right acknowledgement of their sinnes. But the Lord, whose Grace is alwayes undeserved, heard them before they cried, and the afternoone [1] before the day appointed brought him, whom they so much desired, in safety to shore, with divers other faithfull servants of Christ ready armed for the Battell. The day was turned to a day of rejoycing, and blessing the Lord, even the mighty God of Jacob, the God of Armies is for us a refuge high. *Shela.*

The yeare 1633. the honoured John Winthrope Esquire, was chosen Governour againe, and Thomas Dudly Esq. Deputy Governour, the number of Freemen added, or Souldiers listed was 46. The Winters Frost being extracted forth the Earth, they fall to tearing up the Roots, and Bushes with their Howes; even such men as scarce ever set hand to labour before, men of good birth and breeding, but comming through the strength of Christ to war their warfare, readily rush through all difficulties. Cutting down of the Woods, they inclose Corne fields, the Lord having mitigated their labours by the Indians frequent fiering of the woods, (that they may not be hindered in hunting Venson, and Beares in the Winter season) which makes them thin of Timber in many places, like our Parkes in England. The chiefest Corne they planted before they had Plowes was Indian Graine, whose increase is very much beyond all other, to the great refreshing of the poore servants of Christ, in their low beginnings. All kinde of Gardens Fruits grew very well, and let no man make a jest at Pumpkins, for with this fruit the Lord was pleased to feed his people to their good content, till Corne and Cattell were increased.

And here the Lords mercy appeared much in that those, who had beene formerly brought up tender, could now contentedly feed on bare and meane Diet, amongst whom the Honoured and upright hearted in this worke of Christ, Mr. Increase Nowell,[2] shall not be forgotten, having a diligent hand therein from the first beginning.

[1] Of May 26, 1632.

[2] Increase Nowell was one of the original grantees named in the Massachusetts patent, an assistant from 1629 to his death in 1655, and secretary of the colony from 1639 to 1650.

Increase shalt thou, with honour now, in this thy undertaking,
  Thou hast remain'd as yet unstaind, all errors foule forsaking;
To poore and rich, thy Justice much hath manifested bin:
  Like Samuel, Nathanaell, Christ hath thee fram'd within;
Thy faithfulnesse, people expresse, and Secretary they
  Chose thee each year, by which appeare, their love with thee doth
    stay.
Now Nowell see, Christ call'd hath thee, and work thou must for him,
  In beating down the triple Crown, and all that his foes ben.
Thus doest thou stand by Christ fraile man, to tell his might can make
  Dust do his will, with graces fill, till dust to him he take.

Chap. XXVII.

*Of the gratious goodnesse of God, in hearing his peoples prayers
    in times of need, and of the Ship-loades of goods the Lord
    sent them in.*

Here againe the admirable Providence of the Lord is to be
noted, That whereas the Country is naturally subject to
drought, even to the withering of their summers Fruits, the
Lord was pleased, during these yeares of scarcity, to blesse
that small quantity of Land they planted with seasonable
showers, and that many times to the great admiration of the
Heathen, for thus it befell: the extreame parching heate of
the Sun (by reason of a more constant clearnesse of the Aire
then usually is in England) began to scorch the Herbs and
Fruits, which was the chiefest meanes of their livelyhood.
They beholding the Hand of the Lord stretched out against
them, like tender hearted Children, they fell down on their
knees, begging mercy of the Lord, for their Saviours sake,
urging this as a chiefe argument, that the malignant adver-
sary would rejoyce in their destruction, and blaspheme the
pure Ordinances of Christ, trampling down his Kingly Commands with their owne inventions, and in uttering these
words, their eyes dropped down many teares, their affections
prevailing so strong, that they could not refraine in the
Church-Assembly. Here admire and be strong in the Grace
of Christ, all you that hopefully belong unto him, for as they
powred out water before the Lord, so at that very instant,
the Lord showred down water on their Gardens and Fields,

which with great industry they had planted, and now had not
the Lord caused it to raine speedily, their hope of food had
beene lost: but at this these poore wormes were so exceedingly
taken, that the Lord should show himselfe so neere unto their
Prayers, that as the drops from Heaven fell thicker, and faster,
so the teares from their eyes by reason of the sudden mixture
of joy and sorrow, and verily they were exceedingly stirred in
their affections, being unable to resolve themselves, which
mercy was greatest, to have a humble begging heart given
them of God, or to have their request so suddenly answered.

The Indians hearing hereof, and seeing the sweet raine
that fell, were much taken with Englishmens God, but the
Lord seeing his poore peoples hearts were to narrow to beg,
his bounties exceeds toward them at this time, as indeed hee
ever hitherto hath done for this Wildernesse-People, not onely
giving the full of their requests, but beyond all their thoughts,
as witnesse his great worke in England of late, in which the
prayers of Gods people in New England have had a great
stroke; These people now rising from their knees to receive
the rich mercies of Christ, in the refreshed fruits of the Earth,
Behold the Sea also bringing in whole Ship-loades of mercies,
more being filled with fresh forces, for furthering this wonderfull worke of Christ, and indeed this yeare came in many
pretious ones, whom Christ in his grace hath made much use
of in these his Churches, and Common-wealth, insomuch that
these people were even almost over-ballanced with the great
income of their present possessed mercies, yet they addresse
themselves to the Sea shore, where they courteously welcom
the famous servant of Christ, grave godly and judicious
Hooker, and the honoured servant of Christ, M. John Haynes,
as also the Reverend and much desired Mr. John Cotton, and
the Retoricall Mr. Stone,[1] with divers others of the sincere
servants of Christ, comming with their young, and with their
old, and with their whole substance, to doe him service in this

---

[1] Hooker, Cotton, and Stone are commemorated more amply on subsequent
pages, pp. 90, 88, 93, respectively. John Haynes, who came with them in
the *Griffin*, arriving in September, 1633, was a gentleman of large estate in Essex.
In May, 1635, he was chosen governor; he served one year. In 1637 he removed to Connecticut, and was the first governor of that colony, serving in 1639
and seven other years.

Desart wildernesse. Thus this poore people having now tasted liberally of the salvation of the Lord every way, they deeme it high time to take up the Cup of thankfulnesse, and pay their vowes to the most high God, by whom they were holpen to this purpose of heart, and accordingly set apart the 16. day of October (which they call the eighth Moneth,[1] not out of any pevish humor of singularity, as some are ready to censor them with, but of purpose to prevent the Heathenish and Popish observation of Dayes, Moneths and Yeares, that they may be forgotten among the people of the Lord). This day was solemnly kept by all the seven Churches, rejoycing in the Lord, and rendering thanks for all their benefits.

Here must not be omitted the indeared affections Mr. John Wilson had to the worke in hand, exceedingly setting forth (in his Sermon this day) the Grace of Christ in providing such meet helps for furthering thereof, really esteeming them beyond so many Ship-loading of Gold; manifesting the great humility Christ had wrought in him, not complementing, but in very deede prefering the Reverend Mr. John Cotton,[2] many hundreds before himselfe, whom they within a very little time after called to the Office of a Teaching Elder of the Church of Christ at Boston, where hee now remaines, of whom as followeth:

When Christ intends his glorious Kingdome shall
    Exalted be on Earth, he Earth doth take,
Even sinfull Man to make his worthies all;
    Then praise I Man, no, Christ this Man doth make.

[1] The early New England writers, e. g., Winthrop in his *Journal*, usually count March the first month of the year.

[2] John Cotton (1585–1653), fellow of Emmanuel College, Cambridge, then vicar of St. Botolph's, Boston, fled from England before persecution by the Court of High Commission, and became the leading minister of Massachusetts. Of his many books, published in London, those alluded to in the ensuing verses seem to be *The Churches Resurrection, or the Opening of the Fift and Sixt Verses of the 20th Chap. of the Revelation* (1642), *The Powring Out of the Seven Vials* (1642), *A Briefe Exposition of the Whole Book of Canticles or Song of Solomon* (1642, second ed. 1648), *The Keyes of the Kingdom of Heaven* (1644), *The Way of the Churches of Christ in New England* (1645), and *The Way of Congregational Churches Cleared* (1648). The allusion in the last lines is to the fact that at first he was not ill affected toward Anne Hutchinson's teachings, though later, under pressure, he repudiated them and joined in silencing her.

Sage, sober, grave, and learned Cotten, thou,
  Mighty in Scripture, without Booke repeat it,
Annatomise the sence, and shew Man how
  Great mysteries in sentence short are seated,
Gods Word with's word comparing oft unfould
  The secret truths.   Johns Revelations hath
By thee been open'd, as nere was of old;
  Shewes cleere and neere 'gainst Romes whore is Gods wrath.
Then Churches of Christ, rejoyce and sing,
  John Cotten hath Gods minde, I dare believe,
Since he from Gods Word doth his witnesse bring;
  Saints cries are heard, they shall no longer grieve.
That song of songs, 'twixt Christ and's Church thou hast
  Twice taught to all, and sweetly shewed the way,
Christ would his Churches should in truth stand fast,
  And cast off mans inventions even for aye.
Thy labours great have met with catching cheats,
  Mixing their Brasse with thy bright Gold, for why?
Thy great esteeme must cover their ill feates;
  Some soile thou gett'st, by comming them so nie,
But it's wipt off, and thou Christs Champion left.
  The Faith to fight for, Christ hath arm'd thee well,
His worthies would not, thou shoulds be bereft
  Of honours here thy Crown shall soon excell.

These people of God having received these farther helps,
to instruct, and build them up in the holy things of Christ,
being now greatly incouraged, seeing the Lord was pleased
to set such a broad Seale to their Commission for the worke
in hand, not onely by his Word and Spirit moving thereunto,
but also by his Providence in adding such able instruments
for furthering this great worke of Reformation, and advancing the Kingdome of Christ, for which they spent this day of
rejoycing, and sure the Lord would have all that hear of it
know, their joy lay not in the increase of Corne, or Wine, or
Oyle, for of all these they had but very little at this time,
yet did they not spare to lend such as they had unto the
poore, who could not provide, and verily the joy ended not
with the day, for these active instruments of Christ, Preaching
with all instancy the glad Tidings of the Gospell of Jesus
Christ, rejoyced the Heart of this People much.

CHAP. XXVIII.

Of the Eighth Church of Christ, gathered at Cambridge, 1633.

At this time those who were in place of civill Government, having some addition Pillars to under-prop the building, began to thinke of a place of more safety in the eyes of Man, then the two frontire Towns of Charles Towne and Boston were for the habitation of such as the Lord had prepared to Governe this Pilgrim People. Wherefore they rather made choice to enter farther among the Indians, then hazard the fury of malignant adversaries, who in a rage might pursue them, and therefore chose a place scituate on Charles River, betweene Charles Towne, and Water-Towne, where they erected a Towne called New Towne, now named Cambridge,[1] being in forme like a list cut off from the Broad-cloath of the two fore-named Towns, where this wandering Race of Jacobits gathered the eighth Church of Christ. This Town is compact closely within it selfe, till of late yeares some few stragling houses have been built. The Liberties of this Town have been inlarged of late in length,[2] reaching from the most Northerly part of Charles River, to the most Southerly part of Merrimeck River. It hath well ordered streets and comly pompleated [compleated] with the faire building of Harver Colledge. Their first Pastor was the faithfull and laborious Mr. Hooker,[3] whose Bookes are of great request among the faithfull people of Christ; Yee shall not misse of a few lines in remembrance of him.

> Come, Hooker, come forth of thy native soile:
> Christ, I will run, sayes Hooker, thou hast set
> My feet at large, here spend thy last dayes toile;
> Thy Rhetorick shall peoples affections whet.

[1] The name was changed in 1638, on account of the founding of the college in 1636.

[2] In 1644, by the grant of Shawshin.

[3] Thomas Hooker (1586–1647), fellow of Emmanuel and lecturer at Chelmsford, fled from persecution to New England, and became one of the chief of the New England divines, of tendencies more liberal than those of Cotton and Wilson. In 1636 he and his colleague Stone took a leading part in the great migra-

Thy Golden Tongue and Pen Christ caus'd to be
   The blazing of his golden truths profound,
Thou sorry worme, its Christ wrought this in thee;
   What Christ hath wrought must needs be very sound.
Then looke one [on] Hookers workes, they follow him
   To Grave, this worthy resteth there a while:
Die shall he not that hath Christs warrier bin;
   Much lesse Christs Truth, cleer'd by his peoples toile.
Thou Angell bright, by Christ for light now made,
   Throughout the World as seasoning salt to be,
Although in dust thy body mouldering fade,
   Thy Head's in Heaven, and hath a crown for thee.

The people of this Church and Towne have hitherto had
the chiefest share in spirituall blessings, the Ministry of the
Word, by more than ordinary instruments as in due time and
place (God willing) you shall farther heare, yet are they at
this day in a thriving condition in outward things also, both
Corne and Cattell, Neate and Sheepe, of which they have a
good flocke, which the Lord hath caused to thrive much in
these latter dayes then formerly.

This Towne was appointed to be the seate of Government,
but it continued not long. This yeare a small gleane of Rye
was brought to the Court as the first fruits of English graine,[1]
at which this poore people greatly rejoyced to see the Land
would beare it, but now the Lords blessing that way hath
exceeded all peoples expectation, cloathing the Earth with
plenty of all kinde of graine. Here minde I must the Reader
of the admirable acts of Christs Providence toward this people,
that although they were in such great straites for foode, that
many of them eate their Bread by waight, and had little

---

tion from Newtown to the Connecticut valley, and in the foundation of the colony
of Connecticut. As minister in Hartford, he exerted almost unbounded influence in that colony till his death, while his *Survey of the Summe of Church-Dis-*
cipline (London, 1648), posthumously published, remained the classical exposition of the Congregational polity of New England.

   [1] But Wood, who left New England August 15, 1633, says, *New Englands*
Prospect, p. 14: "there hath as good English Corne [*i. e.*, grain] growne there, as
could be desired; especially Rie and Oates, and Barly: there hath beene no great
tryall as yet of Wheate, and Beanes"; and Winthrop, I. 90, speaks of twenty
acres of barley and oats at Lynn in 1632.

hopes of the Earths fruitfullnesse, yet the Lord Christ was pleased to refresh their spirits with such quickning grace, and lively affections to this Temple-worke, that they did not desert the place; and that which was more remarkable, when they had scarce houses to shelter themselves, and no doores to hinder the Indians accesse to all they had in them, yet did the Lord so awe their hearts, that although they frequented the Englishmens places of aboade, where their whole substance, weake Wives and little ones lay open to their plunder; during their absence, being whole dayes at Sabbath-Assemblies, yet had they none of their food or stuffe diminished, neither Children nor Wives hurt in the least measure, although the Indians came commonly to them at those times, much hungry belly (as they use to say) and were then in number and strength beyond the English by far.

Yet further see the great and noble Acts of Christ toward this his wandering people; feeling againe the scarcity of foode, and being constrained to come to a small pittance daily, the Lord to provide for them, causeth the Deputy of Ireland to set forth a great Ship unknowne to this people, and indeed small reason in his own apprehensions why he should so do (but Christ will have it so.) This Ship ariving, being filled with food, the godly Governors did so order it that each Town sent two men aboard of her, who tooke up their Townes allowance, it being appointed before hand, what their portion should be, to this end that some might not by [buy] all, and others be left destitute of food. In the vernall of the yeare 1634, This people being increased, and having among them many pretious esteemed instruments for furthering this wonderous worke of Christ, they began to thinke of fortifying a small Island about two miles distant from Boston to Seaward, to which all the Vessells come in usually and passe. To this end the honoured Mr. John Winthrope, with some 8. or 10. persons of note, tooke boate and arrived on the said Island in a warme Sunshine day, just at the breaking up of Winter as they deemed, but being they were sudden surprised with a cold North-west storme (which is the sharpest winde in this Country) freezing very vehemently for a day and a night, that they could not get off the Island, but were forced to lodge there, and lie in a heape one upon another (on the ground) to keepe themselves from freezing.[1]

This yeare 1634. the much honoured Thomas Dudly Esquire, was chosen Governor, and Mr. Roger Ludlow Deputy Governor, the Freemen added to this little Common-wealth this year were about two hundred and foure.[2]   About this time a sincere servant of Christ Mr. Stone [3] was added to the Church of Christ at New-towne, as a meet helpe to instruct the People of Christ there, with the above named Mr. Hooker, and as he hath hetherto bin (through the blessing of God) an able instrument in his hands to further the worke, So let him be incourraged with the Word of the Lord in the spirit of his might to go on.

> Thou well smoth'd Stone Christs work-manship to be,
>   In's Church new laid his weake ones to support,
> With's word of might his foes are foild by thee;
>   Thou daily dost to godlinesse exhort.
> The Lordly Prelates people do deny
>   Christs Kingly power Hosanna to proclaime,
> Mens mouths are stopt, but Stone poore dust doth try,
>   Throughout his Churches none but Christ must raigne.
> Mourne not Oh Man, thy youth and learning's spent
>   In desert Land, My Muse is bold to say,
> For glorious workes Christ his hath hither sent;
>   Like that great worke of Resurrection day.

Chap. XXIX.

Of the Lords remarkable providence toward his indeared servants M. Norton and Mr. Shepherd.

Now my loving Reader, let mee lead thee by the hand to our Native Land, although it was not intended to speake in particulars of any of these peoples departure from thence,

[1] The episode is related somewhat differently, and doubtless more correctly, by Winthrop, *Journal*, I. 98, who gives the date as February 21, 1633, and the place to be examined as Nantasket, not Castle Island, fortification of which was begun in the summer of 1634.

[2] More exactly, 232.

[3] Samuel Stone, of Hertford in England, and of Emmanuel College, came out in the same ship with Hooker, was his colleague at Newtown (Cambridge), and removed with him to Connecticut, where Hartford was named after his birthplace. He died there in 1663.

purposing a generall relation should serve the turne, yet come
with mee and behold the wonderous worke of Christ in preserving two of his most valiant Souldiers, namely Mr. John
Norton, and that soule ravishing Minister Mr. Thomas Shepheard,[1] who came this yeare to Yarmouth to ship themselves
for New England, where the people of God resorted privately
unto them to hear them Preach.   During the time of their
aboade the Enemies of Christs Kingdome were not wanting
to use all meanes possible to intrap them, in which perilous
condition they remained about two months, waiting for the
Ships readinesse, in which time some persons eagerly hunting
for Mr. Thomas Shepheard, began to plot (for apprehending
of him) with a Boy of sixteene or seventeene yeares of Age,
who lived in the House where hee Lodged, to open the doore
for them at a certaine houre in the night; But the Lord Christ,
who is the Shepheard of Israel, kept a most sure watch over
his indeared servants, for thus it befell, the sweet words of
grace falling from the lips of this Reverend and godly Mr.
Thomas Shepheard in the hearing of the Boy (the Lords
working withall) hee was perswaded this was an holy man of
God, and therefore with many troubled thoughts, began to
relate [repent?] his former practice, although hee had a great
some of money promised him, onely to let them in at the houre
and time appointed; but the Boy, the more neere the time
came, grew more pensive and sad, insomuch that his Master
taking notice thereof began to question him about the cause of
his heavinesse, who being unwilling to reveale the matter,
held of[f] from confessing a long time, till by urgent and insinuating search of his godly Master, with teares hee tells
that on such a night hee had agreed to let in Men to apprehend the godly Preacher.   The good Man of the house forthwith gave notice thereof unto them, who with the helpe of
some well-affected persons was convay'd away by boate

----

[1] John Norton became minister in Ipswich (see p. 103, *post*), and later succeeded John Cotton in the Boston church. Of the early life and emigration of
Thomas Shepard, a minister for whom Johnson had a particular affection, there
is a most interesting account in his autobiography, printed in Young's *Chronicles
of Massachusetts*, pp. 497–558. After graduating at Emmanuel College he had
served as lecturer (independent preacher) at several different places till the
Laudian persecution drove him to New England.

through a back Lane. The men at the time appointed came to the house, where finding not the doore open (when they lifted up the Latch) as they expected, they thrust their staves under it to lift it from the hookes, but being followed by some persons, whom the good man of the house had appointed for that end: yet were they boulstred out in this their wicked act by those who set them one [on] worke. Notwithstanding they were greatly ashamed when they mist of their end.

But the Lord Christ intending to make his New England Souldiers the very wonder of this Age, brought them into greater straites, that this [his] *Wonder working Providence* might the more appeare in their deliverance, for comming a shipboard, and hoiseing saile to accomplish their Voyage, in little time after they were tossed and sore beaten with a contrary winde, to the losse of the Ships upper worke, with which losse and great perill they were driven back againe, the Lord Christ intending to confirme their Faith in shewing them, that although they were brought back, as it were into the mouth of their enemies, yet hee could hide them from the hand of the Hunter, for the space of six moneths longer or thereabout, even till the Spring of the yeare following, at which time (God willing) you shall hear of them againe. In the meane time the Master, and other Sea men made a strange construction of the sore storme they met withall, saying, their Ship was bewitched, and therefore made use of the common Charme ignorant people use, nailing two red hot horse-shoos to their maine mast. But assuredly it was the Lord Christ, who hath command both of Winds and Seas, and now would have his people know he hath delivered, and will deliver from so great a death.

CHAP. XXX.

Of the Ninth Church of Christ, gathered at Ipswitch.

This year [1] came over a farther supply of Eminent instruments for furthering this admirable Worke of his, amongst whom the Reverend and judicious servant of Christ Mr. Nathaniel Ward, who tooke up his station at the Towne of

---

[1] *I. e.*, 1634.

Ipswich, where the faithfull servants of Christ gathered the Ninth Church of his. This Towne is scituated on a faire and delightfull River, whose first rise or spring begins about five and twenty Miles farther up in the Countrey, issuing forth a very pleasant pond. But soone after it betakes its course through a most hideous swamp of large extent, even for many Miles, being a great Harbour for Beares: after its comming forth this place, it groweth larger by the income of many small Rivers, and issues forth in the Sea, due East over against the Island of Sholes, a great place of fishing for our English Nation. The peopling of this Towne is by men of good ranke and quality, many of them having the yearly Revenue of large Lands in England before they came to this Wildernesse, but their Estates being imployed for Christ, and left in banke, as you have formerly heard, they are well content till Christ shall be pleased to restore it againe to them or theirs, which in all reason should be out of the Prelates Lands in England. Let all those, whom it concernes (to judge) consider it well, and do Justice herein.

This Towne lies in the Saggamooreship, or Earldome of Aggawam, now by our English Nation called Essex.[1] It is a very good Haven Towne, yet a little barr'd up at the Mouth of the River, some Marchants here are, (but Boston, being the chiefest place of resort of Shipping, carries away all the Trade). They have very good Land for Husbandry, where Rocks hinder not the course of the Plow: the Lord hath been pleased to increase them in Corne and Cattell of late; Insomuch that they have many hundred quarters to spare yearly, and feed, at the latter end of Summer, the Towne of Boston with good Beefe: their Houses are many of them very faire built with pleasant Gardens and Orchards, consisting of about one hundred and forty Families. Their meeting-house is a very good prospect to a great part of the Towne, and beautifully built; the Church of Christ here consists of about one hundred and sixty soules, being exact in their conversation, and free from the Epidemicall Disease of all Reforming Churches, which under Christ is procured by their pious Learned and

---

[1] The General Court in 1643 organized four shires or counties, Essex (northward from Boston to the Merrimac), Middlesex, Norfolk (northward from the Merrimac to the Piscataqua), and Suffolk (present Suffolk and Norfolk).

Orthodox Ministery, as in due place (God willing) shall be declared, in the meane time, look on the following Meeters concerning that Souldier of Christ Master Nathaniel Ward.[1]

> Thou ancient Sage, come Ward among
>   Christs folke, take part in this great worke of his,
> Why do'st thou stand and gaze about so long?
>   Do'st war in jest? why, Christ in earnest is,
> And hath thee arm'd with weapons for that end,
>   To wound and heale his enemies submitting,
> Not carnally; then to this worke attend.
>   Thou hast prevail'd the hearts of many hitting.
> Although the Presbytery unpleasant jar,
>   And errors daily in their braines new coyne,
> Despayer not; Christs truth they shall not mar,
>   But with his helpe such drosse from Gold refine.
> What, Man, dost meane to lay thy Trumpet downe,
>   Because thy son like Warrier is become?
> Hold out or sure lesse bright will be thy crowne;
>   Till death Christs servants labour is not done.

At this time came over the much honoured Mr. Richard Bellingham,[2] whose Estate and person did much further the civill Government of this wandering people, hee being learned in the Lawes of England, and experimentally fitted for the worke, of whom I am bold to say as followeth:

Richardus now arise must thou, Christ seed [feed?] hath thee to plead
  His peoples cause, with equall Laws, in wildernesse them lead;
Though slow of speech,[3] thy counsell reach, shall each occation well,
  Sure thy sterne looke it cannot brook those wickedly rebell.

---

[1] Nathaniel Ward, the celebrated and humorous author of *The Simple Cobler of Aggawam* (London, 1647), was another Emmanuel College man, and another victim of Laud. He resigned his Ipswich pastorate in 1636. Trained in youth as a lawyer, he was the author of the *Body of Liberties*, the first Massachusetts code of laws. In 1647 he returned to England, and died there. His son John, also of Emmanuel, became pastor of Haverhill in 1645; see *post*, bk. III., ch. I.

[2] Bellingham was recorder (municipal judge) of Boston, England, from 1625 to 1633, and was chosen governor of Massachusetts in 1641, in 1654, and in 1665. He was a learned lawyer, and useful to the colony, but difficult in temper. He was one of the original grantees of the patent.

[3] The historian Hubbard says that he was "like a vessel whose vent holdeth no good proportion with its capacity."

With labours might, thy pen indite doth Lawes for peoples learning,
  That judge with skill, and not with will, unarbitrate discerning;
Bellingham thou, on valiant now, stop not in discontent,
  For Christ with crown, will thee renown, then spend for him, be spent;
As thou hast done thy race still run till death, no death shall stay
  Christs work of might, till Scripture light bring Resurection day.

As also about this time for further incouragement in this
work of Christ, hee sent over the Reverend servant of his Mr.
Lothrop [1] to helpe on with the planting of Plimoth, which increased but little all this time, although shee be the elder
sister of all the united Colonies; Some reasons in due place
may be rendered. This Reverend Minister was soone called
to Office by the Church of Christ at Scicuate [Scituate].

CHAP. XXXI.

Of the Church of Christ gathered at Newberry.

In the latter end of this yeare, two sincere servants of
Christ, inabled by him with gifts to declare his minde unto his
people, came over this broad Ocean, and began to build the
Tenth Church of Christ at a Towne called Newberry, their
names being Mr. James Noise, and Mr. Thomas Parker,[2]
somewhat differing from all the former, and after mentioned
Churches in the preheminence of their Presbytery, and it
were to be wished that all persons, who have had any hand in
those hot contentions, which have fallen out since about
Presbyterian and Independent Government in Churches,[3]
would have looked on this Example, comparing it with the
Word of God, and assuredly it would have stayed (all the godly
at lest) of either part from such unworthy expressions as have

[1] Rev. John Lothrop, ancestor of John Lothrop Motley.

[2] Noyes and Parker were cousins, from Newbury in England. They upheld
at Newbury a partially Presbyterian polity, but not factiously. The book of
Parker's to which allusion is made in the ensuing verses is probably *The Visions
and Prophecies of Daniel Expounded* (London, 1646).

[3] The sessions of the Westminster Assembly, beginning in 1643, and the subsequent struggles between the Presbyterians in Parliament and the Independents
of the army gave rise to the controversial literature here alluded to—Ruther-
ford's *Due Right of Presbyteries* on the one hand, Cotton's and Hooker's treatises
on the other, etc.

passed, to the grief of many of Gods people; And I doubt not but this History will take of[f] that unjust accusation, and slanderous imputation of the rise of that floud of errors and false Doctrines sprung up of late, as flowing from the Independent or rather congregationall Churches. But to follow on, this Town is scituate about twelve miles from Ipswitch, neere upon the wide venting streames of Merrimeck River, whose strong current is such, that it hath forced its passage through the mighty Rocks, which causeth some sudden falls, and hinders Shipping from having any accesse far into the Land. Her bankes are in many places stored with Oken Timber of all sorts, of which, that which they commonly call'd white Oke, is not inferiour to our English Timber; in this River lie some few Islands of fertill Land. This Towne is stored with Meddow and upland, which hath caused some Gentlemen, (who brought over good Estates, and finding then no better way to improve them) to set upon husbandry, amongst whom that Religious and sincere hearted servant of Christ Mr. Richard Dummer, sometime a Magistrate in this little Common-wealth, hath holpen on this Town. Their houses are built very scattering, which hath caused some contending about removall of their place for Sabbath-Assemblies. Their Cattell are about foure hundred head, with store of Corne-land in tillage. It consists of about seventy Families, the soules in Church fellowship are about an hundred; the teaching Elders of this Congregation have carried it very lovingly toward their people, permitting of them to assist in admitting of persons into Church-society, and in Church-censures, so long as they Act regularly, but in case of their male-administration, they assume the power wholly to themselves. Their godly life and conversation hath hitherto been very amiable, and their paines and care over their flock not inferiour to many others, and being bound together in a more stricter band of love then ordinary with promise to spend their dayes together (if the Lord please) and therefore shall not be disunited in the following Verse:

> Loe here Loves twinnes by Christ are sent to Preach
>   In wildernesse his little flock among;
> Though Christs Church-way you fully cannot reach,
>   So far hold fast as you in's word are strong.

Parker thy paines with Pen, and Preaching hath
    Roomes buildings left in Prelacy cast downe,
Though 'gainst her thou defer Gods finall wrath,
    Keepe warring still, and sure thou shalt have crowne.
Thy Brother thou, oh Noise, hast holpe to guide
    Christ tender Lambs within his fold to gather,
From East to West, thou dost Christs Warrier bide;
    Faint not at last, increase thy fighting rather.

Chap. XXXII.

*Of good supply, and seasonable helpes the Lord Christ was
pleased to send to further his Wildernesse worke, and particular for his Churches of Charles Towne, and Ipswich,
and Dorchester.*

Yet farther for the incouragement of the people of Christ
in these their weak beginnings, he daily brings them in
fresh supplies, adding this yeare also the reverend and pain-
full Minister of his Gospell Mr. Zachary Simmes,[1] who was
invited soone after his comming over to assist in planting of
another Church of Christ, but the place being remote from
the pretious servants of Christ already setled, he chose rather
to joyne with some Church among them, and in a short space
after hee was called to the Office of a Teaching Elder in the
Church of Christ at Charles Towne, together with Mr. James,
who was then their Pastor, as you have formerly heard.
Among all the godly Women that came through the perilous
Seas to war their warfare, the wife of this zealous Teacher,
Mrs. Sarah Simmes shall not be omitted, nor any other, but
to avoid tediousnesse, the vertuous Woman, indued by Christ
with graces fit for a Wildernesse condition, her courage exceeding her stature, with much cheerfulnesse did undergoe
all the difficulties of these times of straites, her God through
Faith in Christ supplying all her wants with great industry,
nurturing up her young Children in the feare of the Lord,
their number being ten both Sons and Daughters, a certaine

[1] A Canterbury man, son of a clergyman, born there in the same year as
Johnson, and for whom the latter as a Charlestown parishioner had a special
affection.

signe of the Lords intent to people this vast Wildernesse:
God grant they may be valiant in Faith against Sin, Satan
and all the enemies of Christs Kingdome, following the example of their Father, and Grandfather, who have both suffered for the same, in remembrance of whom these following
lines are placed.

> Come Zachary, thou must reedifie
>   Christ Churches in this Desart Land of his,
> With Moses zeale stampt unto dust defie
>   All crooked wayes that Christ true worship misse.
> With spirits sword and armor girt about,
>   Thou lay'st on load proud Prelates crowne to crack,
> And wilt not suffer Wolfes thy flock to rout,
>   Though close they creepe, with sheepe skins on their back.
> Thy Fathers spirit doubled is upon
>   Thee Simmes, then war, thy Father fighting died,
> In prayer then prove thou like Champion;
>   Hold out till death, and Christ will crown provide.

After these poore people had welcomed with great joy their
newcome Guests, all of a sudden they spy two tall Ships,
whose colours shewed them to be some forrein Nation, at which
time this little handfull of people began to be much troubled,
deeming them to be Rovers, they gathered together such
forces as their present condition would afford, very ill-
fitted as then to rescue an enemy, but their Lord and Master
Christ Jesus would not suffer any such to come, and instead
of enemies brought in friends, even Dutchmen to furnish them
with farther necessary Provision.[1]

For the yeare 1635. the honoured Mr. John Haines was
chosen Governour, and the honoured Mr. Richard Bellingham Deputy Governour, the number of Free-men added to
this little Common-wealth, were about one hundred forty
and five. The time now approaching, wherein the Lord
Christ would have his people come from the Flaile to the Fan,
threshing out much this yeare, increasing the number of his
Troopes, and valiant Leaders, the Ships came thicker and
faster filled with many worthy personages; Insomuch that
the former people began to forget their Poverty, and verily

[1] See Winthrop, I., 151, 152.

could Purity, Peace and Plenty run all in one channell, Gods
people here should sure have met with none other, but the
still waters of Peace and Plenty for back and belly soone
contract much mudde, as you shall heare (God willing) in
the following History: this yeare came in the honoured Sir
Henry Vaine,[1] who aboad not long in this worthy worke, yet
mind him I will in the following Lines.

*Sir Henry Vaine once Governour of the English People in New
England.*

Thy Parents, Vaine, of worthy fame, in Christ and thou for him
    Through Ocean wide in new world tri[e]d a while his warrior bin.
With small defeat thou didst retreat to Brittaine ground againe,
    There stand thou stout, for Christ hold out, Christs Champion ay
        remaine.

Also at this time Christ sent over the much honoured
and upright hearted servant of his Richard Saltingstall
Esquire, Son to the before-named Sir Richard Saltingstall,
who being weary of this Wildernesse worke, returned home
againe not long before,[2] and now his Son being chose to the
Office of a Magistrate, continued for some good space of time,
helping on the affaires of this little Common-wealth, to the
honour of Christ, who hath called him: both Father and Son
are here remembred.

Thou worthy Knight, Saltingstall hight, her's gaine doth go.d exceed,
    Then trifle not, its to be got, if thou can'st see thy neede.
Why wilt thou back, and leave as wreck, this worthy worke begun,
    Art thou back-bore, Christ will send more, and raise instead thy son.
His Fathers gon, young Richard on here valiantly doth War,
    For Christ his truth, to their great Ruth, Heathens opposers are:
To study thou thy mind dost bow, and daily good promote,
    Saltingstall why then dost thou fly, let all Gods people note

---

[1] Sir Henry Vane the younger (1612–1662), son of a diplomatist and statesman, came to Massachusetts, a very young man, in 1635. A few months later he
was elected governor. In the Antinomian controversy he took the other side
from Winthrop and the orthodox majority. Defeated in a closely contested
election in the spring of 1637, he went home that summer. His career in the
Long Parliament was a brilliant and noble one, and finally he came to be its
chief leader. He was executed as a regicide after the accession of Charles II.

[2] See p. 74. The younger Saltonstall became an assistant in 1637.

That thou wilt stand in thy own Land, Christ there then strengthen
    thee,
  With grace thee heate, that thy retreate may for his glory be:
At ending day, he thee array with Glory will not faile,
  Breaking graves bands, with his strong hands, and free dust from
    death's goale [gaol].

    Among these Troopes of Christs Souldiers, came at this
time, the godly servant of Christ Mr. Roger Harlackenden,[1]
a young Gentleman valiant in Faith, and appointed by Christ
to assist his people in this Desart, he was chose to the Office
of a Magistrate, as also to be a choise Leader of their Military
Forces, which as yet were but in a strange posture; And
therefore till the yeare 1644. (at which time the Countrey was
really placed in a posture of War, to be in a readinesse at all
times) there shall not be any thing spoken concerning their
Military Discipline [2] the continuance of this Souldier of Christ
was but short, the Lord taking him to rest with himselfe.

Harlackenden, among these men of note Christ hath thee seated:
  In warlike way Christ thee aray with zeal, and love well heated.
As generall belov'd of all, Christ Souldiers honour thee:
  In thy young yeares, courage appeares, and kinde benignity.
Short are thy days spent to his praise, whose Church work thou must
    aid,
  His work shall bide, silver tride, but thine by death is staid.

    The number of Ministers that came over this yeare was
about eleaven, and many other like faithfull servants of Christ,
among whom arrived those two Reverend and laborious servants of his Mr. Norton, and Mr. Shepheard, of whose narrow
escape you have heard the last yeare: Mr. Norton was called
to the Office of a Teaching Elder, at the Towne of Ipswich to
the Church of Christ there, where Mr. Warde as yet remained
in Office. Also the learned labours of this Souldier of Christ
are obvious to our Countreymen; hee Preaching there, the
blessing of God hath not onely built up many in the Knowledge of Christ, but also been the meanes of converting diverse

    [1] A son of a rich landholder at Earl's Colne in Essex, where Shepard had
been minister, assistant from 1636 till his death in 1638, and chosen in 1636
lieutenant-colonel of the Middlesex regiment.
    [2] See bk. ii., ch. xxvi.

soules, turning them from the power of Satan to Faith in Christ, whom the Lord long continue; you shall further hear of Christs gratious assisting of him in the first and last Synod holden here at Cambridge, and in the meane time let no man be offended that the Author quickens up his own dull affections, in telling how largely the Lord hath bestowed his Graces upon these Instruments of his, although sinfull dust and ashes.

Thou Noble Norton, who art honoured by
    Thy Christ, with learned Arguments doth fill
Thy mouth with might new errors to destroy,
    And force deceivers silently to yeild.
Weake dust, waite on thy Christ for further strength,
    Who doth his Davids make as Angels bright,
To trample down his enemies at length;
    All breake or bow unto his Kingdomes might
Illettered Men and Women that doe love
    Preheminence, condemne thy learned skill,
But Christ hath given his blessing from above
    Unto thy workes the World with light to fill.
Christs faithfull servants met in Synod, take
    Thee for their Pen-men [Pen-man] Scriptures light to cleere,
With Scripture shew what Government Christ gave
    To's Churches till himselfe againe appeare.[1]

Here my indeared Reader, I must mind thee of the industrious servant of Christ Mr. John Wilson, who this yeare landed the third time upon this American shore from his Native Country, where now againe by the Divine Providence of Christ, hee narrowly escaped the Hunters hands, being cloathed in a Country-mans habit, passing from place to place, declared to the people of God, what great Workes Christ had already done for his people in New England, which made many Christian soules long to see these admirable Acts of Christ, although it were not to be injoyed, but by passing through an Ocean of troubles, Voyaging night and day upon the great deep, which this zealous servant of Christ had now five times passed over: at this time came over the Sage,

[1] The allusion is to Norton's reply to Rev. William Apollonius of Middelburg in Zeeland, which Norton wrote at the request of the Cambridge Synod of 1647, *Responsio ad Totam Quæstionum Syllogen à clarissimo Viro Dom. Guilielmo Apollonio propositam* (London, 1648).

grave, reverend and faithfull servant of Christ M. Richard Mather,[1] indued by the Lord with many Heavenly gifts, of a plaine and upright spirit, apt to teach, full of gratious expressions, and Resolvedly bent to follow the truth, as it is in Jesus, hee was anon after his comming called to Office in the Church of Christ at the Towne of Dorchester, to assist in the Worke of the Lord, with Mr. Mavareck, whose worke not long after was ended by death, leaving Mr. Mather alone to continue the same.

With cheerfull face Mather doth toile indure,
  In wildernesse spending the prime of's age,
To build Christs Churches, and soules health procure;
  In battell thou dost deepe thyselfe ingage.
Marvell not Man that Mather through an host
  Of enemies doth breake, and fighting stands,
It's Christ him keepes, of him is all his boast,
  Who power gives to do, and then commands.
With gratious speech thy Masters Message thou
  Declarest to all, and wouldst have submit,
That to his Kingdome every knee might bow;
  But those resist his sword shall surely hit.
Till age doth crown thy head with hory hairs,
  Well hast thou warr'd, till Mathers young againe,
Thy son in fight his Fathers strength repayers;
  Father and Son beate down Christs foes amaine.

Chap. XXXIII.

Of the beginning of the Churches of Christ, to be planted at Canectico, and first of the Church of Christ removall to Hartford, 1635.

This yeare the servants of Christ, who peopled the Towne of Cambridge, were put upon thoughts of removing, hearing of a very fertill place upon the River of Canectico,[2] low Land, and well stored with Meddow, which is greatly in esteeme

---

[1] Richard Mather, minister at Toxteth, near Liverpool, from 1618 to 1634, and at Dorchester, Massachusetts, from 1636 to 1669, was the father of Increase Mather, president of Harvard College, and grandfather of Cotton Mather (whose maternal grandfather was John Cotton). He has left an interesting account of his voyage to New England, printed in Young's *Chronicles of Massachusetts*.

[2] Connecticut.

with the people of New England, by reason the Winters are
very long. This people seeing that Tillage went but little on,
Resolved to remove, and breed up store of Cattell, which were
then at eight and twenty pound a Cow, or neare upon,[1] but
assuredly the Lord intended far greater matters than man
purposes, but God disposes. These men, having their hearts
gone from the Lord [Land], on which they were seated, soone
tooke dislike at every little matter; the Plowable plaines
were too dry and sandy for them, and the Rocky places, although more fruitfull, yet to eate their bread with toile of
hand and how [hoe] they deemed it unsupportable; And
therefore they onely waited now for a people of stronger
Faith then themselves were to purchase their Houses and
Land, which in conceipt they could no longer live upon, and
accordingly they met with Chapmen,[2] a people new come,
who having bought their possessions, they highed them away
to their new Plantation. With whom went the Grave and
Reverend servant of Christ Mr. Hooker, and Mr. Stone, for
indeed the whole Church removed, as also the much honoured Mr. Haynes and divers other men of note. For the
place, being out of the Mattacusets Patten, they erected
another Government, called by the Indian name, Canectico,
being farther incouraged by two honourable personages, the
Lord Say, and Lord Brookes, who built a Forrest [Fort]
at the mouth of the River, and called it Say-brook Forrest
[Fort]: passing up the River, they began to build a Towne,
which they called Hartford, where this Church of Christ sat
down their station.[3] There went to these parts also the
Reverend Mr. Wareham, and divers from the Towne of
Dorchester. The place of setling themselves, and erecting
a Towne was far up on the River, the part next the Sea
being very Rocky, but on the banke of this River they
planted the good Towne of Hartford, and established
civill Government: of their gathering into a Church, you
have formerly heard. Onely here minde the gratious servant of Christ, Mr. Wareham, whose long labours in this
worke are exprest.

---

[1] See also Bradford, p. 347, and Winthrop, I., 112.   [2] Purchasers.

[3] The founders of Hartford went overland to the Connecticut valley; and
the fort at Saybrook was built after their migration, not before.

With length of dayes Christ crowned hath thy head.
　In Wildernesse to manage his great War,
'Gainst Antichrist by strength of him art lead
　With steady hand to sling thy stone from far,
That groveling in his gore may lie smit downe
　This mighty Monster, that the Earth hath taken,
With's poysons sweet in cup of Gold drunke down;
　Dead drunke those lie whom Christ doth not awaken.
But Wareham thou by him art sent to save,
　With's word of truth Christ to their soules apply,
That deadly sin hath laid in rotting Grave
　Dead, live in Christ here, and Eternally.

CHAP. XXXIV.

*Of Cambridge second Church, being the 11. of Christ gathered
in the Mattacusets, and of further supply for Salem Church.*

These people and Church of Christ being thus departed
from New-towne, the godly people, who came in their roomes,
gathered the eleaventh Church of Christ, and called to the Office
of a Pastor, that gratious sweete Heavenly minded, and soule-
ravishing Minister, Mr. Thomas Shepheard, in whose soule
the Lord shed abroad his love so abundantly, that thousands
of souls have cause to blesse God for him, even at this very
day, who are the Seale of his Ministrey, and hee a man of a
thousand, indued with abundance of true saving knowledge
for himselfe and others, yet his naturall Parts were weake,
but spent to the full as followeth:

No hungry Hawkes poore Patridge to devoure
　More eager is, then Prelates Nimrod power
Thomas to hunt, my Shephard sweet pursue
　To seas brinke, but Christ saves his soule for you;
Sending thee, Shepheard, safe through Seas awaie,
　To feede his flock unto thy ending day,
Where (sheepe seek wolves) thy bosome lambs would catch;
　But night and day thou ceasest not to watch
And warne with teares thy flock of cheaters vile,
　Who in sheepes cloathing would the weak beguile;
With dropping dewes from thy lips Christ hath made
　Thy hearers eyes oft water springing blade.

With pierced hearts they cry aloud and say,
  Shew us, sweet Shepheard, our salvations way,
Thy lovely speech such ravishment doth bring;
  Christ gives thee power to heale as well as sting.
Thou gates sets ope for Christ thy King to enter,
  In hearts of many spirits joy to center,
But mourne my Muse, hang downe thy head with woe,
  With teares, sighs, sobs lament thy Shepheard so.[1]
(Why?) hee's in Heaven, but I one [on] Earth am left,
  More Earthly, 'cause of him I am bereft.
Oh Christ why dost thou Shepheard take away,
  In erring times when sheepe most apt to stray.

The many Souldiers and Officers of Christ that came
over this yeare, moved some wonder in the mindes of those,
whom he had beene pleased to give a great measure of
discerning, yet here they fell abundantly short, deeming
almost an impossibility of improving their Talents in this
Wildernesse, the Indian-people being uncapable of understanding their Language, the Englishe congregations that
were already set downe being fully furnished with Teaching Elders, and that which was most strange they were
perswaded they should meet with no enemies to oppose
them, as if Christ would lead them forth into the Field
in vaine. But Christ Jesus, having the hearts of all Men
opened before him, soon shewed them their worke, and
withall made roome for them to set downe, I [ay] and many
more beside, yea, and beyond expectation made this poore
barren Wildernesse become a fruitfull Land unto them that
waited on him for the accomplishing thereof, feeding them
with the flower of Wheat, as in its time and place (God
willing) shall be shewed, although it pleased him this yeare
to visit them, and try them againe with a great scarcity
of Bread, by reason of the multitude that came brought
somewhat shorter Provisions then ordinary, which caused them
to be in some straites. But their Lord Christ gives out a
Word of command to those, who occupy their businesse in
the great deepe, to furnish from Ireland some Ships laden
with food for his people.

----

[1] Shepard died in 1649.

Also hee commands the Winds and the Seas to beare up these Ships, and blow them forth on their way, till they arrive among his people in New England, whose appetities were now sharpeset for Bread. One poore man among others deeming hee had found out some forsaken Barnes of the Indians (whose manner is to lay up their Corne in the Earth), lighted one [on] a grave where finding bones of the dead instead of Corne, hee was taken with feare of this, as a sad omen that hee should then die for want of food, but in this hee proved no true Prophet, for the Lord was pleased to bring in seasonable supply, and the man is living at this very day. This yeere came over the Famous servant of Christ M. Hugh Peters,[1] whose courage was not inferiour to any of these transported servants of Christ, but because his native Soile hath had the greatest share of his labours, the lesse will be said of him here; hee was called to Office by the Church of Christ, at Salem, their former Pastor the Reverend M. Higgingson, having ended his labours resting with the Lord.

With courage bold Peters a Souldier stout
  In Wildernesse for Christ begins to war,
Much worke he finds 'mongst people, yet hold out;
  With fluent tongue he stops phantastick jar.
Swift Torrent stayes of liberties large vent,
  Through crooked wayes of error daily flowing,
Shiloes soft streames to bath in would all bent;
  Should he while they in Christian freedome growing.
But back thou must, thy Tallents Christ will have
  Improved for him, his glory is thy crowne,
And thou base dust till he thee honour gave;
  It matters not though the world on thee do frown.

[1] Rev. Hugh Peter or Peters was already a famous man at the time of his arrival in New England. He had lately been pastor of the English church in Rotterdam. His six years in the colony were marked by activity and influence on the illiberal side in church controversies, but also by great energy in the promotion of practical schemes for the economic betterment of the colony. Returning to England in 1641, he took a leading part, as preacher and politician, among the Independents. In 1660, after the return of Charles II., he was executed for high treason as having been concerned in the beheading of Charles I.

Chap. XXXV.

Of the Twelfth Church of Christ gathered at Concord.

Yet further at this time entered the Field two more valiant Leaders of Christs Souldiers, holy men of God, Mr. Buckly and M. Jones, penetrating further into this Wildernesse then any formerly had done, with divers other servants of Christ: they build an Inland Towne which they called Concord, named from the occasion of the present time, as you shall after heare:¹ this Towne is seated upon a faire fresh River, whose Rivulets are filled with fresh Marsh, and her streames with Fish, it being a branch of that large River of Merrimeck. Allwifes and Shad in their season come up to this Towne, but Salmon and Daice cannot come up by reason of the Rocky falles, which causeth their Meddowes to lie much covered with water, the which these people together with their Neighbour Towne, have severall times assayed to cut through but cannot, yet it may be turned another way with an hundred pound charge, as it appeared. This Towne was more populated once then now it is. Some faint-hearted Souldiers among them fearing the Land would prove barren, sold their possessions for little, and removed to a new Plantation, (which have most commonly a great prize set on them). The number of Families at present are about 50. their buildings are conveniently placed chiefly in one straite streame [streete] under a sunny banke in a low levell, their heard of great Cattell are about 300. The Church of Christ here consists of about seventy soules, their teaching Elders were Mr. Buckly,² and Mr. Jones, who removed from them with that part of the people, who went away, so that onely the reverend grave and godly Mr. Buckly remaines.

> Riches and honours Buckly layes aside
>   To please his Christ, for whom he now doth war,
> Why Buckly thou hast Riches that will bide,
>   And honours that exceeds Earths honour far.

---

¹ The name is understood to have been given to the town on account of the peaceful agreement with the Indians for its purchase.

² Rev. Peter Bulkley, fellow of St. John's College, and a minister silenced for non-conformity, had, says Cotton Mather, "a good benefice, added unto the estate of a gentleman, left him by his father," a doctor of divinity in Bedford-

Thy bodies [body's] worne, and dayes in Desert spent
   To feede a few of Christs poore scattered sheepe;
Like Christ's bright body, thy poore body, rent,
   With Saints and Angells company shall keepe.
Thy Tongue, and Pen doth to the World declare
   Christs covenant with his flock shall firmly stand,
When Heavens and Earth by him dissolved are;
   Then who can hold from this his worke at hand?
Two Bucklies more Christ by his grace hath taken,
   And sent abroad to manage his great wars.
It's Buklies joy that Christ his sons new making,
   Hath placest [placed] in's churches for to shine as Stars.

This holy and sincere servant of Christ was put upon the greater tryall, by reason he and his were tenderly brought up, and now by the provident hand of Christ were carried far into this desert land, where they met with some hardships for a long time; till the place was well peopled, they lived barely.

Chap. XXXVI.

Of the laborious worke Christ's people have in planting this wildernesse, set forth in the building the Towne of Concord, being the first in-land Towne.

Now because it is one of the admirable acts of Christ['s] Providence in leading his people forth into these Westerne Fields, in his providing of Huts for them, to defend them from the bitter stormes this place is subject unto, therefore here is a short Epitome of the manner how they placed downe their dwellings in this Desart Wildernesse, the Lord being pleased to hide from the Eyes of his people the difficulties they are to encounter withall in a new Plantation, that they might not thereby be hindered from taking the worke in hand; upon some inquiry of the Indians, who lived to the North-west of the Bay, one Captaine Simon Willard being acquainted with

shire. The book alluded to in the verses is *The Gospel Covenant, or the Covenant of Grace Opened* (London, 1646); the two sons (he had twelve), Rev. Edward Bulkley, his successor in the Concord church, and Rev. John Bulkley, who after graduating in the first class of Harvard College (1642) went to England and ministered to a church in Essex till deprived by the Act of Uniformity.

them, by reason of his Trade, became a chiefe instrument in erecting this Town, the land they purchase of the Indians, and with much difficulties traveling through unknowne woods, and through watery scrampes [swampes], they discover the fitnesse of the place, sometimes passing through the Thickets, where their hands are forced to make way for their bodies passage, and their feete clambering over the crossed Trees, which when they missed they sunke into an uncertaine bottome in water, and wade up to the knees, tumbling sometimes higher and sometimes lower, wearied with this toile, they at end of this meete with a scorching plaine, yet not so plaine, but that the ragged Bushes scratch their legs fouly, even to wearing their stockings to their bare skin in two or three houres; if they be not otherwise well defended with Bootes, or Buskings, their flesh will be torne: (that some being forced to passe on without further provision) have had the bloud trickle downe at every step, and in the time of Summer the Sun casts such a reflecting heate from the sweet Ferne, whose scent is very strong so that some herewith have beene very nere fainting, although very able bodies to undergoe much travell, and this not to be indured for one day, but for many, and verily did not the Lord incourage their naturall parts (with hopes of a new and strange discovery, expecting every houre to see some rare sight never seene before) they were never able to hold out, and breake through: but above all, the thirsting desires these servants of Christ have had to Plant his Churches, among whom the forenamed Mr. Jones [1] shall not be forgotten.

> In Desart's depth where Wolves and Beares abide,
>   There Jones sits down a wary watch to keepe,
> O're Christs deare flock, who now are wandered wide;
>   But not from him, whose eyes ne're close with sleepe.
> Surely it sutes thy melancholly minde,
>   Thus solitary for to spend thy dayes,
> Much more thy soule in Christ content doth finde,
>   To worke for him, who thee to joy will raise.

[1] After about eight years John Jones, pastor of the Concord church (which had found it difficult to maintain two "teaching elders"), removed to Fairfield, Connecticut, where he died in 1665. His son John (A. B. Harvard, 1643) went to preach in the island of Nevis in the West Indies.

Leading thy son to Land, yet more remote,
To feede his flock upon this Westerne wast:
Exhort him then Christs Kingdome to promote;
That he with thee of lasting joyes may tast.

Yet farther to tell of the hard labours this people found in Planting this Wildernesse, after some dayes spent in search, toyling in the day time as formerly is said; like true Jacob, its [1] they rest them one [on] the Rocks where the night takes them, their short repast is some small pittance of Bread, if it hold out, but as for Drinke they have plenty, the Countrey being well watered in all places that yet are found out. Their farther hardship is to travell, sometimes they know not whether, bewildred indeed without sight of Sun, their compasse miscarrying in crouding through the Bushes, they sadly search up and down for a known way, the Indians paths being not above one foot broad, so that a man may travell many dayes and never find one. But to be sure the directing Providence of Christ hath beene better unto them than many paths, as might here be inserted, did not hast call my Pen away to more waighty matters; yet by the way a touch thus, it befell with a servant maide, who was travelling about three or foure miles from one Towne to another, loosing her selfe in the Woods, had very diligent search made after her for the space of three dayes, and could not possible be found, then being given over as quite lost, after three dayes and nights, the Lord was pleased to bring her feeble body to her own home in safety, to the great admiration of all that heard of it.[2] This intricate worke no whit daunted these resolved servants of Christ to goe on with the worke in hand, but lying in the open aire, while the watery Clouds poure down all the night season, and sometimes the driving Snow dissolving on their backs, they keep their wet cloathes warme with a continued fire, till the renewed morning give fresh opportunity of further travell; after they have thus found out a place of aboad, they burrow themselves in the Earth for their first shelter under some Hill-side, casting the Earth aloft upon Timber; they make a smoaky fire against the Earth at the highest side,

[1] Misprint for Jacobites. See p. 74, n. 1, ante.
[2] See Winthrop's *Journal*, I. 98.

and thus these poore servants of Christ provide shelter for themselves, their Wives and little ones, keeping off the short showers from their Lodgings, but the long raines penetrate through, to their great disturbance in the night season: yet in these poore Wigwames they sing Psalmes, pray and praise their God, till they can provide them houses, which ordinarily was not wont to be with many till the Earth, by the Lords blessing, brought forth Bread to feed them, their Wives and little ones, which with sore labours they attaine every one that can lift a hawe [hoe] to strike it into the Earth, standing stoutly to their labours, and teare up the Rootes and Bushes, which the first yeare beares them a very thin crop, till the soard [sward] of the Earth be rotten, and therefore they have been forced to cut their bread very thin for a long season. But the Lord is pleased to provide for them great store of Fish in the spring time, and especially Alewives about the bignesse of a Herring; many thousands of these, they used to put under their Indian Corne, which they plant in Hills five foote asunder, and assuredly when the Lord created this Corne, hee had a speciall eye to supply these his peoples wants with it, for ordinarily five or six graines doth produce six hundred.

As for flesh they looked not for any in those times (although now they have plenty) unlesse they could barter with the Indians for Venison or Rockoons,[1] whose flesh is not much inferiour unto Lambe, the toile of a new Plantation being like the labours of Hercules never at an end, yet are none so barbarously bent (under the Mattacusets especially) but with a new Plantation they ordinarily gather into Church-fellowship, so that Pastors and people suffer the inconveniences together, which is a great meanes to season the sore labours they undergoe, and verily the edge of their appetite was greater to spirituall duties at their first comming in time of wants, than afterward: many in new Plantations have been forced to go barefoot, and bareleg, till these latter dayes, and some in time of Frost and Snow: Yet were they then very healthy more then now they are: in this Wildernesse-worke men of Estates speed no better than others, and some much worse for want of being inured to such hard labour,

---

[1] Raccoons.

having laid out their estate upon cattell at five and twenty
pound a Cow, when they came to winter them with in-land
Hay, and feed upon such wild Fother as was never cut before,
they could not hold out the Winter, but ordinarily the first
or second yeare after their comming up to a new Plantation,
many of their Cattell died, especially if they wanted Salt-
marshes: and also those, who supposed they should feed upon
Swines flesh were cut short, the Wolves commonly feasting
themselves before them, who never leave neither flesh nor
bones, if they be not scared away before they have made an
end of their meale. As for those who laid out their Estate
upon Sheepe, they speed worst of any at the beginning (although some have sped the best of any now) for untill the
Land be often fed with other Cattell Sheepe cannot live;
And therefore they never thrived till these latter dayes:
Horse had then no better successe, which made many an honest
Gentleman travell a foot for a long time, and some have even
perished with extreame heate in their travells: as also the
want of English graine, Wheate, Barly and Rie proved a sore
affliction to some stomacks, who could not live upon Indian
Bread and water, yet were they compelled to it till Cattell
increased, and the Plowes could but goe: instead of Apples
and Peares, they had Pomkins and Squashes of divers kinds.
Their lonesome condition was very grievous to some, which
was much aggravated by continuall feare of the Indians approach, whose cruelties were much spoken of, and more especially during the time of the Peqot wars.

Thus this poore people populate this howling Desart, march-
ing manfully on (the Lord assisting) through the greatest difficulties, and forest labours that ever any with such weak means
have done.

CHAP. XXXVII.

Of the Thirteenth Church of Christ gathered at Hingham, 1636.[1]

At this time also came to shore the servant of Christ
Master Peter Hubbord, whom the Lord was pleased to make
use of for feeding his people in this Wildernesse, being called

[1] The gathering of the Hingham church took place in September, 1635,
preceding by ten months that of the church of Concord, July, 1636. The name

to Office by the Church of Christ at the Town of Hingham,
which is scituate upon the Sea coasts South-east of Charles
River, being a place nothing inferiour to their Neighbours
for scituation, and the people have much profited themselves
by transporting Timber, Planke and Mast for Shipping to the
Town of Boston, as also Ceder and Pine-board to supply the
wants of other Townes, and also to remote parts, even as far
as Barbadoes. They want not for Fish for themselves and
others also.

This Towne consisted of about sixty Families, the forme is
somewhat intricate to describe, by reason of the Seas wasting
crookes, where it beates upon a mouldering shore, yet have
they compleat streetes in some places. The people joyned
in Church covenant in this place, were much about an hundred
soules, but have been lessened by a sad unbrotherly contention, which fell out among them, wasting them every way,
continued already for seven yeares space,[1] to the great griefe
of all other Churches, who held out the right hand of fellowship unto them in Brotherly communion, which may (the
Lord helping) demonstate to all the true Churches of Christ
the World throughout, although they be distanced by place
or Nation, yet ought they never to take up such an Independent way, as to reject the advise and counsell of each other,
for although the Lord Christ have compleated his commission
in giving full power to every particular Church to exercise all
his Ordinances in and toward their owne body, yet hath the
Lord so dispensed his gifts, that when the one want, the other
shall abound both in spirituall and temporall, that by giving
and receiving mutuall love may be maintained, the intire
truthes of Christ continued, the Churches of Christ supported,
superiority of any may be avoided, and all such as raise dis-
cord among Brethren may be retarded, the downfall of Anti-

was given because the pastor, Hobart, and many of the flock came from Hingham
in Norfolk, England. He was of Magdalene College, Cambridge, and was for
nearly forty-five years pastor of this church.

[1] A dispute broke out in Hingham in 1645, about a militia election. Trivial
in itself, it raised important questions concerning the authority of the magistrates of the colony and the liberties of the people. Winthrop was involved, and
his account of the matter, *Journal*, II. 229-245, including his "little speech" on
liberty, shows him at his best. Hobart's tendency to Presbyterianism aided, as
is intimated in the ensuing phrases and in the verses below, to prolong the dispute.

christ, and restauration of that antient people of the Lord furthered, through the Unity of Christs Churches the World throughout: this Church I hope will give signall to others (the Lord assisting) that they split not upon the Rock. Of their Pastors I shall say no more, but this at present.

> Oh Hubbard! why do'st leave thy native soile?
>   Is't not to war 'mongst Christ's true worthies here?
> What, wilt give out? thou'lt loose thy former toile
>   And starve Christs flock, which he hath purchast deare.
> What would's thou have, speake plaine, truth bides the light:
>   To Gods word goe, it's that must triall be,
> Hath cruell sword, not het one [hit on] thy side right,
>   Increase in love, and thou wilt Justice see.
> With humble, holy, learned men converse,
>   Thee and thy flock they would in one unite,
> And all the fogs of selfe conceit disperse;
>   Thee and thy sons the Lord Christ guide aright.

Some other of the Ministers of Christ arrived this yeare 1635. As Mr. Flint,[1] Mr. Carter, and Mr. Walton and some others, of whom we shall speake (by the Lord assistance) in due time and place, in the meane time here is to be remembred Mr. Thomas Flint a sincere servant of Christ, who had a faire yearly Revenue in England, but having improved it for Christ, by casting it in the common Treasury,[2] as it appeares in the former part of this History, he waites on the Lord for doubling his Talent, if it shall seeme good unto him so to doe, and the meane time spending his person for the good of his people in the Office of a Magistrate.

> At Christs commands, thou leav'st thy lands, and native habitation:
>   His folke to aid, in Desart straid, for Gospells Exaltation,
> Flint Hardy thou, wilt not allow, the underminding Fox,
>   With subtill skill, Christs vines to spill, thy sword shall give them
>   knocks.
> Yet thou base dust, and all thou hast, is Christ's, and by him thou
> Art made to be, such as we see, hold fast for ever now.

---

[1] Henry Flint, afterward teacher of the church at Braintree; see p. 197, *post.* Thomas Carter became Johnson's pastor at Woburn; see pp. 215–218.

[2] He brought £2,000 to the colony, but died a poor man.

Chap. XXXVIII

Of the placing down of many Souldiers of Christ, and gathering
the Church of Christ at Sandwitch in Plimouth patten,[1] and
further supply for the Churches of Ipswich and Linne.

This yeare 1636. Sir Henry Vaine, was chosen Governour,
and John Winthrope Esquire Deputy Governour, the number
of Freemen added were about eighty three.[2]   This yeare came
over the much honoured Mr. Fenwick [3] a godly and able instrument to assist in helping to uphold the civill Government
of the second and third Colonies here planted, by the Divine
Providence of the most high God, hee having purchased the
Plantation of Saybrooke-Fort, became a good incourager to
the Church of Christ at Hartford, where the reverend Mr.
Hooker, and Mr. Stone were Officers.   In remembrance of
whom a few lines take here.

Fenwick among this Christian throng, to wildernesse doth flee:
   There learn'd hast thou, yet further how, Christ should advanced be.
Who for that end, doth back thee send, their Senator to sit; [4]
   In native soile for him still toile, while thou hast season fit.
His Churches peace, do not thou cease, with their increase to bring,
   That they and thee, in lasting Glee, may Hallelujah sing.

The beginning of this yeare was spent in accommodating
these new come Guests in the former yeare, whose numbers
was neer about three thousand, and now they began to be
perswaded they should be a setled people, not minding the
present dangers they were in, as you shall hear anon, onely
in the meane time take notice of further supply the Lord Christ
was pleased to send before the cattell increased to its strength,
among whom the aged, and long continued Souldiers of Christ
Jesus Mr. Partrich, as also Mr. Nathaniel Rogers an able dis-

---

[1] Duxbury in Plymouth patent.   [2] Actually, 96.

[3] George Fenwick, previously a barrister of Gray's Inn, and subsequently
a colonel in the Parliamentary army, visited New England in 1636 as agent of
Lord Saye and Sele and Lord Brooke, Puritan lords who had obtained a patent
from the Earl of Warwick.   Coming again in 1639 he founded a settlement at
Saybrook, which in 1644 he transferred to the colony of Connecticut.

[4] He sat in the Long Parliament and the Parliaments of the Protectorate,
from 1645 to the time of his death in 1656.

putant, whose mouth the Lord was pleased to fill with many arguments for the defence of his truth, Mr. Samuel Whiting, who hath also, with keeping to the patterne of sound and wholesome Doctrine, much stopped the spreading Leaven of the Pharises.   Mr. Partrich was called to Office at a Towne then named Dukes Berry [1] in Plimoth Government, scituated upon the Sea-coast, where the people of Christ being gathered into a Church, Ordained him to be their Pastor.

> In thine owne soile well rooted in the truth,
>   Thou didst stand fast by Prelates power unbow'd,
> But Laude layes load on Gods folke to his Ruth,
>   By whom thou mayst no longer be alow'd.
> Then Partrich thou thy wings begins to spread
>   Of Faith and Love to flie these long Seas o're,
> To wildernesse where thou Christs Lambs hast fed
>   With's sincere Milke this fourteene yeare and more.
> But now with age thy Almon Tree doth flourish,
>   Yet spreading like the Palme Tree dost thou stand,
> I'th'house of God, Christ Roote thy Boughs do nourish;
>   And for thy head he hath a Crowne in's hand.

Mr. Nathaniel Rogers being landed, after a long and tedious Voyage at Sea,[2] was welcomed by the Church of Christ at Ipswitch, where the Reverened and Judicious Mr. Nathaniel Ward, although a very able Preacher, and much desired, yet for some naturall infirmity (himselfe being best privy unto) desired to be unbound of his ingagement with his people in point of Office: that being left to his liberty, hee might Preach more seldom, in whose stead the Church called to Office this Reverend and Holy Man of God Mr. Nathaniel Rogers, whose labours in this Westerne World, have been very much: a very sweet heavenly minded man, of whom the Author is bold to say as followeth:

> Through boystrous Seas thy brittle frame of Man
>   It safely is in Christ's sweet armes infold,
> No wonder then thou weake dust stotly [stoutly] can
>   Preach Christs in's truths, why he doth thee uphold?

---

[1] Duxbury, where Rev. Ralph Partridge, the most influential minister in the Plymouth colony, served nearly twenty-two years.

[2] See Winthrop, I. 199, 200.

Why Rogers he thee over-Sea hath sett
    Against the day of Battell, now at hand,
No sooner are thy feet one [on] those shores set,
    But Leaders do Christ truth withstand.
Undaunted thou these Westerne Fields dost enter,
    Filld with the spirit's ready sword at hand,
Ingage thou wilt thy selfe, 'mongst hardships venter;
    Valiant thou foughtst under thy Christ's command
And yet with all men wouldst have peace thy aime,
    If deepe to wound, and sweetly then to say,
Come to my Christ, hee'l heale your wounds againe;
    Canst but submit hee'l never say thee nay.
With learned Method thou Gods Word divides:
    Long labouring that each soule may take his part,
Thy gratious speech with grave impression bides;
    Thus Christ by thee is pleas'd to win the heart.
My Muse lament, Nathaniel is decaying:[1]
    Why dost thou grutch him Heaven, such toile hath had,
In Christ his Vineyard rather be thou praying;
    That in Christs armes he resting may be glad.

Mr. Samuel Whiting[2] was well welcomed by the Church of
Christ at Cawgust [Saugus], which Towne, being now of age to
receive an English name, was called Linne, where this Reverend man now hath his aboade.

Thy ardent Love, the countlesse Ocean's measure
    Quench cannot, for thy love on him is set,
Who of true love hath aie the depthlesse Treasure,
    Doth thine increase, least thou should'st his forget.
Love Christ in's truths, my Whiting, thou hast done:
    Thou wilt not suffer with their leaven sower,
False Doctrines 'mongst thy tender flock to run;
    Timely cut off wilt thou all those devour.
Samuel mourne not thy strength in Desart's spent:
    Rather rejoyce thy Christ makes use of thee
Soules to convert, his Kingdomes large extent
    From East to West shall shortly setled be.

[1] He died in 1655.
[2] Whiting, son of a mayor of Boston, in Lincolnshire, and a graduate of
Emmanuel College, had been for some years a preacher at Lynn, England.

Thine Eyes and Eares have seen and heard great things
Done by thy Christ, shewes he thy toile accepts;
Though thy weake flesh weaker to dust hee'l bring,
Thy quickned spirit increast in his joy leaps.

CHAP. XXXIX.

*Of the first appearing in the Field, of the enemies of Christs
people in point of Reformation.*

And now to follow our first simile of a Souldier, the Lord
Christ having safely landed many a valiant Souldier of his
on these Westerne shores, drawes hither also the common
enemies to Reformation, both in Doctrine and Discipline;
But it was for like end, as the Lord sometime drew Sisera the
Captaine of Jabins army to the River Kishon for their destruction,[1] onely herein was a wide difference; there Sisera was
delivered into the hands of a Woman, and here Sisera was a
woman; their weapons and warre was carnall, these spirituall;
there Jabin was but a man, here Jabin was the common
enemy of mans salvation.

In the yeare 1636. the Angels of the severall Churches of
Christ in N. England sounding forth their silver Trumpets,
heard ever and anon the jarring sound of ratling Drums in
their eares, striking up an alarum to the battell, it being a
frequent thing publikely to oppose the pure and perfect truths
of Christ (delivered by the mouth of his Ministers) and that
by way of question as the Pharises, Sadduces and Herodians
did Christ.   But to bring this disorderly worke of theirs into
some order, for assuredly could the Author come up to relate
the full of the matter in hand, it would through the mercy of
Christ make much for the good of Gods people the World
throughout, and helpe to discover the last (I hope) but most
subtile practices of Satan to hinder the Restauration of the
purity of Christs Ordinances in his Churches in all places;
As also used by him and his instruments to divert the hands
of those, to whom it belongs, from pulling downe Antichrist,
to which end he stirreth up some of his instruments (well

[1] Judges iv. and v.

educated in the Masking schoole of Hippocrisy) to take upon them this long Voyage, giving them in charge by all meanes to carry it more close, then his Jesuites had done, and for their paines they should have the honours to be counted such as were of a sharper sight, and deeper discerning then any others. Satan, knowing right well that at the fall of Antichrist hee must be chained up for a thousand years, strives with all the wicked craft his long experienced maliciousnesse could possibly invent, to uphold the same, having already perswaded many that his Kingdome was wholly ruinated with our English Nation, and so diswaded them a long time from further prosecuting against him. But Antichrists Kingdome, as it plainly appeares by Scripture, consists chiefly in two parts, his deceaveible Doctrines, and his Kingly power. The first of these being in measure abolished, the latter was still retained by the Prelacy, and some Lording Presbytery in greater or lesser measure, as they could attaine unto it.

Now Satan, who is daily walking to and fro compassing the Earth, seeing how these resolved Souldiers of Christ in New England with indefatigable paines laboured, not onely the finall ruine of Antichrist, in both, but also the advance of Christs Kingdome, in seting up daily Churches according to his first institution. Wherefore he sets upon a new way to stop (if it were possible) this worke of Reformation, and seeing no other way will serve, he stirs up instruments to cry down Antichrist as much as the most, I [ay] and more too, but by this project they should leade people as much out of the way on the other hand, and in the Doctrinall part of Antichrists Kingdome, fall to more horrid Blasphemies then the Papist, as (God willing) you shall heare some of them did, namely the Gortenist, who most blasphemously professe themselves to be personally the Christ: and as for the other part of his Kingdome, namely the power or Dominion of the beast, this they should with all violence batter downe also, but it must be none other then to make way for their owne exaltation, and pay them their wages in the former page promised them, as also withall to overthrow the authority Christ hath ordained to be continued in his Chūrches, in and under him, and furthermore to lock up the Sword of Civill Government for ever, especially in matters that concerne the foure first Commands of God,[1] a cunning way to save the beasts head whole.

You have now heard of the intention, you shall now see their actions. The Lord Christ in his boundlesse mercy give all his people eyes to see, and hearts to believe, that after they have in measure escaped the filthy pollutions of the beast, they may not againe be intangled with these damnabled Doctrines, stealing away their hearts by degrees, under a seeming shew of pulling down Antichrist. The Embassadors of Christ Jesus, having full liberty to deliver their masters minde, Preach unto all the Doctrine of Free grace, beseeching them to be reconciled unto God in Christ, and that the revealed will of God is, that all should be saved, and come to the knowledge of the truth, and that God hath given his onely begotten Son, That whosoever believeth in him should not perish, but have everlasting Life. Yet withall minding them that Faith is the gift of God, and none can come unto Christ, but such as the Father drawes, and withall that the whole will not see any need of the Phisicians, but the sick, adding also that none can come to the sight of his sicknesse or dead condition but by the Law of God, unlesse they be quicker sighted then the Apostle; They indevour also to build up others in their holy Faith, that they might come to see the Love of God in Christ which passeth knowledge, and to this end they shew them the fruits of Faith which worketh by love, and that love will be obedient to all the commands of Christ, who saith, if you love me keepe my Commandements; And further that Faith purifies the heart, and that a constant supply must be had from Christ. With these and the like sound and wholsome truths the Ministers of Christ feeds their severall flocks in New England, drawing their Doctrines plainly from their Text, and substantially backing them with store of Scripture, and undeniable reason, and then delivering to every man his portion.

[1] Classing the first four Commandments as those prescribing man's duty to God (the "First Table"), and the remaining six as those prescribing his duty to his neighbor (the "Second Table"), the Massachusetts government maintained, and dissentients like Roger Williams denied, the right of the magistrates to punish for infractions of the First Table.

But this good old way would not serve the turne with certaine Sectaries that were hither come,[1] who like cunning Sophisters, seeing the bent of the peoples hearts (after so many mercies received) was to magnifie the rich Grace of God in Christ; they began to tell the people (yet very privately) that the most, if not all the Ministers among them Preached a Covenant of workes, either course or fine, and with a what doe you say to this, They begin to spread their Errors and Heresies, laying the foundation of them as nere the truth as possible they can, the easier to deceive, but in the prosecution, to be sure they ran far enough from it, but to begin; First, they quarrell with the Doctrine of Faith in Christ, and say, a Soule is justified without it.

Chap. XL.

Of the cunning policy of Satan in that machevillian Principle, divide and overcome, and of the two first dividing Principles, by which many errors were brought in.

And verily Satans policy here (as in all places where the Lord Christ is acknowledged) was to keepe men from that one right way, by the which hee applies himselfe to the soule, no marvell then if so many Errours arise, like those fained heads

---

[1] We are not to expect that one of Johnson's temperament should give us a perfectly fair account of those who opposed the standing order in Massachusetts, the theocracy so sacred in his eyes and so infallible. The gainsaying which he is about to describe is that of the so-called Antinomians, who, led by Mrs. Anne Hutchinson and Rev. John Wheelwright, maintained that saving grace went only to such as were "justified by faith"; that, this grace once received, the recipient was above law, above the "Covenant of Works"; and that no works, no degree of sanctification, could prove that one was the possessor of saving grace. Mrs. Hutchinson carried a majority of the Boston church with her for a time, and Cotton partially. After a bitter and dangerous struggle the orthodox prevailed, dissent was suppressed, sectaries were banished; and Johnson, as we shall see, thinks it advisable, for the peace of Zion, to suppress the names alike of those who led, of those who fell, and of those who wavered. For his own part, he has plainly had no doubts; he is moved only to indignation mingled with mirth by the talk of those who presume "in thought's abstractest forms to seem to see"— and do not see as constituted authority sees. The best account of the whole affair is that in Mr. Charles Francis Adams's *Three Episodes of Massachusetts History.*

of Hidra, as fast as one is cut off two stand up in the roome,
and chiefly about the uniting of a soule to Christ by Faith.
Their Errors in this point they reported to be the judgement
of the Reverend and Judicious Mr. John Cotten; But hee
having spoken for himselfe in his answer to Mr. Baily,[1] I forbeare, onely this by the way, take notice of these subtill Pro-
jectors, the Erronist I meane, who perceiving this holy man
of God Mr. Cotten was and yet is in great esteeme with the
people of God, for the great grace Christ hath bestowed upon
him in his deepe discerning the mysteries of godlinesse, as
also discerning some little difference betweene him and the
other Elders about this point, comment upon it, and inlarge
at their pleasure, and then in daily venting their deceivable
Doctrines, like subtill Logicians, bring in this as their strongest
argument in the last place. I'le tell you Friend, Neighbour,
Brother, if you will forbeare to speake of it till you hear
farther, this is the judgement of M. Cotten, when he, it may
be, had never heard of it, or at least wise, when they brought
this their bastardly brat to him, they put another vizard on the
face of it: but that you may understand their way of broach-
ing their abominable errors, it was in dividing those things
the Lord hath united in his worke of conversion continued,
carrying on a Soule to Heaven in these foure Particulars.

First, in dividing betweene the word and the word, under
pretence of a legall Gospell, perswading the people their
Ministers were legall Preachers, teaching them little better
then Popery, and unfit for Gospell Churches, denying them
to be any Ministers of Christ that Preach any preparation
worke,[2] by shewing men what the Law requires. Here's
nothing, sayes one of them, but Preaching out of the Law and
the Prophets, truly sayes another of them I have not heard a
pure Gospell Sermon from any of them, but sure they were
both troubled with the Lethargy, or read not the Gospell
themselves, for they may finde the Apostles, yes, and Christ
himselfe, Preached good Gospell sure, out of the Law and the
Prophets.

[1] Cotton's *The Way of the Churches of Christ in New England* (London,
1645), was an answer to Robert Baillie's *Dissuasive from the Errours of the
Time (do.).*

[2] Work on the part of man, preparing him for the reception of God's grace.

Secondly, in separating Christ and his Graces, in manifesting himselfe to be in the Soule, and this they say makes
much for the magnifying of Free-grace, and indeed they made
it so free, that the soule that receives it shall never taste any
of it by their consent, but remaine still a dry branch as before;
these legall Pharises, says one of them, tell us of a thing they
call inherent grace, and of a man being made a new creature,
but I am sure the best of them goe on in their legall duties
and performances still, sorrowing for sinne, hearing of Sermons,
observing duty Morning and Evening, and many such like
matters. Tush man, sayes another of them, you shall hear
more then this, I was discoursing with one of their Scholas-
ticall Preachers Disciples, a professed convert, and yet when
he came to pray, he beg'd for forgivenesse of his sins, I asked
him why he used that vaine repetition, since hee did believe
he was justified by Christ already, and hee made me an answer
not worth repeating, but when I told him God could see no
sinne in his people, no more than I could see that which was
covered close from my eye-sight; hee told mee I spake little
lesse then blasphemy, so ignorant are these men, and their
learned guides also; who perswade them the more they have
of the in-dwelling of the Spirit of Christ, the better they shall
be inabled to these legall duties. Nay, quoth the other, I
can tell you more then all this, they make it an evidence of
their good estate, even their sanctification, and yet these men
would make people believe they are against Popery.

By this discourse of theirs, you may see the manner how
these Erronious, and Hereticall persons batter off the fruit
from the goodly branches of Christs vines and make bare the
flourishing trees planted in the house of the Lord, and yet
professe themselves to be Schollars of the upper forme, that
have learned as far as their Masters can teach them, but let
me tell you friends you'l prove but trewants if you fall thus
to Robbing of Orchards, and its an offence far beyond petty
Larceny, to rob Christs Garden, let your pretences be what
they will: can it possible be for the magnifying of Christs
Grace that the branches growing upon his root should remaine
fruitlesse? no assuredly, herein God is glorified that his people
bring forth much fruit, yet many of these new Gospellers had
another plea, hypocrites have a seeming shew of Saints graces

by which they deceive themselves and others; And therefore because Felons and Traytors coyne counterfeit Gold, therefore true Gold should not passe for current, but the intent of the Author is to prosecute the History, these errours being confuted already by the able servants of Christ, whom the Lord in his mercy brought hither for that purpose.

Chap. XLI.

Of the two latter dividing Principles under which these Erronists fought.

The third dividing tenent, by which these persons prosecuted their errors at this time, was betweene the Word of God, and the Spirit of God, and here these Sectaries had many prety knacks to delude withall, and especially to please the Femall Sex, they told of rare Revelations of things to come from the spirit (as they say); it was onely devised to weaken the Word of the Lord in the mouth of his Ministers, and withall to put both ignorant and unlettered Men and Women, in a posture of Preaching to a multitude, that they might be praised for their able Tongue. Come along with me, says one of them, i'le bring you to a Woman[1] that Preaches better Gospell then any of your black-coates that have been at the Ninneversity, a Woman of another kinde of spirit, who hath had many Revelations of things to come, and for my part, saith hee, I had rather hear such a one that speakes from the meere motion of the spirit, without any study at all, then any of your learned Scollers, although they may be fuller of Scripture (I) [ay] and admit they may speake by the helpe of the spirit, yet the other goes beyond them. Gentle Reader, thinke not these things fained, because I name not the parties, or that here is no witnesse to prove them, should I so do: neither of both is the cause I assure you, but being somewhat acquainted with my own weakenesse, should the Lord withdraw the light of his word, and also I verily believe some of them are truly turned againe to the truth, the which I wish to all, yet by relating the story all men may see what a spirit of giddinesse they were given up to, and some of them to strong

---

[1] Meaning Mrs. Hutchinson.

delusions, even to most horrid and damnable blasphemies, having itching eares, or rather proud desires to become Teachers of others, when they grosly erred in the first Principles of Religion themselves. There was a man in one of the farthest Townes of the Mattacusets Government, where they had no Ministers for the present, he being much desirous to shew himselfe some body in talking to as many as hee could get to hear him one [on] the Sabbath day, missing some of his Auditors, he meets with one of them some few dayes after, they passing over the water together, where were you quoth he on the Sabbath day that you were not at the meeting? we had a notable piece of Prophecy. Quoth the man that was missing, who was it that Preached? The other replying not: his Wife being in presence, answered; it was my husband. Nay wife, quoth he, thou shoulds not have told him, teach him to stay at home another time.

By this and divers other such like matters, which might be here inserted, you may see how these Sectaries love the preheminence, and for this end seeke to deprive the Ministers of Christ, inveigling as many as they can in the head, that they take to much upon them (just like the rebellious Korath, Dathan, and Abiram) [1] scoffing at their Scholler-like way of Preaching, wherein the grosse dissimulation of these erronious persons hath appeared exceedingly, as for instance first of a Woman, even the grand Mistris of all the rest, who denied the Resurrection from the dead, shee and her consorts mightily rayling against learning, perswading all they could to take heed of being spoyled by it, and in the meane time, shee her selfe would dispute (forsooth) and to shew her skill that way, here is a falacy quoth she in this syllogisme: as also one of the Gortonists, as shallow a pated Scholler as my selfe, far from understanding Latine, much lesse any other Language the Scriptures were writ in, yet when hee would hold out some of the best of his false Doctrines, as namely, that there were no other Devills but wicked men, nor no such thing as sin, Quoth he, that place in the fourth Psalme, where men commonly read, *stand in awe and sin not,* in the originall it is read *stand in awe and misse not.* But to go on, at this time

[1] See Numbers xvi.

there were many strange Revelations told both of Men and Women, as true some of them said as the Scripture, so that surely had this Sect gone on awhile, they would have made a new Bible, and their chief Mistris when she was shipt for N. England, what will you say, quoth she, and it hath beene revealed to me that we shall be there in six weekes, and one of the femall Gortonists said, she was a Prophetesse, and it was revealed unto her, that shee must prophecy unto the People in the same words the Prophet Ezekiel did, as also a lusty big man to defend this tenent held forth to his Pastor before the whole Congregation, that the spirit of Revelation came to him as he was drinking a pipe of Tobacco.[1]

The fourth dividing way to bring in their Heresies, was to devide betweene Christ and his Ordinances, and here they plaid their game to purpose, even to casting down of all Ordinances as carnall, and that because they were polluted by the Ordinance of man, as some of these Sectaries have said to the Minister of Christ, you have cast off the crosse in Baptisme, but you should do well to cast off Baptisme it selfe; as also for the Sacrament of the Lords Supper, for to make use of Bread, or the juce of a silly Grape to represent the Body and Bloud of Christ, they accounted it as bad as Negromancy in the Ministers of Christ to performe it.   But seeing there will be occasion to bring in a bed-roule [2] of these Blasphemies in the yeare (43) and (44) take the lesse here; onely minde that these persons being first bewildred in the deniall of Infants being Baptized, could neither finde right faith to be Baptized into, nor yet any person rightly constituted to Baptize.   Remaining Seekers, they came to this, but yet here must not be omitted the slights these Erronists had to shoulder out the Officers Christ hath ordained, and set up in

---

[1] This is probably a reminiscence of the saying attributed (1638) to that scandalous hypocrite, Captain John Underhill, that "he had lain under a spirit of bondage and a legal way five years, and could get no assurance, till at length, as he was taking a pipe of tobacco, the Spirit set home an absolute promise of free grace with such assurance and joy, as he never since doubted of his good estate, neither should he, though he should fall into sin" (which he was lamentably prone to do); or of his argument before the Boston church the next Lord's Day, that the Lord might readily "manifest Himself to him as he was taking the moderate use of the creature called tobacco."   Winthrop, I. 275, 276.

[2] Bead-roll, catalogue.

his Churches; and verily in this point they sided directly with the Papist and Prelates, although in most of the other they went directly out of the way on the other hand. Ignorance say the Papist is the Mother of devotion, its better say the Protestant Prelates to have a blind sir John,[1] one that cannot tell how to Preach, provided he will conforme to our Ceremonies, than to have one that will Preach constantly, and not conforme also: these Erronist, shewing themselves to be whelps of the same litter, Cry out against a learned Presbitery, as the onely way to captivate liberty, and herein the transformed Devill came to shew his Hornes, for why, his errors would not take where the people were followers of their seeing guids, and if it be well noted, here is the Masterpiece of all their knavery, the which comes in after this manner, The Lording Prelacy, Popes, Cardinalls, Bishops, Deanes, etc., were ordinarily brought up at the University to learning, and have most tyrannically abused it, usurping over the People of Christ, and exercised most inhumane and barbarous cruelty upon them; as also the Presbyterian Kirke by these Provinciall Classes, men of learning having robbed the particular Congregations of their just and lawfull priviledges, which Christ hath purchased for them, Each Congregation of his being invested with full power to Administer all the Ordinances he hath ordained, in and toward their owne Members; and further learned men in some places, feeding the people for their Tith-sake in a Parishioniall way, desire the upholding thereof, lest their fat Benefices should grow leane.

Now the Redemption of the people of Christ out of all these bondages, being full of difficulty to attaine, as is abundantly witnessed in the great hardship Gods people have undergon in this Wildernesse-worke; as also much more by that bloudy war so long continued in our Native Country, and the two adjacent Kingdomes, This makes a very faire bottome for those to build upon, who would have the sluce of authority in the Officers of Christs Churches plucked up, that so their errors might flow in like a floud; And therefore they impannell a Jury of their own Sectaries to passe upon all such as put a higher esteem upon their Pastors and Teachers

---

[1] A cant name for a priest, for Sir, besides its other uses, was employed as a title for a bachelor of arts, and hence for a clergyman.

(in point of discerning the holy things of God) then upon other men, who returne in their Verdit as finding them guilty of the crime above expressed, either as party, or privy abetters unto them. Upon this the Vote goes for advancing such men as will let them out line enough, for such as will worke without wages, and give to every man liberty to exercise a large conscience, provided it be his own, and as for authority, they would have none used, as being a thing two opposite to liberty. My friend, cast off as much of thy owne power as thou canst, and beware of Lording it over Gods Heritage, but I pray thee let Christ alone with his, which he hath given to his Pastors and Teachers in administring the holy things of God, peculiar to their Office, and tremble all you Presbyterians, who to please the people prostrate the authority Christ hath put upon the Eldrs of his Churches as Officers, to the resolute liberty of man: the people may and ought to call them to Office, to the which Christ hath united double honour and authority, and appointed them to be had in high esteeme for their workesake, being Embassadors of Christ Jesus. This may no man take from them, nor yet they themselves cast off, and yet all this makes nothing for the Papall, Prelaticall, Classicall or Parishionall authority of the Presbitery, for it holds onely in their ruling well, while they rule for Christ, they must and shall have the power hee hath put upon their Office. From these foure dividing Tenents by the cunning art of these deceivers, were forescore grosse errours [1] broached secretly, sliding in the darke like the Plague, proving very infectious to some of the Churches of Christ in their Members.

Chap. XLII.

Of sad effects of the pitifull and erronious Doctrines broached by the Sectuaries.

The number of these infectious persons increasing now, haveing drawn a great party on their side, and some considerable persons, they grow bold, and dare question the sound and wholesome truths delivered in publick by the Ministers

---

[1] The number eighty (more exactly eighty-two) is taken from the catalogue of these errors which was drawn up by the assembly of ministers which sat at Cambridge in 1637.

of Christ. Their Church-meetings are full of Disputes in points of difference, and their love-Feasts are not free from spots, in their Courts of civill Justice some men utter their Speeches in matters of Religion very ambiguously, and among all sorts of persons a great talke of new light, but verily it proved but old darknesse, such as sometime over-shadowed the City of Munster; [1] But blessed be the Lord Christ, who now declared himselfe to be a helpe at hand for his poore New England Churches, being now in their infancy, whose condition at present was very dolorous, and full of difficulties, insomuch that the better part of this new transported people stood still many of them gazing one upon another, like Sheepe let loose to feed on fresh pasture, being stopped and startled in their course by a Kennell of devouring Wolves. The weaker fort wavered much, and such as were more growne Christians hardly durst discover the truth they held one unto another. The fogs of errour increasing, the bright beames of the glorious Gospell of our Lord Christ in the Mouth of his Ministers could not be discerned through this thick mist by many, and that sweete refreshing warmth that was formerly felt from the spirits influence, was now turned (in these Erronists) to a hot inflamation of their owne conceited Revelations, ulcerating and bringing little lesse then frenzy or madnesse to the patient, the Congregation of the people of God began to be forsaken, and the weaker Sex prevailed so farre, that they set up a Priest of their own Profession and Sex, who was much thronged after, abominably wresting the Scriptures to their own destruction: this Master-piece of Womens wit, drew many Disciples after her, and to that end boldly insinuated her selfe into the favour of none of the meanest, being also backed with the Sorcery of a second, who had much converse with the Devill by her own confession,[2] and did, to the admiration of those that heard her, utter many speeches in the Latine Tongue, as it were in a trance. This Woman was wonted to

[1] At Münster in western Germany, in 1534, occurred an outbreak of the visionary and revolutionary Anabaptists, who, carrying to an extreme the processes of the Reformation, set up the reign of the saints in a form which speedily developed into tyranny and the wildest license. In 1535, after a long siege, the city was subdued; but the name of Münster remained for more than a century a bugbear to the upholders of constituted religious and civil authority.

[2] Jane Hawkins the midwife. See Winthrop, *Journal*, I. 266, 268; II. 8.

give drinkes to other Women to cause them to conceive, how they wrought I know not, but sure there were Monsters borne not long after, as you shall hear in the following History.

Oh yee New England Men and Women, who hath bewitched you that you should not obey the truth? And indeed Satan, to make sure worke with semblance of Preaching the Doctrine of Free-grace by his instruments, makes shew of out-bidding all the Orthodox and godly Ministers in the Countrey, pretending their Preaching to be but a Covenant of workes, supposing by this meanes to silence them without a Bishop, and lest the civill power should stand up for their aid, they threaten them with the high displeasure of Christ for persecuting his people, which as they said these erronious persons with their new light, were the onely Men and Women that were pure Gospell Preachers. Thus the poore people of Christ, who kept close to his antient truths, invironed with many straites, having expended their Estates to voyage far through the perillous Seas, that their eyes might behold their Teachers, and that they might injoy the protection of a godly civill Government, began to deeme themselves in a more dolorous condition then when they were in the Commissaries Court, and Prelates Prisons. The hideous waves in which their brittle Barques were sometimes covered, as they passed hither, were nothing so terrible in the apprehension of some as was this floud of errors violently beating against the bankes of Church and civill Government. The wants of this Wildernesse, and pinching penury in misse of Bread, put them to no such paine by gnawing on their empty stomacks, with feare of famishing, as did the misse of the Administration of Christ in his Word and Ordinances, leaving the soule in a languishing condition for want of a continuall supply of Christ in his Graces.

Chap. XLIII.

Of the sorrowfull condition of the people of Christ, when they were incountred with these erronists at their first landing.

But to end this dismall yeare of sixteene hundred thirty six, take here the sorrowfull complaint of a poore Soule in misse of its expectation at landing, who being incountered

with some of these Erronists at his first landing,[1] when he saw
that good old way of Christ rejected by them, and hee could
not skill in that new light, which was the common theame of
every mans Discourse, hee betooke him to a narrow Indian
path,[2] in which his serious Meditations soone led him, where
none but sencelesse Trees and eccohing Rocks make answer
to his heart-easeing mone. Oh quoth he where am I become,
is this the place where those Reverend Preachers are fled,
that Christ was pleased to make use of to rouse up his rich
graces in many a drooping soule; here I have met with some
that tell mee, I must take a naked Christ. Oh, woe is mee if
Christ be naked to mee, wherewith shall I be cloathed, but
methinks I most wonder they tell me of casting of all godly
sorrow for sin as unbeseeming a Soule, that is united to Christ
by Faith, and there was a little nimbled tongued Woman
among them, who said she could bring me acquainted with
one of her own Sex that would shew me a way, if I could attaine it, even Revelations, full of such ravishing joy that I
should never have cause to be sorry for sinne, so long as I
live, and as for her part shee had attained it already: a company of legall Professors,[3] quoth she, lie poring on the Law
which Christ hath abolished, and when you breake it then
you breake your joy, and now no way will serve your turne,
but a deepe sorrow. These and divers other expressions in-
timate unto men [me?], that here I shall finde little increase
in the Graces of Christ, through the hearing of his word
Preached, and other of his blessed Ordinances. Oh cunning
Devill, the Lord Christ rebuke thee, that under pretence of a
free and ample Gospell shuts out the Soule from partaking
with the Divine Nature of Christ, in that mysticall Union of
his Blessed Spirit, creating and continuing his Graces in the
Soule: my deare Christ, it was thy worke that moved me

---

[1] It should be borne in mind that Johnson, on his second coming to New
England (see the Introduction), arrived in 1636, in October of which year the
Antinomian troubles began.

[2] The path from Charlestown, where Johnson at first dwelt, to Cambridge,
where his admired Thomas Shepard preached, would answer to the description
and to what follows.

[3] Not professors of law, be it understood, but professors of religion in whom
the free course of faith was hampered by undue regard to the legal aspects of
God's relation to man.

hither to come, hoping to finde thy powerfull presence in the Preaching of the Word, although administred by sorry men, subject to like infirmities with others of Gods people, and also by the glasse of the Law to have my sinfull corrupt nature discovered daily more and more, and my utter inabillity of any thing that is good, magnifying hereby the free grace of Christ; who of his good will and pleasure worketh in us to will, and to doe, working all our works in us, and for us.

But here they tell me of a naked Christ, what is the whole life of a Christian upon this Earth? But through the power of Christ to die to sinne, and live to holinesse and righteousnesse, and for that end to be diligent in the use of meanes: at the uttering of this word he starts up from the greene bed of his complaint with resolution to hear some one of these able Ministers Preach (whom report had so valued) before his will should make choyce of any one principle, though of crossing the broade Seas back againe; then turning his face to the Sun, he steered his course toward the next Town, and after some small travell hee came to a large plaine. No sooner was hee entred thereon, but hearing the sound of a Drum he was directed toward it by a broade beaten way. Following this rode he demands of the next man he met what the signall of the Drum ment, the reply was made they had as yet no Bell to call men to meeting; and therefore made use of a Drum.[1] Who is it, quoth hee, Lectures at this Towne? The other replies, I see you are a stranger, new come over, seeing you know not the man, it is one Mr. Shepheard. Verily quoth the other, you hit the right, I am new come over indeed, and have been told since I came most of your Ministers are legall Preachers, onely if I mistake not they told me this man Preached a finer covenant of workes then the other, but however, I shall make what hast I can to heare him. Fare you well. Then hasting thither hee croudeth through the thickest, where having stayed while the glasse was turned up twice,[2]

---

[1] The usual mode in the New England churches at this time. Rasieres noted it at Plymouth. *Narratives of New Netherland*, in this series, p. 112.

[2] Public worship in Massachusetts at this period consisted of extemporaneous prayers, the singing of the Psalms in a metrical version, without instrumental accompaniment, and preaching without notes. The length of the sermon was

the man was metamorphosed, and was faine to hang down
the head often, least his watry eyes should blab abroad
the secret conjunction of his affections, his heart crying
loud to the Lords ecchoing answer, to his blessed spirit, that
caused the Speech of a poore weake pale complectioned
man to take such impression in his soule at present, by
applying the word so aptly, as if hee had beene his Privy
Counseller, cleering Christs worke of grace in the soule from
all those false Doctrines, which the erronious party had
afrighted him withall, and now he resolves (the Lord willing)
to live and die with the Ministers of New England; whom
hee now saw the Lord had not onely made zealous to stand
for the truth of his Discipline, but also of the Doctrine,
and not to give ground one inch.

Chap. XLIIII.

*The Congregationall Churches of Christ are neither favourers
of sinfull opinions, nor the Lords over any, or many Churches,
or mens Consciences.*

And here, Christian Reader, the Author according to his
former practice, must minde thee of the admirable providence
of Christ toward his New England Churches, in preserving
them from these erronious spirits, that have hitherto in all
places dog'd the sincere servants of Christ, when ever they
have set upon a through Reformation, as stories doe abundantly testify, which thing the reverend Calvine and divers
others, have declared. But seeing the boasting Prelates in
these times are ready to say their Lordly power kept these
errours under, it's plaine otherwise: for Satan saw while
people were under their yoake of humane inventions, they
were far enough from exalting the Kingdome of Christ; And
therefore he reserved these errours, for his last shifts, and
further you shall see in the following story that the Lord
Christ reserved this honour for those, whose love hee had
inlarged to follow him in a dezart wildernesse, even with the

measured by the hour-glass. Commonly it was one hour. In this case, as we
see, it was at least two hours, while at the founding of the Woburn church, pp. 215,
218 *post*, Mr. Symmes and Mr. Carter "exercised" at still greater length.

sharpe sword of the Word, timely to cut off the heads of this
Hidra; but yet there are two sorts of persons in our Native
Country, whom the Elders and Brethren here do highly honour
in Christ, and prefer before themselves, namely the godly
Prebyterian party, and the Congregationall sincere servants
of Christ, both which the Author could wish, that (with
bowells of compassion, sweet simpathising affection of Brethren
knit together in that transcendent love of Christ, which couples
all his distanced flockes together) they would seriously ponder
this History, which through the Authors weakenesse wants
much of measure, but nothing of the truth of things, so far as
a shallow capacity can reach. Of the first sort named, I
could wish the Reverend Mr. Ruterford, Mr. Bayle, Mr.
Rathbone, Mr. Paget, Mr. Ball, etc.[1] would but informe
themselves further by the truth of this History, supposing
they cannot chuse but in a good measure be satisfied already
with the pacificatory and meeke answers of as many Reverend
and godly Elders of ours.[2]

Now that I would they should take notice of is, that the
Churches of Christ in New England, and their Officers have
hitherto been so far from imbracing the erronious Doctrines
of these times, that through the powers of Christ they have
valiantly defended the truth, and cut down all deceivable
Doctrine; the like hath not been done for many ages heretofore. Reverend and beloved in Christ, could your eyes but
behold the efficacy of loving counsell in the Communion of
congregationall Churches, and the reverend respect, honour
and love, given to all Teaching Elders, charity commands
me to thinke you would never stand for Classicall injunc-

---

[1] Samuel Rutherfurd, *The Due Right of Presbyteries* (London, 1644); Robert
Baillie, *A Dissuasive from the Errours of the Time* (1645); William Rathband,
*A Most Grave and Modest Confutation of the Errours of the Sect called Brownists
or Separatists* (1644); John Paget, *A Defence of Church-Government exercised in
Presbyteriall, Classicall and Synodicall Assemblies* (1641); John Ball, *A Trial
of the New Church Way in New England and in Old* (1640). The debates in
Parliament and in the Westminster Assembly had given rise to a large controversial literature on the respective merits of the Presbyterian and Congregational
systems.

[2] *Church-Government and Church-Covenant Discussed, in an Answer of the
Elders of the severall Churches in New-England to two and thirty Questions sent
over to them by divers Ministers in England* (London, 1643).

tions[1] any more, neither Diocesan, nor Provinciall authority can possible reach so far as this royall Law of love in communion of Churches: verily its more universall then the Papall power, and assuredly the dayes are at hand, wherein both Jew and Gentile Churches shall exercise this old Modell of Church Government, and send their Church salutations and admonitions from one end of the World unto another, when the Kingdomes of the Earth are become our Lord Christs; Then shall the exhortation of one Church to another prevaile more to Reformation, then all the thundering Bulls, excomunicating Lordly censures, and shamefull penalties of all the Lording Churches in the World, and such shall be and is the efficacy of this intire love one to another, that the withdrawing of any one Church of Christ, according to the Rule of the word, from those that walke inordinatly, will be more terrible to the Church or Churches so forsaken, then an Army with Banners: yea, and it may be added, because civill Government is like to turne nurse in more places then one, this royall Law of love shall become the Law of Nations, and none will suffer their subjects to rebell against it.

But to our beloved brethren in England on the other hand, the Reverend Mr. Burroughs, Mr. Goodwin etc.[2] This seemeth you have apprehended our Churches and civill Government, to be too strict in dealing with persons for their sinfull opinions, I wish the offenders be none of your intelligencers, who to be sure will make the worst of things. I know you are in charity with us; And therefore a few words will satisfie, which I hope you want not from your good friends our Reverend Elders, who could wish you as much happinesse as our selves to expell error before it grew to that height to cry downe the sound and wholesome truths, casting durt on

---

[1] *I. e.*, injunctions of the classis or presbytery, the local assembly of elders of churches which, in the Presbyterian system, stood midway between the church session of the individual church and the provincial synod. The Presbyterian contention was that Congregationalism provided insufficient means for preserving unity and maintaining uniform standards of orthodoxy by regular organs of governmental control. Johnson's contention is that in the Congregational system this is sufficiently achieved by the occasional councils of churches.

[2] Jeremiah Burroughs and Thomas Goodwin, President of Magdalen College, Oxford, were two of the five noteworthy Independent divines in the Westminster Assembly.

our Orthodox and godly Ministery. I wish you open your mouths wide enough to be filled with this blessing; the Lord hath done great, and unexpected things for you, and why not this? one and twenty yeares experience hath taught us that Errors and Heresies are not broached, and held out here by tender consciences, such as are weak in the Faith, but by such as think them Scholers of the upper forme, such as would teach the most ablest Christian among us another Gospell, and further we finde our Erronist[s], wanting a common enemy to contend withall, as you, have fallen foule of our godly Magistrates and Ministers, and will not suffer us quietly to injoy the Ordinance of Christ, for which wee hither came, buzzing our people in the eare with a thing they call liberty, which when any have tasted a smack of, they can no more indure to hear of a Synod or gathering together of able, and Orthodox Christians, nor yet of communion of Churches, but would be independant to purpose, and as for civill Government they deem Religion to be a thing beyond their Sphere.

Chap. XLV.

Of the civill Government in N. England, and their nurture of the people upon their tender knees.

The vernall of the yeare 1637. being now in his prime, and as the season of the yeare grew hotter, so the minds of many were hot in the eager pursuite of their selfe conceited opinions, and verily had not authority stept in, it was much to be doubted they would have proceeded from words to blowes. Great hold and keepe there was about choice of Magistrates this yeare, the choyce being retarded by a paper call'd a Petition, but indeed a meere device to hinder the election, till the erronious party were strengthened, their number increasing daily, but the Lord Christ gratiously providing for the peace of his people toward the end of the day the honoured John Winthrope Esquire, was chosen Governour, and Thomas Dudly Esq. Deputy Governor: the number of free-men added this year was about 125.[1]

[1] In fact, 102.   For the history of this exciting election, see Winthrop, I. 215.

Here according to promise the Reader shall have an accoumpt of the civill Government of this little Commonwealth. As their whole aime in their removall from their Native Country, was to injoy the liberties of the Gospell of Christ, so in serving up civill Government, they daily direct their choice to make use of such men as mostly indeavour to keepe the truths of Christ pure and unspotted, and assuredly they can digest any wrongs or injuries done them in their estates, or trade, better then the wresting of their right in the freedome of the Gospell, out of their hands, and this the Erronist knowing right well (to save their heads whole) perswade men it is not for civill Government to meddle with matters of Religion; and also to helpe out with their damnable Doctrines, they report it in all places, where they be come, that New England Government doth persecute the people and Churches of Christ; which to speake truth they have hitherto beene so far from, that they have indeavoured to expell all such beasts of prey, (who will not be reclaimed) that here might be none left to hurt or destroy in all Gods holy Mountaine, and therefore are ready to put the Churches of Christ in minde of their duty herein; yea, and sometimes going before them in their civill censures that they may not onely professe the truth, but also hate every false way, not that they would compell men to believe by the power of the Sword, but to indeavour all may answer their profession, whether in Church Covenant or otherwise, by knowing they bare not the Sword in vaine. Neither doe they exercise civill power to bring all under their obedience to a uniformity in every poynt of Religion, but to keepe them in the unity of the spirit, and the bond of peace, nor yet have they ever mixed their civill powers with the authority peculiarly given by Christ to his Churches and Officers of them, but from time to time have laboured to uphold their priviledges, and only communion one with another.[1]

The chiefe Court or supreame power of this little Commonwealth, consists of a mixt company, part Aristocracy, and part Democracy of Magistrates, that are yearly chosen by the major Vote of the whole body of the Free-men through-

---

[1] It cannot be necessary to point out the artless speciousness of this defence.

out the Country; and Deputies chosen by the severall Townes. They have hitherto had about 12. or 13. Magistrates in the Colony of the Mattacusets, the other Colonies have not above five or six, they have hitherto beene Volunteers, governing without pay from the people, onely the Governor of the Mattacusets hath some yeares 100 *l.* allowed him, and some years lesse. Many of the Magistrates are already remembred, yet with some of the first came hither Mr. Simon Brodestreet,[2] in this short Meeter is he remembred.

Now Simon yong, step in among, these worthies take thy place:
  All day to toile in vinyard, while Christ thee upholds with grace;
Thee wisdom grave betime he gave, and tongue to utter it,
  That thou mightst be a blessing free, and for this calling fit.
Thy counsell well advis'd dost tell, with words ordered compleat,
  Thy memory, doth amplifie, meeting with matters great.
Broad liberty, do thou deny, Brodstreet Christ would thee have
  For's truth contend, strong reason spend, it from aspersion save.
He furnish't thee with these gifts free, to last he must them make,
  Still adding more, to thy old store, till he thee to him take.

The Lord was pleased to furnish these his people with some able instruments in most of their Townes, that were skill'd in Common-wealth work, out of which they chose their Deputies, whose number was ordinarily between 30. and 40. Some of them there will be occasion to speake of among their Military Men, but see here the *Wonder-working Providence of Sions Saviour* appears much in gathering together stones to build up the walls of Jerusalem (that his Sion may be surrounded with Bulworkes and Towres). With a whispering

---

[1] In saying that the magistrates, or court of assistants, were "a mixt company, part Aristocracy and part Democracy," Johnson perhaps refers to the fact that, though they were annually elected by the whole body of the freemen, the constant custom of re-election, and of choosing only those who had the standing of gentlemen, made the board in some sense an oligarchy. Of the deputies, two were chosen for and by each town. Since 1644 the two bodies had sat as separate houses of a legislature. The governor, deputy-governor, and assistants also had executive and judicial powers not shared with the deputies.

[2] See p. 65, note 1. The verses seem to contain a gentle rebuke to Bradstreet for his action on the side of liberty in 1646, when he dissented openly from the action of his fellow-magistrates in fining Dr. Robert Child and his associates who petitioned on behalf of the unenfranchised citizens.

word in the eares of his servants, he crosses the Angles of
England from Cornewall to Kent, from Dover to Barwick, not
leaving out Scotland and Wales; Wise men are perswaded to
the worke without arguing like Elisha, when Elias cast his
mantle on him, so these men make no stop, but say suffer me
onely to sell my inheritance, and I will away for New England.
And now I could wish our Brethren in England would not be
angry with us for making such hast. Brethren, you know
how the case stood with our Ministers, as it was with Gideon,[1]
who could thresh out no Corne, but hee must doe it secretly
to hide it from the Midianites, who spread the Land like
Grashoppers, no more could they thresh and cleane up any
Wheate for the Lords Garner, but the Prelates would presently be upon their backs, and plow long furrowes there, and
you may believe it, if you will (for it is certaine) many, had
not this little number gone forth to blow their Trumpets, and
breake their Pitchers, making the brightnesse of their Lamps
appeare, surely the host of the Midianites had never been put
to flight, and if still any of our Brethren shall contend with
us, wee answer with Gideon, the Lord hath delivered into your
hands the chiefe Princes of Midian, and what were we able to
do in comparison of you; yet shall we not cease to follow on
the worke of Reformation, although weake and faint, till the
Lord be pleased to free his Israel from all their enemies; and
verily England hath not wanted the Prayers of the poore
people of Christ here. And also some of our chiefe helpes
both for Church-worke, Military and common-wealth-worke;[2]
yet through the Lords mercy, we still retaine among our

[1] Judges vi. 11.

[2] When the Civil War broke out in England, in 1642, emigration to New
England halted, and many importan[t] men went back to take part in the conflict
or to share in the new liberty which they foresaw. Of those who are named below as remaining in the colony and taking a prominent part in the work of the
House of Deputies, Hathorne (ancestor of Nathaniel Hawthorne) was speaker
of the House six times, Russell five times, Atherton, Gookin, and Hill each once.
Duncan was auditor-general from 1645. Gookin, a notable Virginian planter,
retired from Virginia in 1644 when the Puritans were persecuted, was superin-
tendent of the Massachusetts Indians for thirty years, and wrote a most interesting account of them. He was major-general of the colony from 1681 to 1687,
Atherton from 1654 to 1661. Edward Rawson was its secretary from 1650 to
the end of government under the old charter in 1686. William Hubbard was the
father of the historian.

Democracy the godly Captaine William Hathorn, whom the Lord hath indued with a quick apprehension, strong memory, and rhetorick, volubillity of speech, which hath caused the people to make use of him often in publick service, especially when they have had to do with any forrein Government; Mr. Nathaniel Duncan, learned in the Latine and French tongue, a very good accountant, Wherefore he is called to the place of Auditor Generall for the County [Country]; Mr. John Glovar, a man strong for the truth, a plaine sincere godly man, and of good abilities; Captaine Daniel Gogkin, who was drawen hither from Virginia, by having his affection strongly set on the truths of Christ, and his pure Ordinances; being indued by the Lord with good understanding; Captaine William Tinge, sometime Treasurour for the County [Country], but being absent for some space of time in England, Mr. Richard Russell was chosen in his roome; Mr. Edward Rawson, a young man, yet imployed in Common-wealth affaires a long time, being well beloved of the inhabitants of Newbery, having had a large hand in her Foundation; but of late he being of a ripe capacity, a good yeoman [penman] and eloquent inditer, hath beene chosen Secretary for the Country; Mr. William Hubbard of Iphshwich, a learned man, being well read in state matters: of a very affable and humble behaviour; who hath expended much of his Estate to helpe on this worke; although he be slow of speech, yet is hee down right for the businesse; Captaine Umphry Atherton, one of a cheerfull spirit, and intire for the Count[r]y; Mr. Edward Jackson, one who cannot indure to see the truths of Christ trampled under foot by the erronious party, Eleazar Lusher one of the right stamp, and pure mettle, a gratious, humble and heavenly minded man; Mr. Joseph Hill, a man active for to bring the Lawes of the Count[r]y in order;[1] Mr. Whipple, one whose godly sincerity is much approved; Mr. Francis Norton, one of a cheerfull spirit, and full of love to the truth; Mr. Robert Paine, a right godly man, and one whose estate hath holpe on well with the worke of this little Common-wealth; Mr. William Torry, a good penman and skild in the Latine tongue, usually Clarke of the Deputies; the Survayor Generall

---

[1] He was on committees with Johnson, for the work described in book III., chap. v., and perhaps had the leading part in it.

of the Armies [Armes] of the Country, John Johnson, of an undanted spirit; Mr. William Parker [Parkes], a man of a pregnant understanding, and very usefull in his place. Many more would be named, but for tediousnesse, neither will it please the men more to be named, then not, for all are very willing to acknowledge their inability for the worke, and the best are not without many imperfections.

The Authors end in naming some few is for none other end, but to make good the title of this Book and to incourage all the servants of Christ for time to come, wholely to rely upon him, when they go about any difficult work, which may tend to the glory of his Name. Who could have told these men, being scattered abroad throughout the Island of Great Brittaine, they should meete on a Wildernesse nine hundred Leagues remote, and there keep Court together to study the preservation of Christs poore scattered flockes? nay brethren, when you first tooke book in hand to learne your Letters, you would have been very dull pates, but for this worke; assuredly, how you came by large inheritances, some of you, and estates of hundreds, and thousands, your selves best know, but believe it, the Lord intended it for this very work, The Earth is the Lords, and the fulnesse of it, then let none of the people of Christ mourn that they have spent their wealth in this Wildernesse, if it have holpe on the worke, rather rejoyce that Christ hath betrusted thee to be Steward for the King of Kings, and that in so noble an achievement the worthiest worke that the memory of our selves, and our fore-fathers can reach unto.

And brethren, as for the good parts and gifts the Author hath commended you for, but for the edifying of the body of Christ, and assisting his people in this work, you had been empty of all good.

And now seeing it is the opinion of many in these dayes of Reformation, that all sorts of Sectaries (that acknowledge a Christ) should be tolerated by civill Government, except Papist, and this Government hath hitherto, and is for future time resolved to practice otherwise (the Lord assisting) having met already with more blasphemous Sectaries, then are Papists; wherefore it will not be amisse if our Countrymen be acquainted with the one and twenty yeares experience of this

Wildernesse worke, in point of Government. First, it is their judgment, and that from Scripture taught them, that those, who are chose to place of government, must be men truly fearing God, wise and learned in the truths of Christ, (if so) as hitherto it hath been New Englands practice, then surely such will be utterly unfit to tolerate all sorts of Sectaries, as because they have taken up Joshuas resolution, to serve the Lord [1] and a man cannot serve two Masters, much lesse many Masters; Then surely such as would have all sorts of sinfull opinions upheld by the civill government, must be sure to make choise of the most Atheisticall persons they can finde to governe, such as are right Gallios: [2] for N. E. hath found by experience that every man will most favour his own way of Profession, and labor tooth and naile to maintaine it, and if any have complied with other that have been of a contrary sinfull opinion to their own, it hath been, because they would have their own scape scot free, but assuredly the Lord Christ will allow of no such wayes for the favouring the professors of his truths, nor may any Magistrate doe evill that good may come of it, in favouring dangerous and deceivable doctrines, that others may favour the true servants of Christ, neither is there any such need, for it is their honours (if the will of God be so) to suffer, nor can the people of N. England (I meane the better part) be perswaded to set up any other to governe, but such are zealous for the maintainance of the truths of Christ; yet of late there is a buzzing noise, as if it were injury to the Churches for civill power to medle in matters of Religion, but to be sure there are many that strive for a Toleration, yet the people of Christ, who are the naturall Mothers of this Government, resolve never to see their living child so divided, looking at such a government to be no better to them, a living child divided in twaine; and therefore desires their loving Countrymen to beare with them in this point, and if any notwithstanding shall force it to be so, we shall shew our natural affection, and leave all to them, chusing rather to dwell on the backside of this Desert (a place as yet unaccessible) knowing assuredly our God will appeare for our deliverance. Yet let them also know the Souldiers of Christ in N E. are not of

---

[1] Joshua xxiv. 15.   [2] Acts xxiii. 17.

such a pusillanimous spirit, but resolve as that valiant Jeptha [1]
did to keep in possession, the Towns his God had given them,
so we are resolved (the Lord willing) to keepe the government
our God hath given us, and for witnesse hee hath so done, let
this History manifest: for we chose not the place for the
Land, but for the government, that our Lord Christ might
raigne over us, both in Churches and Common-wealth, and
although the Lord have been pleased by an extraordinary
blessing upon his peoples industry to make the place fruitfull
(as at this day indeed it is) yet all may know the land in it
selfe is very sterrill, but the upholding of the truths of Christ,
is chiefe cause why many have hitherto come: and further if
the servants of Christ be not much mistaken, the downfall of
Antichrist is at hand, and then the Kingdome[s] of the Earth
shall become the Kingdome of our Lord Christ in a more
peculiar manner, then now they are, and surely godly civill
government shall have a great share in that worke, for they are
exhorted to fill her double of the Cup, shee hath given to them;
and also know our Magistrates, being conscious of ruling for
Christ, dare not admit of any bastardly brood to be nurst up
upon their tender knees, neither will any Christian of a sound
judgement vote for any, but such as earnestly contend for
the Faith, although the increase of Trade, and traffique may
be a great inducement to some.

[1] Judges xi. 24.

WONDER–WORKING PROVIDENCE OF SIONS SAVIOUR, IN NEW ENGLAND.

[Book II.]

CHAP. I.

The beginning of the relation of the Pequot war, and the great straites these wandering Jacobites were in.

THE great Jehovah, minding to manifest the multitude of his Mercies to the wandering Jacobites, and make an introduction to his following wonders, causeth the darke clouds of calamities to gather about them, presaging some terrible tempest to follow, With eyes full of anguish, they face to the right, upon the damnable Doctrines, as so many dreadfull Engines set by Satan to intrap their poore soules; Then casting forth a left hand looke, the labour and wants accompaning a Desert, and terrible Wildernesse affright them. Their memories minding them of their former plenty, it much aggravated the present misery, When with thoughts of retreating, they turne their backs about, the experienced incumbrances and deepe distresses of a dangerous Ocean hinders their thoughts of flight, besides the sterne looke of the Lordly Prelates, which would give them a welcome home in a famishing prison. Then purposing to put on more stronger resolution, facing to the Front, behold a Messenger with sorrowfull tidings from their fellow brethren, that inhabited the bankes of the River Canectico,[1] who having audience, informes them of the great insolency, and cruell murthers committed by a barbarous and bloudy people called Peaquods, upon the bodies of their indeared friends, these savage

---

[1] Connecticut.

Indians lying to the South-west of the Mattacusets,[1] were more warlike then their Neighbouring Nations, the Narrowganzet or Niantick Indians, although they exceeded them in number;[2] also Mawhiggins (who were the best friends of the English, and a chiefe instrumentall meanes of their sitting down there) stood much in feare of these Peaquods, which were big, swollen with pride at this time, facing the English Fort built on the mouth of the River[3] in their large Cannowes, with their Bowes and long Shafts, The English being then but weake in number and provision, were unable to manage the war against so numerous a company, being above thirty to one, yet their desires being beyond their meanes, they made some shot at them, forcing them to hast away faster then they willingly would. These Indians trusting in their great Troopes, having feasted their corps in a ravening manner, and leaving their fragments for their Sqawes, they sound an alarum with a full mouth, and lumbring voyce, and soone gather together without presse[4] or pay, their quarrell being as antient as Adams time, propagated from that old enmity betweene the Seede of the Woman, and the Seed of the Serpent,[5] who was the grand signor of this war in hand, and would very gladly have given them a large Commission, had not his own power been limited, neither could he animate them so much as to take off the gastly looke of that King of terror, yet however at his command they arme themselves: casting their quiver at their backs with Bowes ready bent, they troope up some of them, being extraordinarily armed with Guns, which they purchast from the Dutch (who had assuredly paid deare for this their courteous humour, not long since, had not some English Volunteers rescued them from the Indians hands). The most of them were armed also with a small Hatchet on a long handle. They had a small number of Mawhawkes,[6] Hammers, which are made of stone, having a long pike on the

---

[1] The Pequot country was what is now south-eastern Connecticut, from the Thames to the Rhode Island boundary.

[2] The meaning apparently is, that the Narragansetts were more numerous than the Pequots. The latter probably numbered a thousand fighting men.

[3] The fort at Saybrook, built by Lion Gardiner in the preceding winter of 1635–1636.

[4] Impressment.   [5] Genesis iii. 15.   [6] Tomahawks.

one side, and a hole in the handle, which they tie about their
wrists, They neede not provisions follow their Camp; because they are continually at home. But for their mats to
shelter them from Raine or Snow, the Woods are as wellcome
to them as their Wigwams, fire they can make in all places
by chafing two sticks together. Their food is ready drest at
all times, parching Indian Corne in their fire they pound it to
meale, and with foure or five spoonfull of it cast into their
mouths, and a sup or two of water, which they take up with
a leafe of a Tree, this is their common repast, and indeed
their chiefe viaticum. Thus furnisht for the war they troope
away without any goodly equipage, to effect, as they suppose,
some great designe, but within some few Miles of the Towne
of Hartford, they were discovered by one of the English, who
having with him a good Horse, hastens away to give intelligence of their approach, and by the way meeting with foure
or five persons, hee advises them to haste away with all speed,
for the Peaquods were at hand. The weaker Sex among them,
being at this time not so credulous as they should have been,
began to dispute the case with him, demanding what Peaquods
they were, and questioning how they should come there;
The horseman deeming it now no time for words, when the
battell followed him so hard at the heeles, rod on his way,
and soone after the sudden approach of the Indians forced
them with feare to Seale to the truth of this evill tidings,
and some of them with their dearest bloud; three Woemen-
kinde they caught, and carried away, but one of them being
more fearfull of their cruell usage afterward then of the losse
of her life at present, being borne away to the thickest of the
company, resisted so stoutly with scratching and biting, that
the Indian, exasperated therewith, cast her downe on the
Earth, and beate out her braines with his Hatchet, the other
two maids they led away and returned, their Commission
reaching no farther at present, having taken these two prisoners they did not offer to abuse their persons, as was verily
deemed they would, questioned them with such broken English, as some of them could speak, to know whether they
could make Gunpowder. Which when they understood they
could not doe, their prize proved nothing so pretious a Pearle
in their eyes as before; for seeing they exceeded not their

own Squawes in Art, their owne thoughts informed them they would fall abundantly short in industry, and as for beauty they esteeme black beyond any colour.

Wherefore their Sqawes use that sinfull art of painting their Faces in the hollow of their Eyes and Nose, with a shining black, out of which their tip of their Nose appeares very deformed, and their cheeke bone, being of a lighter swart black, on which they have a blew crosse dyed very deepe.

This is the beauty esteemed by them, but yet their pride was much increased by this hostile Act of theirs, and the English were more and more contemned of them, notwithstanding the Dutch, who traded with these Indians, procured the Maides liberty againe.

CHAP. II.

Of the couragious resolutions, the Lord indued these his People withall being invironed with many deepe distresses.

After this Message delivered, these brood of Travilers being almost Non-plus't in their grave and sollid Counsells, deem it now high time to follow their old way, of making their complaint to the supreame judge of all the World, by way of Petition, who they knew right well, stood not as an idle spectator beholding his peoples Ruth, and their Enemies rage; But as an Actor in all actions to bring to naught the desires of the wicked, but [put] period to their power, divert their stroaks from his, to their own heads, bring glory to his Name, and good to his people from their most wicked malignity, having also the ordering of every weapon in its first produce, guiding every shaft that flies, leading each bullet to his place of setling, and Weapon to the wound it makes; yet he most righteous and holy in all his actions. To this great Lord Peramount, had these poore afflicted people accesse through the intercession of their Lord Christ, whose worke (though very weake to performe) they were now about, wherefore casting themselves down at his feet in the sense of their owne unworthinesse, that [they] desire him to doe his owne worke in them, and for them, that the Mountaines in

the way of Zerubbabel may become a plaine, and then laying
open the great straites they were in to him, who knew them
far better then themselves, they had this answer returned
them, which if men dare deny, the Lord from Heaven hath,
and shall further witnesse it; But before it be declared, let
all men lay downe their interest they suppose they may have
in procuring it, both English and others, that the glory of our
Lord Christ may appeare in its splendor, to the danting of
every proud heart, and for the perpetuall incouragement of
all the Souldiers of Christ, even the meanest in his Armies:
for the day of his high Power is come, yea, his appointed time
to have mercy upon Sion is at hand, all you whose eyes of pity
so see her in the dust, streame down with pear-like drops of
compassion, a little mixture of the unconceiveable joy for
the glorious worke of Christ, Now, now, I [ay] now in hand
for the exalting of his glorious Kingdome, in preparing his
Churches for himselfe, and with his own blessed hands wiping
away the teares that trickel downe her cheekes, drying her
dankish eyes, and hushing her sorrowfull sobs in his sweete
bosome.   This rightly believed, and meeting in the soule of
any poore Christian, will make the narrow affections of his
body too little to containe the present apprehensions of his
Soule; And therefore wanting a vacuum to containe the
strength of this new Wine, wonder not if it vent it selfe with
swift thrilling teares from the most tender part of the vessell.
And here the Author must needs intreate the charitable
Reader to enlarge in the Closset of his own heart, for his folly
hee confesses in medling so meanly with such waighty matters,
being blinded by eager affection, hee lost the sight of his great
inability to the worke, when hee first set Pen to Paper.   As
the Lord surrounded his chosen Israel with dangers deepe to
make his miraculous deliverance famous throughout, and to
the end of the World, so here behold the Lord Christ, having
egged a small handfull of his people forth in a forlorne Wildernesse, stripping them naked from all humane helps, plunging
them in a gulph of miseries, that they may swim for their
lives through the Ocean of his Mercies, and land themselves
safe in the armes of his compassion.

CHAP. III.

Of the Lords great deliverance of his New England People, from the flouds of Errors that were bursting in among them.

As for the great Mountaine[s] of proud erronious judgement on your right hand, the prayer of Faith shall remove them, and cast them into the depth of the Sea, and for the strengthning of your faith herein, because the Lord will have you depend on him in the use of his meanes, not miracle, hee hath purposely pitcht out for this very worke, some of his most orthodox servants, and chiefe Champions of his truth, able through his mercy to weld [wield] that bright Weapon of his Word prepared by the spirit for this purpose, to bring to the block these Traytours to his truths one by one, and behead them before your eyes.   And for this very end they are to gather together as one Man in a Synodicall way,[1] with a decisive power to undoe all the cunning twisted knots of Satans Malignity to the truths of Christ, opening the Scriptures by the power of his spirit, cleering Scripture by Scripture, that nothing but the pure Word of God may take place; and that you may assuredly believe the Lord hath purposely called his Servants and Souldiers to this place by his Providence to cut off this cursed spirit of Errours and Heresies, which hath but at first dog'd all Reformed Churches of Christ, There are for your further aid herein many more of these sincere Souldiers floating upon the great Ocean toward you, who will be with you before this Synod is set, that you may declare it in the Eares of all posterity, to be the very Finger of God in catching the proud in their owne craftinesse, who had hatch't their devices, thus to cast all the Ministers of Christ, except some one or two, under this censure of being prejudiced against their persons, and for the little remnant to labour with flattery to blinde their eyes, that at least they might not be against them, Seeing they could not procure them to take

---

[1] A general council of the Congregational churches of New England, including both the ministers and representatives of the laity, sat at Cambridge from August 30 to September 22, 1637.   It condemned eighty-two errors attributed to the Hutchinsonian party.

their part, (to be sure when the grossenesse of their Errors were made known, they would not), by this meanes having their hopes exalted (in their owne apprehensions at least) to gaine the most of the people on their side.

The Lord casts them downe from the proud Pinacle of their Machiavilian Plot, by bringing in more men of courage uninterested, yea, unknown to most of their persons, but for their errors, as strong to confute them as any, and more fit to wipe off the filme from the eyes of some of their brethren, which these Erronists by their Syccophancy had clouded.

The time for the meeting of this Synod was to be in the seventh month following, commonly called September. The civill government well approving of their desires herein, were very willing to further them all they could, and in the meane time it was the worke of these valiant of the Lord, to search out, not for men and Womens persons, but their errors, which they gathered up from all parts, willing all that would or could defend them to use their best meanes, like as Jehu when he was to execute the judgements of the Lord upon Ahabs bloudy household, would have had his servants defend their Masters Children if they could,[1] onely you must understand there was but 70. Sons, and here was 80. Errors, of which you shall further hear when the time comes.

CHAP. IV.

Of the abundant mercies of Christ in providing liberall supply for his New England People, in regard of their outward man, Food, Rayment and all other necessaries and conveniencies.

Now for the hardships on the left hand, they had as good an answer as in the former; their Christ had not saved their lives from the raging Seas to slay them in the Wildernesse with Famine; your life is much more pretious in the eyes of the Lord then food, and your bodies then rayment: yea, the Lord of Heaven, who hath honoured you so far as to imploy you in this glorious worke of his, knowes you must have these

---

[1] II Kings x. 1–3.

things, and it was not you, deare hearts, that chose this place,
but the Lord, as seeing it most fit to doe his worke in, knowing
that had you met with a Rich Land filled with all plenty,
your heart would have beene taken off this worke, which he
must have done. But to strengthen your Faith in this point
also, you shall see hee who commanded the Fruits to spring
out of the Earth, when none were, can much more cause this
corner of the Earth to be fruitfull to you, and this you shall
attaine by meanes; although hee have caused the Foules of
the Aire, the Grasse of the Field to depend upon him in a
more immediate manner, yet you hath he taught to Sow,
Reape, carry into Barnes, and Spin, and indeed herein the
Lord hath answered his people abundantly to the wonder of
all that see or hear of it; And that whereas at their first comming it was a rare matter for a man to have foure or five
Acres of Corne, now many have four or five score, and to prevent men from Sacrificing to their Nets, the Lord hath taught
them to labour with more ease: to great admiration also in-
larg'd it, for it was with sore labour that on [one] man could
Plant and tend foure Acres of Indians Graine, and now with
two Oxen hee can Plant and tend 30.   Besides the Lord hath
of late altered the very course of the Heavens in the season of
the weather, that all kinde of graine growes much better then
heretofore; Insomuch that Marchandizing being stopped at
present, they begin question what to do with their Corne.

CHAP. V.

*Of the wonderfull deliverance wrought by the Lord Christ, for his
poore New England Churches, in freing them from the fear
of their Malignant adversaries, who forc't them to this
Wildernesse.*

And now to the third and great distresse, which lay behind them by reason of their back friends, the Lording Bishops,
and other Malignant adversaries, being daily exasperated
against them, and in especiall at this time by one Morton, who
named himselfe the Host of Merrimount, who wanted not
malice, could he possible have attained meanes to effect it;
But the Lord Christ prevented both him and his Masters,

whom with flattery he sought to please with scurrillous deriding the servants of Christ, to bring them into contempt,[1]
yet the Lord prevented all, and delivered this wretched fellow
into his peoples hands againe after all this, who dealt as fa-
vourably with him as David did with Shimmei.[2]   Besides this,
the evill usage that many of the beloved servants of Christ
had from the hands of those in office at their departure, declared plainely, that there were some, who would willingly
have pursued them to bring them under bondage againe.
Herein their answer was that they should stand still, and see
the salvation of the Lord, who was now resolved to fight for
them against his and their implacable enemies; although
more mighty than they: and indeed all meanes of resistance
in the hand of man being so small, that it could not possible
bee discerned by any mortall eye; yet will the Lord worke by
means and not by miracle; when the Lord called forth Joshua
to fight with Amaleck, his Moses must be in the Mount at
Prayers; seeing this answer deeply concernes the dearly beloved of our Lord Christ remaining in England, let them listen
to the answer.[3]

Also how came it to passe that the Lord put it into your
hearts to set upon a Reformation, was it not by prayer attained?   You are not excluded, although the Churches of
Christ here are for the present in the Mount, and you in the
Vally fighting, yet surely they had neede of helpe to hold up
their hands, whereas the nerenesse of the danger to you in the
enemies overcoming, is a great motive to keepe up yours stedy,
yet may you say rightly to the Churches of Christ here, as

---

[1] The allusion is to Thomas Morton's *New English Canaan* (London, 1637),
which gives an amusing but scurrilous account of the Puritan *régime* in New
England and of what the graceless author suffered at Puritan hands.

[2] II Samuel xix. 18–22.   The parallel is none too close.   David pardoned
Shimei for his sedition.   When Thomas Morton injudiciously came within reach
of the magistrates of Massachusetts, six years after the publication of his book,
they kept him in prison for a year and fined him a hundred pounds.

[3] Exodus xvii. 8–13.   The voluble harangue which fills the remainder of
the chapter is such an intricate mosaic of Scripture texts that to identify them all
in foot-notes would be cumbersome and probably useless.   Its main purport,
as may easily be seen, is to express the sympathy of the New England Puritans
with those of Old England in the successful struggle the latter had waged against
prelacy.

Mordachy to Hester the Queene, if you hold your peace deliverance shall come another way, and thinke not to escape, because you are in New England; Assuredly the Lord is doing great things, and waites for the prayers of his people that he may be gratious unto them, and verily the poore Churches of Christ heere cannot but take notice of the great workes the Lord hath done for you of late, which are famous throughout the whole World; And should they not take them as an answer of these weake prayers, they feare they should neglect to magnify his mercy toward you, and them: the noble acts of the Lord Christ, for the freedome of his people from that intolerable Prelaticall bondage, are almost miraculously committed to memory by the able servants of Christ, whom hee hath stirred up for that very end, yet must you not shut out the valiant souldiers of Christ (disciplin'd in this unwonted Wildernesse) from having share with you in the worke, yet no farther but that Christ may be all in all: who hath caused the Midianites to fight against Midian, till the true Israelites had gathered themselves together, hee it is that hath brought the counsells of the wicked to naught, hee it is that hath discovered the secret plottings of the King of Assyria, even in his Bedchamber; Hee it is that hath declared himself to be with your mighty men of valour, and assuredly all you valiant Souldiers of Christ, both in one England and the other, the Lord hath shewed you as great signes and wonders for the strengthening of your faith, as was the wetting and drying of the fleece to Gedeon, onely beware of setting up an Ephod in the latter end; Let the Churches of Christ be set up according to his first institution, or you will make double worke, for all may see by what is done already, there is nothing too hard for him. Hee will downe with all againe and againe, till his Kingdom alone be exalted, for the which all the Israel of God fight, wrastle, pray, and here you may see the servants of Christ fighting at 900 leagues distant.

Oh you proud Bishops, that would have all the World stoope to your Lordly power, the heathen Romans your predecessors, after they had banished John to the Isle of Pathmos, suffered him quietly to injoy the Revelation of Jesus Christ there; here is a people that have betaken themselves to a newfound World, distanced from you with the widest

Ocean the World affords, and yet you grudge them the purity of Christs Ordinances there. No wonder then, nay wonder all the World at the sudden and unexpected downfall of these domineering Lords, who had Princes to protect them, armes to defend them, and almost three whole Kingdomes at their command; and no enemy of theirs in sight, onely there appeares a little cloud about the bignesse of a mans hand out of the Westerne Ocean, I [ay] but the Lord Christ is in it, out of Sion the perfection of beauty hath God shined. Our God shall come, and shall not keepe silence, a Fire shall devour afore him, and mighty tempests shall be moved round about him. Now gather together you King-like Bishops, and make use of all the Kingly power you can, for the cloud is suddenly come up, he rode upon Cherub and did flie. And now let the Children of Sion rejoyce in their King, for the Lord hath pleasure in his people, hee will make the meeke glorious by deliverance; And that the whole Earth may know it is the Lords owne worke, the Arch-prelate and his complices must begin to war with the Scots, and that implacably; [1] the Prelates desire a Parliament thinking to establish iniquity by a Law, but the iniquity of the Ammorites is already full, and all your cunning counsells shall but contrive your owne destruction; They remonstrant against all Acts of Parliament that passe without their Vote, and by this means wind out themselves for ever voting more,[2] they devise how they may have such persons committed to prison as favour not their proceeding,

But the Lord turned their mischiefe they had conceived upon their own pates, and they themselves were sent to prison by halfe a score at a time; And such was the unsavourynesse of this seeming salt, that it was good for nothing, but to Lord it over others. Their tyranny being taken out of their hands, they could not indure to be commanded by any; And therefore unfit for the war which they stirred up, to recover the

---

[1] The invasion of Scotland by Charles I., in the spring of 1639, to meet the insurrection excited by Archbishop Laud's attempt to re-establish episcopacy in that country.

[2] Twelve protesting bishops declared the nullity of all votes passed by the lords while the prelates were absent through fear of the multitude; whereupon Parliament passed, in February, 1642, an act excluding all the bishops.

people againe under their bondage, yet such was the madnesse of some, that they loved their servitude so well as to
fight for it; but surely such had never rightly knowne the
service of the Lord Christ, which is perfect freedome from all
such tyrannous yoaks, and verily just it is with the Lord to
cause such to be servants unto Shishak,[1] that they may know
the service of the Lord, and the service of the Kingdomes of
the Country.   But however an Army is raised to defend their
Lordly dignity; Let the Saints be joyfull with glory, let the
high Acts of God be in their mouths, and a two edged Sword
in their hands, to bind their Kings in chaines, and their
Nobles in fetters of Iron.   The Charets of the Lord are twenty
thousand thousands of Angells, the Lord is among them as in
Sinai, Kings of Armies did flee apace; and now you that have
borne such a wicked spirit of malignity against the people of
Christ, can your hearts indure, and your hands wax strong in
the day that he shall have to doe with you?   Oh you proud
Prelates that boast so much of your taking the Kings part,
miserable partakers are you; in stead of obeying him, you
have caused him to obey you, its writ in such great capitall
letters that a child may read it: what was the cause of the first
raising war against the Scots which occasioned the Parliament?   When you saw they would not further the war as
you would have them, they were soone traytors in your account, and prosecuted against with Army after army, and
was not all this to make the Scots receive your Injunctions?
A very fayer bottom to build a bloudy war upon, that the
Prelatticall power might Lord it in Scotland, as they of a
long time had done in England: it was your Pithagorian
Phylosophy that caused the King to loose his Life, by perswading him his Kingly power lived in your Lordly dignity,
as a thing subordinate unto it, and he so deeply taken with
this conceit, that it cost the lives of many thousands more
then ever hee, or his Father, would doe for saving or recovering the Pallatine Country.[2]

[1] II Chronicles xii. 8.
[2] In the eyes of the Puritan party it was a most culpable offence on the
part of both James and Charles, that in 1621–1626 they did nothing effectual to
aid James's son-in-law, the Protestant Frederick V., elector palatine and king of
Bohemia, to defend himself and the Palatinate from Austrian and Spanish conquest.

Experience hath taught the savage Indians, among whom we live, that they may and doe daily bring Wolves to be tame, but they cannot breake them of their ravening nature, and I would your Royalist would learne of them to know, that as your Lord Bishops, Deanes, Prebends, etc. be right whelps of the Roman litter, so let them be never so well tam'd, they will retaine their nature still, to Lord it over all kinde of Civill Government; But woe and alasse that ever any of our Countrymen should be so blind, that after they are delivered from so great a bondage by such *Wonder working Providence* of the Lord Christ; Ever and anon to indeavour to make a Captaine over them, that they may returne againe into Egypt, as appeares by the plots which have been discovered, and broken in pieces by the right hand of the most high, and yet for all this their's such a hankering after somewhat of the Prelaticall greatnesse, by the English Clergy, and the Scottish Classis, that many of them could afford to raise another war for it.[1] But brethren I beseech you be more wiser, lest when you are growne hot in your quarrell, the Malignant party come and set you agreed. Stablish peace in righteousnesse, and let the word be your rule, heare one another with meekeness, and the Lord will cleare up the whole truth unto you in his due time; And now to declare plainly how far the Lord hath beene pleased to make use of any of his people in these Westerne parts, about this Worke, for to say truth they have done nothing in holes and corners, but their workes are obvious to all the World: if the sufferings of the Saints be pretious in the eyes of Christ, so as to provoke him in displeasure to cut off the occasioners thereof, then thus his poore unworthy people here have had a great stroake in the downfall of their adversaries to the present possessed truths of Christ, for this wildernesse worke hath not beene carried on without fighthings that have come before him, and Groanes that have entred his eares, and Teares treasured up in his bottles. Againe, if the ardent and strong affections of the people of God, for his glorious comming to advance his Kingdome in the splendor and purity of his Gospell, as to cry with the holy Prophet, "Oh that he would breake the Heavens and come down," be regarded of

---

[1] "New Presbyter is but old Priest writ large," said Milton.

the Lord Christ, so as to remove with his mighty power the very Mountaines out of the way, and hurle them into the deepe; Then hath these weake wormes instrumentally had a share in the great desolation the Lord Christ hath wrought. For this History will plainely declare with what zeale and deepe affection, and unresistable resolutions, these pilgrim people have endeavoured the gathering together his Saints, for the edifying the Body of Christ, that he may raign both Lord and King for ever.

Yet againe, if the prayers of the faithfull people of God availe any thing for the accomplishment of his promises, in the destruction of Antichrist, for the subduing of Armies without striking one stroake; Then assuredly these Jacobites have wrestled with the Lord, not onely (with that good King Jekoshaphat) [1] proclaiming one Fast, but many Fasts, they, their Wives and little ones standing before the Lord; Oh our God wilt thou not judge them for we have no might, etc. Lastly, if the Lord himselfe have roared from Sion, (as in the dayes of the Prophet Amos) [2] so from his Churches in New England, by a great and terrible Earthquake (which happened much about the time the Lordly Prelates were preparing their injunctions for Scotland). [3] Taking rise from the West, it made its progresse to the Eastward, causing the Earth to rise up and downe like the waves of the Sea; having the same effect on the Sea also, causing the Ships that lay in the Harbor to quake, the which, at that very time, was said to be a signe from the Lord to his Churches, that he was purposed to shake the Kingdomes of Europes Earth, and now by his providences brought to passe, all men may reade as much and more: as if he should have said to these his scattered people (yet now againe united in Church Covenant) the Lord is now gathering together his Armies, and that your faith may be strengthened, you shall feele and heare the shakings of the Earth by the might of his power: yea, the Sea also, to shew he will ordaine Armies both by Sea and Land to make Babilon desolate; Things thus concurring as an immediate answer of the Lord to his peoples prayers and endeavours, caused some of this

---

[1] II Chronicles xx. 1–21.   [2] Amos i. 2.

[3] Earthquakes of June 1, 1638, and January 14, 1639. See bk. II., ch. XII., *post*, and Winthrop, I. 270, 292.

little handfull with resolute courage and boldnesse to returne againe to their native Land, that they might (the Lord accepting and assisting them in their endeavours) be helpfull in advancing the Kingdome of Christ, and casting down every strong house of sinne and Satan.   It matters not indeed who be the instruments, if with the eye of faith these that go forth to fight the Lords Battailes, can but see and heare the Lord going out before them against their enemies, with a sound in the tops of the Mulbery Trees.   Here are assuredly evident signes that the Lord Christ is gone forth for his peoples deliverance, and now Frogs, Flies, Lice or Dust, shall serve to destroy those [who] will yet hold his people in bondage, notwithstanding the Lord will honour such as hee hath made strong for himself;   And therefore hee causeth the worthies in Davids time to be recorded, and it is the duty of Gods people to incourage one another in the worke of the Lord, then let all whose hearts are upright for the Lord, ponder well his goings in his Sanctuary, that their hands may be strengthened in the work they goe about, onely be strong and of a good courage.

CHAP. VI.

Of the gratious goodnesse of the Lord Christ, in saving his New England people, from the hand of the barbarous Indians.

Lastly, for the frontispiece of their present distresse, namely the Indian war, they with much meeknesse and great deliberation, wisely contrived how they might best helpe their fellow brethren; hereupon they resolved to send a solemne Embassage to old Cannonicus, chiefe Sachem of the narrow Ganset [1] Indians, who being then well stricken in yeares had caused his nephew Miantinemo to take the Govern-

[1] Narragansett. The embassy to Canonicus is related so minutely and so vividly as to make it reasonable to conclude that Johnson was of the party, though Winthrop names only Edward Gibbons and John Higginson, with Cutshamekin, sagamore of Massachusetts. The Narragansetts dwelt in what is now southern Rhode Island. Their number of fighting men was probably some 1,500 or 2,000. If they had combined with the Pequots against the colonists, the latter might have been exterminated. That they were persuaded not to make this dangerous combination was due largely to the intercession of Roger Williams, whom they much regarded.

ment upon him, who was a very sterne man, and of a great stature, of a cruell nature, causing all his Nobility and such as were his attendance to tremble at his speech. The people under his Government were very numerous, besides the Niantick Indians, whose Prince was of neare aliance unto him; They were able to set forth, as was then supposed, 30000. fighting men. The English sought by all meanes to keepe these at least from confederating with the Pequods, and understanding by intelligence, that the Pequots would send to them for that end, endeavoured to prevent them. Fit and able men being chosen by the English, they hast them to Cannonicus Court, which was about fourescore miles from Boston.

The Indian King hearing of their comming, gathered together his chiefe Counsellors, and a great number of his Subjects to give them entertainment, resolving as then that the young King should receive their message, yet in his hearing. They arriving, were entertain'd royally, with respect to the Indian manner. Boil'd Chesnuts is their White-bread, which are very sweet, as if they were mixt with Sugar; and because they would be extraordinary in their feasting, they strive for variety after the English manner, boyling Puddings made of beaten corne, putting therein great store of black berryes, somewhat like Currants. They having thus nobly feasted them, afterward give them Audience, in a State-house,[1] round, about fifty foot wide, made of long poles stuck in the ground, like your Summer-houses in England, and covered round about, and on the top with Mats, save a small place in the middle of the Roofe, to give light, and let out the smoke.

In this place sate their Sachim, with very great attendance; the English comming to deliver their Message, to manifest the greater state, the Indian Sachim lay along upon the ground, on a Mat, and his Nobility sate on the ground, with their legs doubled up, their knees touching their chin; with much sober

---

[1] An early use of a term the history of which Mr. Albert Matthews has elaborated in the *Publications of the Colonial Society of Massachusetts*, VIII. 14–26. Its development, in the sense in which we now use it (state capitol), has been peculiar to America. The sense in which Johnson uses it, and out of which the modern use grew, is that of "house of state," "house belonging to the body politic," to wit, the tribe of the Narragansetts.

gravity they attend the Interpreters speech. It was matter of much wonderment to the English, to see how solidly and wisely these savage people did consider of the weighty undertaking of a War; especially old Canonicus, who was very discreet in his answers. The young Sachem was indeed of a more lofty spirit, which wrought his ruine, as you may heare, after the decease of the old King. But at this time his answer was, that he did willingly embrace peace with the English, considering right well, that although their number was but small in comparison of his people, and that they were but strangers to the Woods, Swamps, and advantagious places of this Wildernesse, yet withall he knew the English were advantaged by their weapons of War, and especially their Guns, which were of great terror to his people, and also he had heard they came of a more populous Nation by far than all the Indians were, could they be joyn'd together. Also on the other hand, with mature deliberation, he was well advised of the Peaquods cruell disposition and aptnesse to make War, as also their neere neighbourhood to his people, who though they were more numerous, yet were they withall more effeminate, and lesse able to defend themselves from the sudden incursions of the Peaquods, should they fall out with them. Hereupon hee demes it most conducing to his owne and his peoples safety to direct his course in a middle way, holding amity with both. The English returne home, having gained the old Kings favour so farre, as rather to favour them then the Pequods, who perceiving their Neighbouring English [1] had sent forth aid to the Mattacusets government, thought it high time to seeke the winning all the Indians they could on their side, and among others they make their addresse to old Cannonicus, who, instead of taking part with them, labours all he can to hush the War in hand, laying before them the sad effects of War; sometimes proving sad and mournfull to the very Victors themselves, but alwayes to the vanquished, and withall tells them what potent enemies they had to contend with, whose very weapons and Armor were matter of terror, setting their persons a side; as also that English man was no much hoggery yet, and therefore they might soone appease

[1] The Connecticut men, both those at Gardiner's fort of Saybrook and those up the river at Hartford, Windsor, and Wethersfield.

them, by delivering into their hands those persons that had beene the death of any of them, which were much better than that the whole Nation should perish.

For the present the Pequods seemed to be inclinable to the old Sachims counsell, but being returned home againe among their rude multitude (the chief place of cowardly boasting) they soon change their minde; yet the old Sachim sends the English word he had wrought with them, and in very deed, the English had rather make choice of Peace then Warre, provided it may stand with Truth and Righteousnesse: and therefore send forth a band of Souldiers, who arriving in the Peaquod Country, address themselves to have a Treaty with them about delivering up the murtherers; they making shew of willingness so to doe bade them abide awhile and they would bring them, and in the mean time they were conversant among the Souldiers, and viewing their Armie,[1] pointed to divers places where they could hit them with their Arrowes for all their Corslets. But their greatest number lying the while at the other side of a great hill, and anon appearing on the top of the hill, in sight of the English, those Indians that were among the English withdrawing toward them, no sooner were they come to their Companions, but all of a suddaine they gave a great shout, and shewed the English a fair pair of heeles, who seeing it would not availe any thing to follow them (they being farre swifter of foot than the English) made their returne home againe.[2]

This bootlesse voyage incouraged the Indians very much, who insulted over them at the fort, boasting of this their deluding them, and withall, they blasphemed the Lord, saying Englishmans God was all one Flye, and that English man was all one Sqawe, and themselves all one Moor-hawks. Thus by their horrible pride they fitted themselves for destruction. The English hearing this report, were now full assured that the Lord would deliver them into their hands to execute his righteous judgement upon these blasphemous murtherers; and therefore raised fresh Souldiers for the warre, to the num-

[1] Armor.
[2] This first unsuccessful expedition or reconnoissance was made by a body of Massachusetts troops, sent out by Governor Vane in August, 1636, under command of Endicott.

ber of fourscore, or thereabout,[1] out of the severall towns in the Matachusets, and although they were but in their beginnings, yet the Lord, who fore-intended their work, provided for all their wants, and indeed it was much that they had any bisket to carry with them in these times of scarcity, or any vessels to transport their men and ammunition: yet all was provided by the gracious hand of the most high; and the Souldiers, many of them, not onely armed with outward weapons, and armour of defence, but filled with a spirit of courage and magnanimity to resist, not onely men, but Devils; for surely he was more than ordinaryly present with this Indian army, as the sequell will shew: as also for their further incouragement, the reverend and zealously affected servant of Christ, Mr. John Wilson, went with the army, who had treasured up heaps of the experimentall goodnesse of God towards his people. Having formerly passed through perils by Sea, perils by Land, perils among false brethren, etc. he followed the warre purposely to sound an alarum before the Lord with his silver trumpet, that his people might be remembred before him: the Souldiers arriving in safety at the towne of Hartford, where they were encouraged by the reverend Ministers there, with some such speech as followes.

Fellow-Souldiers, Country-men, and Companions in this Wildernesse worke, who are gathered together this day by the inevitable providence of the great Jehovah, not in a tumultuous manner hurried on by the floating fancy of every high hot headed braine, whose actions prove abortive, or if any fruit brought forth, it hath beene rape, theft, and murther, things inconsisting with natures light, then much lesse with a Souldiers valour; but you, my deare hearts, purposely pickt out by the godly grave Fathers of this government, that your prowesse may carry on the work, where there Justice in her righteous course is obstructed, you need not question your authority to execute those whom God, the righteous Judge of all the world, hath condemned for blaspheming his sacred Majesty, and murthering his Servants: every common Souldier among you is now installed a Magistrate; then shew your selves men of courage. I would not

---

[1] The whole Massachusetts levy was 160. There are interesting accounts of the Pequot war, of May, 1637, by each of the three chief commanders against them: Captain John Mason's *Brief History of the Pequod War*, Captain John Underhill's *Newes from New England*, and Lion Gardiner's *Relation of the Pequot Wars*.

draw low the height of your enemies hatred against you, and so debase your valour. This you may expect, their swelling pride hath laid the foundation of large conceptions against you and all the people of Christ in this wildernesse, even as wide as Babels bottome. But, my brave Souldiers, it hath mounted already to the clouds, and therefore it is ripe for confusion; also their crueltie is famously knowne, yet all true-bred Souldiers reserve this as a common maxime, cruelty and cowardize are unseparable companions; and in briefe, there is nothing wanting on your enemies part, that may deprive you of a compleat victory, onely their nimbleness of foot, and the unaccessible swamps and nut-tree woods, forth of which your small numbers may intice, and industry compell them.   And now to you I put the question, who would not fight in such a cause with an agile spirit, and undaunted boldnesse? yet if you look for further encouragement, I have it for you; riches and honour are the next to a good cause eyed by every Souldier, to maintain your owne, and spoile your enemies of theirs; although gold and silver be wanting to either of you, yet have you that to maintaine which is farre more precious, the lives, libertyes, and new purchased freedomes, priviledges, and immunities of the indeared servants of our Lord Christ Jesus, and of your second selves, even your affectionated bosome-mates, together with the chiefe pledges of your love, the comforting contents of harmlesse pratling and smiling babes; and in a word, all the riches of that goodnesse and mercy that attends the people of God in the injoyment of Christ, in his Ordinances, even in this life; and as for honour, David was not to be blamed for enquiring after it, as a due recompence of that true valour the Lord hath bestowed on him: and now the Lord hath prepared this honour for you, oh you couragious Souldiers of his, to execute vengeance upon the heathen, and correction among the people, to binde their Kings in chaines, and Nobles in fetters of Iron, that they may execute upon them the judgements that are written! this honour shall be to all his Saints.   But some of you may suppose deaths stroke may cut you short of this: let every faithfull Souldier of Christ Jesus know, that the cause why some of his indeared Servants are taken away by death in a just warre (as this assuredly is) it is not because they should fall short of the honours accompanying such noble designes, but rather because earths honours are too scant for them, and therefore the everlasting Crown must be set upon their heads forthwith.   Then march on with a cheerfull Christian courage in the strength of the Lord and the power of his might, who will forthwith inclose your enemies in your hands, make their multitudes fall under your warlike weapons, and your feet shall soon be set on their proud necks.

After the Ministers of Christ had, through the grace that was given them, exhorted and encouraged these Souldiers appointed for the work, they being provided with certaine Indian guides, who with the close of the day brought them to a small river, where they could perceive many persons had been dressing of fish; upon the sight thereof, the Indian guides concluded they were now a feasting it at their fort, which was hard at hand.[1] The English calling a Councill of warre, being directed by the speciallest providence of the most high God, they concluded to storm the fort a little before break of day; at which time they supposed the Indians being up late in their jolly feasting, would bee in their deepest sleepe; and surely so it was, for they now slept their last: the English keeping themselves as covertly as they could, approached the fort at the time appointed, which was builded of whole Trees set in the ground fast, and standing up an end about twelve foot high, very large, having pitcht their Wigwams within it, the entrance being on two sides, with intricate Meanders to enter. The chiefe Leaders of the English made some little stand before they offered to enter, but yet boldly they rushed on, and found the passages guarded at each place with an Indian Bow-man, ready on the string, they soone let fly, and wounded the formost of the English in the shoulder, yet having dispatch'd the Porters, they found the winding way in without a Guide, where they soone placed themselves round the Wigwams, and according to direction they made their first shot with the muzzle of their Muskets downe to the ground, knowing the Indian manner is to lie on the ground to sleep, from which they being in this terrible manner awakened, unlesse it were such as were slaine with the shot.

After this some of the English entered the Wigwams, where they received some shot with their Arrowes, yet catching up the fire-brands, they began to fire them, and others of the English Soulders with powder, did the same: the day now

---

[1] The Pequots' fort stood on the western side of the Mystic River, near the present site of Mystic, Conn. Mason, after a demonstration on the western border of their territory, surprised them by making his attack from the eastward, after a march through the neutral territory of the Narragansetts. Underhill gives a diagram of the fort, which may be seen reproduced in Palfrey's *History of New England*, I. 466.

began to break; the Lord intending to have these murtherers know he would looke out of the cloudy pillar upon them: and now these women and children set up a terrible out-cry; the men were smitten down, and slaine, as they came forth with a great slaughter, the Sqawes crying out, oh much winn it [1] English-man, who moved with pitty toward them, saved their lives: and hereupon some young youth cryed, I squaw, I squaw, thinking to finde the like mercy. There were some of these Indians, as is reported, whose bodyes were not to be pierced by their sharp rapiers or swords of [for] a long time, which made some of the Souldiers think the Devil was in them, for there were some Powwowes [2] among them, which work strange things with the help of Satan. But this was very remarkable, one of them being wounded to death, and thrust thorow the neck with a halbert; yet after all, lying groaning upon the ground, he caught the halberts speare in his hand, and wound it quite round. After the English were thus possessed of this first victory, they sent their prisoners to the pinnaces, and prosecute the warre in hand, to the next Battalia of the Indians, which lay on a hill about two miles distant, and indeed their stoutest Souldiers were at this place, and not yet come to the fort; the English being weary with their night worke, and wanting such refreshing as the present worke required, began to grow faint, yet having obtained one victory, they were very desirous of another: and further, they knew right-well, till this cursed crew were utterly rooted out, they should never be at peace; therefore they marched on toward them.[3] Now assuredly, had the Indians knowne how much weakned our Souldiers were at present, they might have born them downe with their multitude, they being very strong and agile of body, had they come to handy-gripes; but the Lord (who would have his people know their work was his, and he onely must order their Counsels, and

---

[1] *Match winnet*, very good.   [2] Medicine-men.

[3] In reality Mason, after the destruction of the fort and the slaughter of several hundred of the Pequots, contented himself with holding in check the second body of Indians encountered and making good his retreat to the fort at Saybrook. The pursuit of the remaining Pequots into the swamp near New Haven, resulting almost in the extermination of the tribe, was the work of a fresh expedi-cion, in July.

war-like work for them) did bring them timely supply from
the vessels, and also gave them a second victory, wherein they
slew many more of their enemies, the residue flying into a
very thick swamp, being unaccessible, by reason of the boggy
holes of water, and thick bushes; the English drawing up their
company beleagered the swamp, and the Indians in the mean
time skulking up and down, and as they saw opportunity
they made shot with their Arrowes at the English, and then
suddainly they would fall flat along in the water to defend
themselves from the retalliation of the Souldiers Muskets.
This lasted not long, for our English being but a small number,
had parted themselves far asunder, but by the providence of
the most high God, some of them spyed an Indian with a
kettle at his back going more inwardly into the swamp, by
which they perceived there was some place of firm land in the
midst thereof, which caused them to make way for the passage
of their Souldiers, which brought this warre to a period: For
although many got away, yet were they no such considerable
number as ever to raise warre any more; the slaine or wounded
of the English were (through the mercy of Christ) but a few:
One of them being shot through the body, neere about the
breast, regarding it not till of a long time after, which caused
the bloud to dry and thicken on either end of the arrow so
that it could not be drawne forth his body without great difficulty and much paine, yet did he scape his life, and the wound
healed. Thus the Lord was pleased to assist his people in
this warre, and deliver them out of the Indians hands, who
were very lusty proper men of their hands, most of them, as
may appear by one passage which I shall here relate: thus it
came to passe, As the Souldiers were uppon their march, close
by a great thicket, where no eye could penetrate farre, as it
often falls out in such wearisom wayes, where neither men nor
beast have beaten out a path; some Souldiers lingering behinde their fellowes, two Indians watching their opportunity,
much like a hungry hauke, when they supposed the last man
was come up, who kept a double distance in his march, they
sudden and swiftly snatched him up in their tallens, hoising
him upon their shoulders, ran into the swamp with him; the
Souldier unwilling to be made a Pope by being borne on mens
shoulders, strove with them all he could to free himselfe from

their hands; but, like a carefull Commander, one Captaine Davenport,[1] then Lieutenant of this company, being diligent in his place to bring up the reare, coming up with them, followed with speed into the swamp after him, having a very severe cutlace tyed to his wrist, and being well able to make it bite sore when he set it on, resolving to make it fall foul on the Indians bones, he soone overtook them, but was prevented by the buckler they held up from hitting them, which was the man they had taken: It was matter of much wonder to see with what dexterity they hurled the poore Souldier about, as if they had been handling a Lacedæmonian shield, so that the nimble Captaine Davenport could not, of a long time, fasten one stroke upon them; yet, at last, dying their tawny skin into a crimson colour, they cast downe their prey, and hasted thorow the thickets for their lives. The Souldier thus redeemed, had no such hard usage, but that he is alive, as I suppose, at this very day: The Lord in mercy toward his poore Churches having thus destroyed these bloudy barbarous Indians, he returnes his people in safety to their vessels, where they take account of their prisoners: the Squawes and some young youths they brought home with them, and finding the men to be deeply guilty of the crimes they undertooke the warre for, they brought away onely their heads as a token of their victory. By this means the Lord strook a trembling terror into all the Indians round about, even to this very day.

Chap. VII.

Of the first Synod holden in New England, whereby the Lord in his mercy did more plainly discover his ancient truths, and confute those cursed errors that ordinarily dogg the reforming Churches of Christ.

The Lord Christ deeming it most expedient for his people to adde some farther help to assist them in cutting downe those cursed errors (that were the next dangerous difficulty they were to meet with) sends in the Reverend and bright

---

[1] Captain Richard Davenport, afterward commander of the fort at Castle Island.

shining light Mr. Davenport, and the cheerfull, grave, and gracious Soldier of his, Mr. Allen, as also Mr. Thompson, Mr. Browne, Mr. Fish, with divers other of the faithfull servants of Christ, the much honoured Mr. Eaton and Mr. Hopkins:[1] and now the time being come, the Synod sate at Cambridge, where was present about 25. Reverend and godly Ministers of Christ, besides many other graciously-eminent servants of his.   A Catalogue of the severall Errors scattered about the Countrey was there produced, to the number of 80. and liberty given to any man to dispute pro or con, and none to be charged to be of that opinion he disputed for, unlesse he should declare himselfe so to be.   The weapons these Souldiers of Christ warred with, was the Sword of the Spirit, even the Word of God, together with earnest prayer to the God of all Truth, that he would open his truths unto them. The clearing of the true sense and meaning of any place of Scripture, it was done by Scripture, for they so discerned by the grace of God that was given them, that the whole Scripture must be attended unto.   Foure sorts of persons I could with a good will have paid their passage out, and home againe to England, that they might have been present at this Synod, so that they would have reported the truth of all the passages thereof to their own Colledges at their return.   The first is the Prelates, who both in Theorie and Practice might have made their owne Eyes Judges in the case, Whether would prevaile most, (to the suppressing of Error, and advancing of Unity in the true worship of God), either their commanding power backt with the subordinate sword of Princes, or the Word of God cleered up by the faithfull labour and indefatigable pains of the sincere servants of the Lord Christ, and mightily declared through the demonstration of his blessed Spirit.   This well waighed, may (through the Lords blessing) stop the yet running fancie in the brains of many, that their Lordly power is the onely means of suppressing Error.

[1] Rev. John Davenport and Theophilus Eaton, founders of New Haven, and Edward Hopkins, are commemorated, in prose and verse, in the next chapter.   The others mentioned are Revs. John Allen, William Thompson, Edmund Browne and John Fisk, who became ministers at Dedham, Braintree, Sudbury, and Wenham respectively, and are commemorated in later chapters narrating the foundation of the churches in those four towns.   All seven arrived in 1637.

Secondly, the Godly and Reverend Presbyterian Party, who had they made their eye-witnesses of this worke, they had assuredly saved themselves much labour, which I dare presume they would have spent worthily otherwayes, then in writing so many books to prove the Congregationall or Independant Churches to be the sluce, through which so many flouds of Error flow in: nay, my deare and reverend brethren, might not so much work of yours in writing, and ours in answering, have been a meanes to have stopt the height of this overflowing floud? and through the Lords assisting have setled Peace and Truth in a great measure throughout the three Nations.

Thirdly, those who with their new stratagems have brought in so much old error; for although they had a party here, yet verily they durst not bring their New Light to the Old Word, for fear it would prove but Old Darknesse, (as indeed they doe.) But here might they have seene the Ministers of Christ (who were so experienced in the Scripture, that some of them could tell you the place, both Chapter and Verse, of most sentences of Scripture could be named unto them) with scriptures light, cleering up the truths of Christ clouded by any of these Errors and Heresies, as had not been done for many Ages before: and verily this great work of Christ must not be lightly over-past. The Author of this History passeth not for the shrewd censures of men: nor, can it be any matter of disparagement to the reverend and highly honoured in Christ, remaining in England, that their fellow brethren have done so worthily here? It is well knowne to all our English Nation, that the most able-preaching Ministers of Christ were most pursued by the lording Clergy, and those that have spent all their dayes, even from a child, in searching the Scriptures, the Lord Christ preparing them by his blessed spirit for this very work. Besides, their continued practice in studying and preaching the wayes of truth; and lastly, their meeting with the opposition of so many crafty, close couched errors, whose first foundation was laid cheke by joule with the most glorious, heavenly, and blessed truths, to dazle the eyes of the beholders, and strike terrour into the hearts of those should lift up their hands against them, for feare they should misse them, and hit their stroke upon the blessed truth; and also to bring up a slanderous and evil report on all the able Orthodox Ministers of Christ that withstand them, perswading men they withstand the holy, heavenly, and blessed truth, which they have lodged there, which this Synod did with strong and undenyable arguments fetch from Scripture, to overthrow and pluck up by the roots, all those Errors, which you have heard mentioned in the former Book, the which they divided for the more full answering of them, among all those valiant Champions of the Truth whom you have heard named, to some six, some five, some foure, etc. It had assuredly been worth the work to have related the particular manner of putting to the sword every one of them: but besides the length of the discourse, there must have been a more able Penman: but however they were so put to death, that they never have stood up in a living manner among us since, but sometimes like Wizards to peepe and mutter out of ground, fit for such people to resort unto, as will goe from the living to the dead.   But blessed be the Lord Christ, who girded his people with strength against this day of battaile, and caused the Heavens to cleere up againe in New-England, after these foggy dayes.

The fourth and last sort of persons, whose presence I could most of all the other three former have desired was, those whose disease lay as chiefly in despising all Physitians, and that upon this ground for one, because some for filthy lucre sake have nourisht Diseases rather than cured them.   Many pamphlets have come from our Countreymen of late, to this purpose, namely, scurrillously to deride all kind of Scholarship, Presbytery, and Synods.   Experience hath taught Gods people here, that such are troubled with some sinfull opinion of their owne, that they would not have touched; but had they been at this Synod, they must, per force, have learned better language, or their speech and their knowledge would fall foule one of the other; here might they have beheld the humility of the most learned of these servants of Christ, condemning the high conceitednesse of their ignorance, and then also the framing of Arguments in a Schollar-like way, did (the Lord assisting) cleare up the truths of Christ more to the meanest capacity in one hour, then could be clouded again in seaven yeare by the new notion of any such as boast so much of their unlettered knowledge. Diversity of languages, although a correcting hand of God upon the whole world, when they joyned together in that proud Edifice,[1] yet now is it blest of God, to retaine the purity of the Scriptures; if any man should goe about to corrupt them in one language, they should remain pure in another; and assuredly, the Lord intending to have the wayes of the Gospel of Christ to be made more manifest at this time, then formerly, not by tradition of our forefathers, or by mans reason, but by the revealed will of God in the holy Scripture, did accordingly prepare Instruments for this work, earthen vessels, men subject to like infirmities with our selves; sorry men, and carrying about with them a body of sinne and death, men subject to erre: yet these did the Lord Christ cause to be train'd up in Learning, and tutor'd at the Universities, and that very young, some of them, as the reverend Mr. John Cotten, at 13. yeares of age. The mighty power of God sanctifyed and ordained them for this work, and made them a defenced city, an iron pillar, a wall of brass against all the opposers of his truth; and now coupled them together in this Synod, to draw in Christs yoke, and warre with the weapons he had furnished them withall, and cause the blessed truths of Christ to shine forth in their splendour and glory, farre more after the dispersing of this smoak, which of a long time hath filled the Temple, and hindered the entring in of those great number of Converts, which shall flow in at the fall of all antichristian Errors; and verily as the Lord Christ had called forth this little handfull to be a model of his glorious work, intended throughout the whole world, so chiefly in this suppressing of Errours, Sects, and Heresies, by the blessed word of his truth, causing his servants in this Synod, mutually to agree; and by his gracious providence, break in pieces a contrived plot of some, who, by misreports, insinuating jealousies, and crafty carriage of matters to the wrong mark, with a writing of thrice twenty strong,[2]

---

[1] The tower of Babel.

[2] Sixty members of the Boston church (which in general, alone among the churches, sustained the Hutchinsonian party) sent in to the General Court of March, 1637, a petition which the General Court of November, after the synod, declared to be seditious, and used as a pretext for banishing all those petitioners who would not recant.

would have drawne away one of the valiant Souldiers of Christ from this worthy worke, who both then, and since, hath been very helpfull to cast downe many a strong fort erected by the Sectaries; but the Lord Christ would not suffer this blow to be given, intending all people (by way of restitution) for their slanderous reports, cast upon his New England Churches (as being the inlet to Errours) shall honour them with this victorious conquest, given them by Christ herein; yet willing they would, their brethren in England might win the prize by out-stripping them, more abundantly in length, bredth and height, which the same God is able to performe, that hath been thus abundantly good to us.

About this time the Churches of Christ began to be diligent in their duty, and the civil government in looking after such as were like to disturb the peace of this new erected government; some persons being so hot headed for maintaining of these sinfull opinions, that they feared breach of peace, even among the Members of the superiour Court, but the Lord blessing them with agreement to prevent the wofull effects of civill broyles; those in place of government caused certain persons to be disarmed in the severall Townes, as in the Towne of Boston, to the number of 58, in the Towne of Salem 6, in the Towne of Newbery 3, in the Towne of Roxbury 5, in the Towne of Ipswitch 2, and Charles Towne 2. Others there were, that through the help of the faithfull servants of Christ, came to see how they had beene misled, and by the power of Christ in his Word, returned againe with an acknowledgement of their sinne; but others there were, who remained obstinate, to the disturbing of the civill power, and were banished, of whom you shall heare farther hereafter. Some of the Churches of Christ being more indulgent, waited long ere they fell upon the work: and here you must tak notice, that the Synod, Civil Government, and the Churches of Christ, kept their proper place, each moving in their own spheare, and acting by their own light, or rather by the revelation of Jesus Christ, witnessed by his Word and Spirit, yet not refusing the help of each other (as some would willingly have it). Some of the Churches prosecuting the Rule of Christ against their hereticall Members, were forced to proceed to excommunication of them, who when they saw whereto it would come, they would have prevented it with lying, but the Lord discovered it; and so they were justly separated from the Churches of Christ for lying: which being done, they fell to their old trade againe.

CHAP. VIII.

Of the planting the fourth Colonie of New Englands godly Government called New-Haven.

The Lord Christ having now in his great mercy taken out of the way these mountains that seemed in the eye of Man to block up his Churches further proceedings, they had now leisure to welcome the living stones that the Lord was pleased to adde unto this building, and with thankfull acknowledgment to give him of his owne for his mercyes multitude, whose was the work in planting, not onely more Churches, but another Colony also; for the honoured Mr. Eaton [1] being accompanied with many worthy persons of note, whom the Lord had furnished with store of substance for this wildernesse-work, although they would willingly have made their abode under the government of the Mattachusets; yet could they finde no place upon the Seacoasts for their settling: the Lord intending to enlarge his peoples border, caused them, after much search, to take up a place somewhat more southwardly, neare the shalles of Cape-cod,[2] where they had very flatt water; yet being entred in, they found a commodious harbour for shipping, and a fit place to erect a Towne, which they built in very little time, with very faire houses, and compleat streets; but in a little time they overstockt it with Chattell, although many of them did follow merchandizing, and Maritime affairs, but their remotenesse from the Mattachusets Bay, where the chiefe traffique lay, hindred them much.

[1] Theophilus Eaton (1590–1658) was a rich London merchant, deputy-governor of the company for the Baltic trade, and had been a diplomatic agent of Charles I. at the court of Denmark. He was a parishioner in London of his school friend Rev. John Davenport. They came out to New England in 1637, arriving in Boston in June, with a company which, disclaiming any definite intention of founding a separate colony, yet wished to maintain itself as a unit. In March, 1638, they settled at Quinipiac, where they founded the New Haven colony, of which Eaton was constantly governor from 1639 to 1658.

[2] It is more than one hundred and fifty miles from Cape Cod.

Here did these godly and sincere servants of Christ, according to the rule of the Word, gather into Church Estate, and called to the office of a Pastor the reverend, judicious, and godly Mr. John Davenport,[1] of whom the Author is bold to say as followeth:

> When Men and Devils 'gainst Christs flock conspire,
>   For them prepar'd a deadly trapping net;
> Then Christ to make all men his work admire,
>   Davenport,[2] he doth thee from thy Country fet
> To sit in Synod, and his folk assist:
>   The filthy vomit of Hels Dragon, deepe
> In earths womb drawn, blest they this poyson mist,[3]
>   And blest the meanes doth us from error keep.
> Thy grave advice and arguments of strength
>   Did much prevaile, the Erronist confound.
> Well hast thou warr'd, Christ drawes thy dayes in length,
>   That thou in learn'd experience maist abound:
> What though thou leave a city stor'd with pleasure,
>   Spend thy prime dayes in heathen desert land,
> Thy joy's in Christ, and not in earthly treasure,
>   Davenport rejoice, Christs Kingdome is at hand;
> Didst ever deem to see such glorious dayes?
>   Though thou decrease with age and earths content,
> Thou live'st in Christ, needs then must thy joy raise;
>   His Kingdome's thine, and that can ne'r be spent.

This Church and Town soon procur'd some Sisters to take part with her, and among them they erected a godly and peaceable Government,[4] and called their frontier towne New-

[1] John Davenport (1597–1670), joined with Eaton as the chief founder of the New Haven colony, was the son of the mayor of Coventry, and was M.A. and B.D. of Oxford. After years of service to an important London congregation, as vicar of St. Stephen's, Coleman Street, he fled to Holland at the end of the year 1633 to escape prosecution by the Court of High Commission. In 1637 he went to New England, where he took a prominent part in the synod or council of churches at Cambridge, and next year in the founding of New Haven. There he was pastor till 1668, then for two years in Boston.

[2] Here, and twelve lines below, the metre makes Davenport a dissyllable; and it was often so pronounced, as the spelling Damport in many letters shows.

[3] The meaning appears to be, "blessed are they who missed, or escaped, this poison."

[4] Guilford and Milford were established as separate colonies, independent of New Haven; Stamford and Southold (Long Island) in partial dependence upon

haven, of which the Government is denominated, being inhabited by many men eminent in gifts for the populating thereof, and managing of affaires both by Sea and Land; they have had some shipping built there, but by the sad losse of Mr. Lambertons ship and goods also,[1] they were much disheartned, but the much honoured Mr. Eaton remaines with them to this very day.

Thou noble thus, Theophilus, before great kings to stand,
   More noble far, for Christ his war thou leav'st thy native land;
With thy rich store thou cam'st on shore Christs Churches to assist;
   What if it wast[e]? thou purchast hast that Pearl that most have mist,
Nay rather he hath purchast thee, and whatsoever thou hast,
   With graces store to govern o're his people, he thee plac't.
Our State affaires thy will repaires, assistant thou hast bin
   Firm league to make, for Gospels sake, four Colonyes within;
With Sweads, French, Dutch, and Indians much, Gods peoples
     peace this bred,[2]
Then Eaton aye remember may the Child that's yet unfed.

This government of New-Haven, although the younger Sister of the foure, yet was she as beautifull as any of this broode of travellers, and most minding the end of her coming hither, to keep close to the rule of Christ both in Doctrine and Discipline; and it were to be wished her elder Sister would follow her example, to nurture up all her children accordingly: here is not to be forgotten the honoured Mr. Hopkins, who came over about this time, a man of zeale and courage for the

it.   In 1643 all joined in a federal union to form the New Haven colony, of which New Haven and the rest were townships, and which, with Branford added, lasted till the absorption into Connecticut effected by the charter of 1662.

[1] Captain George Lamberton sailed out of New Haven harbor in January, 1646, in a new ship carrying seventy persons and a valuable cargo, which it was hoped would retrieve the falling fortunes of New Haven commerce. The ship was never heard of again. The story of the ship returning as a phantom some months later, sailing into the mouth of the harbor, and then vanishing, comes from Cotton Mather's *Magnalia*, bk. i., ch. vi.

[2] That is to say that the formation of the New England Confederation of 1643 much promoted the peace of God's people with the Swedes on the Delaware River, where New Haven had attempted to found a settlement, with the French of Canada, with the Dutch of New Netherland (particularly in respect to the possession of the Dutch fort at Hartford), and with the Indians. Eaton and Hopkins had an important place among the federal commissioners.

truths of Christ, assisting this blessed work, both in person and estate; for the which the Author cannot forget him, being oft in commission for the good of all the united Colonyes.

Hopkins thou must, although weak dust, for this great work prepare,
   Through Ocean large Christ gives thee charge to govern his with care;
What earthen man, in thy short span throughout the world to run
   From East to West at Christs behest, thy worthy work is done:
Unworthy thou acknowledge now, not unto thee at all,
   But to his name be lasting fame, thou to his work doth call.

Chap. IX.

Of the planting the fourteenth Church of Christ under the govern-men of the Mattachusets Bay, called Dedham.

The latter end of this yeare 'twas the Towne of Dedham began, an inland Towne, scituate, about ten miles from Boston, in the County of Suffolk, well watred with many pleasant streames, abounding with Garden fruits fitly to supply the Markets of the most populous Towne, whose coyne and commodities allures the Inhabitants of this Towne to make many a long walk; they consist of about a hundred Families, being generally given to husbandry, and, through the blessing of God, are much encreased, ready to swarme and settle on the building of another Towne more to the Inland; [1] they gather into a Church at their first settling, for indeed, as this was their chiefe errand, so was it the first thing they ordinarily minded; to pitch their Tabernacles neare the Lords Tent: To this end they called to the office of a Pastor, the reverend, humble, and heavenly-minded, Mr. John Allen, a man of a very courteous behaviour, full of sweet Christian love towards all, and with much meeknesse of spirit, contending earnestly for the faith and peace of Christs Churches.

All you so slite Christs sanctifying grace, [2]
   As legall workes, what Gospel-work can be
But sinne cast out, and spirits work in place,
   They justifyed that Christ thus reigning see:

[1] Medfield was set off from Dedham in May, 1650.
[2] The margin says, "M[r]. Allen a great help against the Errors of the time"; and the first four lines of these verses refer, in crabbed phrase, to the refusal of the Antinomians to attach value to sanctification as evidence of justification.

Allen, thou art by Christs free spirit led
  To warre for him in wildernesse awhile;
What, doe for Christ, I [ay] man thou art in's stead,
  Sent to beseech, in's Vineyard thou must toyle.
John Allen, joy, thou sinfull dust art taken
  To spend thy dayes in exile, so remote,
Christs Church to build, of him that's ne'r forsaken,
  Nor thou, for now his truths thou must promote.
He guides thy tongue, thy paper, pen and hands,
  Thy hearts swift motion, and affections choice;
Needs thou thus lead, must doe what he commands,
  And cry aloud when he lifts up thy voice:
Seven yeares compleat twice told, thy work hath bin,
  To feed Christs flock, in desart land them keep,
Both thou and they each day are kept by him;
  Safe maist thou watch, being watcht by him ne'r sleeps.

This Church of Christ hath in its bosome neere about 70.
souls joyned in Covenant together, and being well seasoned
with this savoury salt, have continued in much love and unity
from their first foundation, hitherto t[r]anslating the close,
clouded woods into goodly corn-fields, and adding much comfort to the lonesome travellers, in their solitary journey to
Canectico, by eying the habitation of Gods people in their
way, ready to administer refreshing to the weary.

Chap. X.

*Of the planting of the fifteenth Church of Christ at the Towne
of Waymoth.*

The Towne and Church of Christ at Waymoth had come
in among the other Townes before this, as being an elder
Sister,[1] but onely for her somewhat more than ordinary in-
stability; it is battered with the brinish billows on the East;
Rocks and Swamps to the Southwest, makes it delightfull to

---

[1] Savage counts the Weymouth church as existing from July, 1635. Of the
clergymen mentioned below, Thomas Jenners removed to Saco, Maine, Samuel
Newman to Seekonk. Charles Chauncy was at this time minister at Scituate.
In earlier life he had been professor of Hebrew at Cambridge, England, then
professor of Greek, then vicar of Ware. Afterward he was for eighteen years,
1654–1672, president of Harvard College.

the nimble tripping Deere, as the plowable places of Medow land is to the Inhabitants. This Towne was first founded by some persons that were not so forward to promote the Ordinances of Christ, as many others have been: they desired the reverend Minister of Christ Mr. Gennors, to be helpfull in preaching the Word unto them; who after some little space of time, not liking the place, repaired to the Eastern English: but the people of this place, after his departure, being gathered into a Church, they called to office the reverend and godly Mr. Newman; but many of them unwilling to continue in this Towne, as supposing they had found a fitter place for habitation, removed into the next Government, carrying with them their Pastor; by which means, the people that were left behinde, were now destitute, and having some godly Christians among them, who much desired the sincere milk of the Word, that they might grow thereby: upon diligent use of meanes they found out a young man able gifted for the work, brought up with the reverend and judicious Mr. Chancie, called Mr. Thomas Thatcher. Yet againe, after some few yeares, for want of sufficient maintenance, with mutuall consent they parted with him, and are forced to borrow help of their Neighbours, wherein all of them to [to all of them] the Author is bold to say as followeth:

> Oh people, reason swayes mans actions here,
>   You sanctifyed, o're these long seas doth look,
> With heavenly things your earthly toyle to cheere;
>   Will lose[1] the end for which this toyle you tooke.
> Christ comes in's Word, let their bright feet abide
>   Your Towne, among whose grace and gifts excell
> In preaching Christ, it's he your hearts hath try'd,
>   They want no store that all for him doe sell.
> Gennors, dost love thy Christ? I hope he's deare
>   Belov'd of thee, he honour'd would thee have
> To feed his flock, while thou remainest here;
>   With's Word of truth thy soule and others save.
> With little flock doth Newman pack away;
>   The righteous lips sure might a many feed;
> Remov'st for gaine? it's most where most men stay,
>   Men part for land, why land least helps at need.

---

[1] *I. e.*, you will lose.

Thatcher, what mean'st to leave thy little flock?
    Sure their increase might thee much profit bring:
What, leave Christs Church? it's founded on a rock;
    If rock not left, their ebb may suddain spring;
Pastor and People, have you both forgot
    What parting Paul and Christs deare people had?[1]
Their loves melt teares, it's ve'mently so hot,
    His heart-strings break to see his folk so sad.

This yeare came over, besides the former, for the furthering of this blessed work of Christ, Mr. William Tompson, Mr. Edm: Browne, and Mr. David Frisk,[2] who were called to office in severall Churches, as you shall after hear. And now to end this yeare, that abounded in the wonder-working Providence of Christ, for his Churches, in the exaltation of his truths, that all may take notice the Lord cast in by the by, as it were, a very fruitfull crop, insomuch that from this day forward, their increase was every yeare more and more, till the Country came to feed its owne Inhabitants; and the people who formerly were somewhat pincht with hunger, eat bread to the full, having not onely for their necessity but also for their conveniency and delight.

Chap. XI.

*Of the increase of the people of Christ. Printing brought over,
and the sixteenth Church of Christ planted at Rouly.*

For the yeare 1638 John Winthrope Esq. was chosen Governour, and Tho: Dudly Esq. Deputy Governour; the number of Freemen added were about 130. The peace of this little Common-wealth being now in great measure settled, by the Lords mercy, in overthrowing the Indians, and banishing of certaine turbulent spirits, The Churches of Christ were much edified in their holy faith by their [the] indefatigable pains of their Ministers, in their weekly Lectures extraordinary, as well as by their Sabboth-Assemblies, and continuall visiting of their people from house to house, endeavouring to heale

---

[1] Acts xx. 36–38.
[2] For these ministers, see *post*, pp. 197, 265, 196 and 226, respectively. On this latter page the name of the third is correctly given as John Fisk.

the hurts these false deceivers had made, with double diligence showring downe the sweet dews of the blessed Gospel
of Jesus Christ, to the converting of many a poor soul. And
indeed, now were the glorious days of New England; the
Churches of Christ increase dayly, and his eminent Embassa-
dours resort unto them from our native Country, which as
then lay under the tyranny of the Monarchall Arch-prelates,
which caused the servants of Christ to wander from their
home. This yeare the reverend and judicious M. Jos. Glover
undertook this long voyage; being able both in person and
estate for the work, he provided, for further compleating the
Colonies in Church and Common-wealth-work, a Printer,
which hath been very usefull in many respects; [1] the Lord seeing it meet that this reverend and holy servant of his should
fall short of the shores of New England: but yet at this time
he brought over the zealous affected and judicious servant of
his, Master Ezekiel Rogers,[2] who with a holy and humble
people, made his progress to the North-Eastward, and erected
a Towne about 6. miles from Ipswich, called Rowly, where
wanting room, they purchased some addition of the Town of
Newbery; yet had they a large length of land, onely for the
neere conveniency to the Towne of Ipswich, by the which
meanes they partake of the continued Lectures of either
Towne: these people being very industrious every way, soone
built many houses, to the number of about three-score families, and were the first people that set upon making of Cloth
in this Western World; for which end they built a fulling-
mill, and caused their little-ones to be very diligent in spinning
cotton wooll, many of them having been clothiers in England,
till their zeale to promote the Gospel of Christ caused them to
wander; and therefore they were no lesse industrious, in

[1] The Cambridge printing-press was the first one established north of Mexico
and was for many years the only one in British America. The donor, Rev. Jose
Glover, a suspended English rector, died on the voyage. The printer, whom he
brought over under contract, was Stephen Daye. The first thing printed was the
Freeman's Oath, the second an almanac, the third the Bay Psalm-Book.

[2] Rev. Ezekiel Rogers, cousin of Nathaniel Rogers, the minister of Ipswich
(p. 119, *ante*), had been for twenty years minister of Rowley in Yorkshire, and
many of his congregation came from there. Strong efforts, concerning which
Winthrop speaks with unwonted sharpness, were made to persuade them to
settle in the New Haven jurisdiction.

gathering into Church society, there being scarce a man among them, but such as were meet to be living stones in this building, according to the judgement of man; they called to the office of a Pastor this holy man of God, Mr. Ezekiel Rogers, of whom this may be said:

> Christ for this work Rogers doth riches give,
>   Rich graces fit his people for to feed,
> Wealth to supply his wants whilst here he live,
>   Free thou receiv'st to serve his peoples need.
> England may mourne they thee no longer keep,
>   English rejoice, Christ doth such worthyes raise,
> His Gospel preach, unfold his mysteries deep;
>   Weak dust made strong sets forth his makers praise:
> With fervent zeale, and courage thou hast fought
>   'Gainst that transformed Dragon and his bands,
> Snatcht forth the burning thou poore soules hast caught,
>   And freed thy flock from wolves devouring hands.
> Ezekiel mourn not, thou art severed farre,
>   From thy deare Country, to a desart land;
> Christ call'd hath thee unto this worthy warre;
>   By him o'rcome, he holds thy Crowne in's hand.

For the further assisting of this tender flock of Christ, the reverend Mr. John Miller did abide among them for some space of time, preaching the Word of God unto them also, till it pleased the Lord to call him to be Pastor of the Church of Christ at Yarmouth, in Plimoth patten,[1] where he remaineth at this very day.

> With courage bold Miller through Seas doth venter,
>   To toyl it out in this great Western wast,
> Thy stature low one [on] object high doth center;
>   Higher than Heaven thy faith on Christ is plac't:
> Allarum thou with silver trumpet sound,
>   And tell the world Christs Armyes are at hand,
> With Scripture-truths thou Errors dost confound,
>   And overthrow all Antichristian bands:
> It matters not for th' worlds high reputation;
>   The World must fall and Christ alone must stand;
> Thy Crown's prepar'd in him, then keep thy station,
>   Joy that Christs Kingdome is so neare at hand.

----

[1] Patent.

Chap. XII.

Of the great Earthquake in New England, and of the wofull end of some erronious persons, with the first foundation of Harverd Colledge.

This yeare, the first day of the Fourth Month,[1] about two of the clock in the after-noone, the Lord caus'd a great and terrible Earth-quake, which was generall throughout all the English Plantations; the motion of the Earth was such, that it caused divers men (that had never knowne an Earthquake before) being at worke in the Fields, to cast downe their working-tooles, and run with gastly terrified lookes, to the next company they could meet withall; it came from the Westerne and uninhabited parts of this Wildernesse, and went the direct course this brood of Travellers came. The Ministers of Christ many of them could say at that very time (not from any other Revelation, but what the word holds forth) that if the Churches of New England were Gods house, then suddenly there would follow great alterations in the Kingdomes of Europe.

This yeare the civill government proceeded to censure the residue of those sinfull erroneous persons, who raised much commotion in this little Common-wealth; who being banished, resorted to a place more Southward, some of them sitting down at a place called Providence, others betooke them to an Island about 16. miles distant from the former, called Rode Island,[2] where having Elbow roome enough, none of the Ministers of Christ, nor any other to interrupt their false and deceivable Doctrines, they hamper'd themselves fouly with their owne line, and soone shewed the depthlesse ditches that blinde guides lead into; many among them being much to be pittyed, who were drawne from the truth by the bewitching

---

[1] June 1, 1638.

[2] Providence had been founded by Roger Williams in 1636. The settlement on Rhode Island was founded in 1638 by William Coddington and his companions, banished from Massachusetts in the spring of that year. Johnson's account of the amusing variety of religious opinions in these two plantations is from the hand of an opponent, but is far from being baseless.

tongues of some of them, being very ignorant and easily per-
verted: and although the people were not many in all, yet
were they very diverse in their opinion, and glad where they
could gaine most Disciples to heare them; some were for every
day to be a Sabbath, and therefore kept not any Sabbath-day
at all; others were some for one thing, some for another; and
therefore had their severall meetings, making many a goodly
piece of Preachment; among whom there were some of the
female sexe, who (deeming the Apostle Paul to be too strict
in not permitting a roome [woman] to preach in the publique
Congregation) taught notwithstanding, they having their call
to this office from an ardent desire of being famous, especially
the grand Mistresse of them all, who ordinarily prated every
Sabbath day, till others, who thirsted after honour in the same
way with her selfe, drew away her Auditors, and then she
withdrew her self, her husband, and her family also, to a more
remote place; [1] and assuredly, although the Lord be secret in
all the dispensation of his providences, whether in judgement
or mercy, yet much may be learn'd from all, as sometimes
pointing with the finger to the lesson; as here these persons
withdrawing from the Churches of Christ (wherein he walketh,
and is to be found in his blessed Ordinances) to a first and
second place, where they came to a very sad end; for thus it
came to passe in the latter place, The Indians in those parts
forwarned them of making their abode there; yet this could
be no warning to them, but still they continued, being amongst
a multitude of Indians, boasted they were become all one Indian: and indeed, this woman, who had the chiefe rule of all
the roast, being very bold in her strange Revelations and mis-
applications, tells them, though all nations and people were
cut off round about them, yet should not they; till on a day
certaine Indians coming to her house, discoursing with them,
they wished to tye up her doggs, for they much bit the man,
not mistrusting [2] the Indians guile, did so; the which no

---

[1] From Aquidneck Mrs. Hutchinson, after her husband's death in 1642,
removed to a point in the Dutch jurisdiction, now known as Pelham Neck, near
New Rochelle, New York, where the name of Hutchinson Creek perpetuates her
memory. Here she and nearly all her household were murdered by the Indians
in September, 1643, in an uprising consequent upon "Kieft's war."

[2] Probably the sense is: "for they much bit. The man, not mistrusting," etc.

sooner done, but they cruelly murthered her, taking one of
their daughters away with them, and another of them seeking
to escape is caught, as she was getting over a hedge, and they
drew her back againe by the haire of the head to the stump
of a tree, and there cut off her head with a hatchet; the other
that dwelt by them betook them to boat, and fled, to tell the
sad newes; the rest of their companions, who were rather
hardened in their sinfull way, and blasphemous opinions,
than brought to any sight of their damnable Errours, as you
shall after hear; yet was not this the first loud speaking hand
of God against them; but before this the Lord had poynted
directly to their sinne by a very fearfull Monster, that another
of these women brought forth,[1] they striving to bury it in
oblivion, but the Lord brought it to light, setting forth the
view of their monstrous Errors in this prodigious birth. This
yeare, although the estates of these pilgrim people were much
wasted, yet seeing the benefit that would accrew to the
Churches of Christ and Civil Government, by the Lords blessing, upon learning, they began to erect a Colledge, the Lord
by his provident hand giving his approbation to the work, in
sending over a faithfull and godly servant of his, the reverend
Mr John Harverd, who joyning with the people of Christ at
Charles Towne, suddainly after departed this life, and gave
near a thousand pound toward this work;[2] wherefore the
Government thought it meet to call it Harverd Colledge in
remembrance of him.

> If Harverd had with riches here been taken,
>   He need not then through troublous Seas have past,
> But Christs bright glory hath thine eyes so waken,
>   Nought can content, thy soule of him must tast:

[1] Jane Hawkins. Mrs. Hutchinson bore another.

[2] The college was founded, by vote of the General Court, in October, 1636,
with a grant of £400 from the public treasury. John Harvard, whose bequest of
half his estate, about £800, caused it to be named for him, was the son of Robert
Harvard, butcher, of Southwark, and Katherine Rogers of Stratford-on-Avon,
the daughter of an alderman in that town whose house is still standing, and has
lately been made a Harvard memorial. After taking his M.A. degree at Emmanuel College, Cambridge, in 1635, John Harvard came, in 1637, to Charlestown, where he was minister for a short time, and died in 1638.

Oh tast and tell how sweet his Saints among,
   Christ ravisht hath thy heart with heavenly joyes
To preach and pray with teares affection strong,
   From hearts delight in him who thee imployes.
Scarce hast thou had Christs Churches here in eye,
   But thou art call'd to eye him face to face;
Earths scant contents death drawes thee from, for why?
   Full joy thou wouldst that's onely in heavens place.

Chap. XIII.

Of the coming over of the honoured Mr. Pelham, and the plant-
ing of the seaventeenth Church of Christ at the Towne of
Hampton.

This yeare 1639. John Winthrope Esq. was chosen Governour, and Thomas Dudly Esq. Deputy Governour, the number of freemen added were about 83. This yeare came over
the much honoured Mr. Herbert Pelham,[1] a man of a courteous
behaviour, humble, and heavenly minded.

Harbertus, hye on valiant, why lingerst thou so long?
Christs work hath need of hasty speed, his enemies are strong:
In wildernesse Christ doth thee blesse with vertues, wife, and seed,
To govern thou at length didst bow to serve Christs peoples need;
To thine own soyle thou back dost toyle, then cease not lab'ring there,
But still advance Christs Ordinance, and shrink no where for fear.

Much about this time began the Town of Hampton, in
the County of Northfolk,[2] to have her foundation stone laid,
scituate neare the Sea-coast, not farre from the famous River
of Merimeck. The great store of salt marsh did intice this
people to set downe their habitation there, for as yet Cowes

---

[1] Pelham was an Oxford man, and became the first treasurer of Harvard
College. Governor Bellingham married his sister. The meaning of the fourth
line is probably to allude to his election as assistant in 1645.

[2] The county of Norfolk, established in 1643, should not be confounded
with the present Norfolk County. It lay north of the Merrimac, embracing
Salisbury and Haverhill in present-day Massachusetts, and Dover, Exeter, Hampton, and Strawberry Bank or Portsmouth in present-day New Hampshire. Hampton and Salisbury were founded in 1639. There was violent dissension in the
Hampton church, almost to its disruption, between Timothy Dalton the teacher,
and Stephen Batchellor the pastor (see p. 73), and their respective adherents.

and Cattell of that kinde were not come to the great downfall
in their price, of which they have about 450. head; and for
the form of this Towne, it is like a Flower-de-luce, two streets
of houses wheeling off from the maine body thereof, the land
is fertile, but filled with swamps, and some store of rocks,
The people are about 60. Families; being gathered together
into Church covenant, they called to office the reverend,
grave, and gracious Mr. Doulton, having also for some little
space of time the more ancient Mr. Batchelor (of whom you
have heard in the former Book) to preach unto them also;
here take a short remembrance of the other.

> Doulton, doth teach perspicuously and sound,
>   With wholsome truths of Christ thy flock dost feed;
> Thy honour with thy labour doth abound;
>   Age crownes thy head in righteousnesse, proceed
> To batter downe, root up, and quite destroy
>   All Heresies, and Errors, that draw back
> Unto perdition, and Christs folk annoy;
>   To warre for him thou weapons dost not lack;
> Long dayes to see, that long'd for day to come
>   Of Babels fall, and Israels quiet peace—
> Thou yet maist live of dayes so great a sum
>   To see this work, let not thy warfare cease.

Chap. XIV.

Of the planting the eighteenth Church of Christ at the Towne of Salsbury

For further perfecting this Wildernesse-work, not far
from the Towne of Hampton was erected another Towne,
called Salsbury, being brought forth as Twins, sometime
contending for eldership: This being seated upon the broade
swift torrent of Merrimeck, a very goodly River to behold,[1]
were it not blockt up with some suddaine falls through the
rocks; over against this Towne lyeth the Towne of Newberry, on the Southern side of the River, a constant Ferry
being kept between; for although the River be about half a

---

[1] It was doubtless the largest river our author had ever seen.

mile broad, yet, by reason of an Island that lies in the midst thereof, it is the better passed in troublesom weather: the people of this Towne have of late placed their dwellings so much distanced the one from the other, that they are like to divide into two Churches; the scituation of this Towne is very pleasant, were the Rivers Navigable farre up, the branches thereof abound in faire and goodly medowes with good store of stately Timber upon the uplands in many places. This Towne is full as fruitfull in her Land, Chattell, and Inhabitants, as her Sister Hampton; the people joyned in Church-relation or brotherhood, nere about the time the other did, and have desired and obtained the reverend and graciously godly M. Thomas Woster to be their Pastor.

> With mickle labour and distressed wants,
> Woster, thou hast in desart's depth remain'd
> Thy chiefest dayes, Christs Gospel there to plant,
> And water well; such toyle shall yeild great gaine.
> Oh happy day! may Woster say, that I
> Was singled out for this great work in hand;
> Christ by distresse doth Gold for's Temple try;
> Thrice blest are they may in his Presence stand.
> But more, thou art by him reserved yet,
> To see on earth Christ's Kingdom's exaltation:
> More yet, thou art by him prepared fit
> To help it on, among our English Nation.

Chap. XV.

Of further supply for the Church of Christ at Waterton. And a sad accident fell out in Boston Towne.

The Lord intending to strengthen his poore Churches here, and after the overthrow of these damnable Errors, to trample Satan under their feet, he manifesteth his mindeful-ness of them, in sending over fresh supplyes againe and againe: although weak and sory men in themselves, yet strong in the Lord, and the power of his might. The last that this yeare is to be named, is the reverend, judicious, and godly-affected Mr. John Knowles, who was desired of the Church of Christ

at Waterton, to be a two-fold cord unto them, in the office
of a teaching Elder, with the reverend Mr. Phillips, of whom
you have heard in the former Book.

> With courage bold and arguments of strength,
>   Knowles doth apply Gods word his flock unto,
> Christ furnisht hath (to shew his bountyes length)
>   Thee with rich gifts, that thou his work mayst do:
> New England is too scant, for thy desire
>   Inkindled is, Christs truths abroad to spread,
> Virginia may his grace to them admire,
>   That thee through Seas for their instruction led;
> Thy labours Knowles are great, far greater hee,
>   Not onely thee, but all his valiant made,
> Forth sinfull dust, his Saints and Warriers be;[1]
>   He thee upheld, thy strength shall never fade.
> John come thou forth, behold what Christ hath wrought
>   In these thy dayes; great works are yet behinde;
> Then toyle it out till all to passe be brought,
>   Christ crowne will thee, thou then his glory minde.

To end this yeare 1639. the Lord was pleased to send a
very sharp winter, and more especially in strong storms of
weekly snows, with very bitter blasts: And here the Reader
may take notice of the sad hand of the Lord against two persons, who were taken in a storme of snow, as they were passing from Boston to Roxbury, it being much about a mile
distant, and a very plaine way. One of Roxbury sending to
Boston his servant maid for a Barber-Chirurgion, to draw
his tooth, they lost their way in their passage between, and
were not found till many dayes after, and then the maid was
found in one place, and the man in another, both of them
frozen to death; in which sad accident, this was taken into
consideration by divers people, that this Barber was more
then ordinary laborious to draw men to those sinfull Errors,
that were formerly so frequent, and now newly overthrowne
by the blessing of the Lord, upon the endeavour of his faithfull servants (with the word of truth). He having a fit oppor-

---

[1] *I. e.,* "far greater is He who hath made not only thee but all His valiant
ones, from sinful dust, to be His saints and warriors." For Knowles's mission
to Virginia, see p. 265, *post.*

tunity, by reason of his trade, so soone as any were set downe in his chaire, he would commonly be cutting of their haire and the truth together; notwithstanding some report bette: of the man, the example is for the living, the dead is judged of the Lord alone.

Chap. XVI.

The great supply of godly Ministers for the good of his People in New England.

For to govern and rule this little Common wealth, was this year chosen the valiant Champion, for the advance of Christs truth, Thomas Dudly Esq. and Richard Bellingham Esq. Deputy-Governour; the freemen added to the former were about 192.[1] This yeare the reverend Mr. Burr [2] (a holy, heavenly-minded man, and able gifted to preach the Word of God) was exercised therein for some space of time, in the Church of Christ at Dorchester, where they were about calling him to the office of a teaching Elder; but in a very little time after his coming over he departed this life, yet minde you may in the following Meetre.

Well didst thou minde thy worke, which caus'd thee venter
    (Through Ocean large) thy Christ in's Word to preach,
Exhorting all their faith on him to center;
    Soules ravisht are by him in thy sweet speech.
Thy speech bewrayes thy heart for heaven doth look;
    Christ to enjoy Burr from the earth is taken;
Thy words remaine, though thou hast us forsook,
    In dust sleep sound till Christ thy body waken.

There are divers others of the faithfull Ministers of Christ that came over for to further this his work, somewhat before this time, as the godly and reverend Mr. Rayner,[3] who was

[1] Misprint, probably, for 162.

[2] Jonathan Burr was one of those whom Johnson's church at Woburn had endeavored to secure as pastor.

[3] John Rayner was teacher of the Plymouth church from 1636 to 1654, then minister at Dover, N. H. The worthies commemorated below are: William Hooke and Samuel Eaton of New Haven; President Chauncy (see p. 180, *supra*);

called to office in the Church of Christ at Plimoth, and there
remaines preaching the Word instantly, with great paines
and care over that flock, as also the reverend and faithfull
servant of Christ Jesus, Mr. William Hook, who was for some
space of time at the Church in Taunton, but now remaines
called to office in the Church of Christ at Newhaven, a man,
who hath received of Christ many gracious gifts, fit for so
high a calling, with a very amiable and gracious speech labouring in the Lord; and here also the Reader may minde how
the Lord was pleased to reach out his large hand of bounty
toward his N. England people, in supplying them abundantly
with Teachers, able and powerfull to break the bread of life
unto them, so long as their desires continued hot and zealous;
but after here grew a fulnesse in some, even to slight, if not
loath the honey comb; many returned for England, and the
Lord was pleased to take away others by death, although
very few, considering the number; but let N. England beware
of an after-clap, and provoke the Lord no longer. But seeing
this yeare proved the last of the yeares of transportation of
God's people, only for enjoyment of exercising the Ordinances
of Christ, and enlargement of his Kingdome (there being hopes
of great good opportunity that way at home) it will be expedient onely to name some others in the Southwest parts,
among the lesser Colonyes, and so passe on to the story:
And first, not to forget the reverend Mr. Eaton, a man of love
and peace, and yet godly zealous, he came over with those
who planted the Colony of Newhaven, spending his labours
in the Lord with them in Plimoth Plantation:[1] also here is

Ephraim Hewett, pastor of the church in Windsor, Conn.; Henry Smith of
Wethersfield; Henry Whitefield of Guilford, whose stone house in that town is
still standing, and is interestingly figured in Palfrey's *History of New England*,
II. 59–61; Robert Peck of Hingham in England, teacher of the church in the
Massachusetts Hingham; Peter Saxton of Scituate; and Richard Denton, who,
after service in Watertown, Wethersfield, and Stamford, withdrew from New
England in 1644 on account of Presbyterianism, and was for more than a dozen
years minister under the Dutch at Hempstead, Long Island. Of these, Hooke,
Eaton, Whitefield, Peck, Saxton, and Denton returned finally to England, where
Hooke enjoyed much favor with the Lord Protector, while Whitefield was a
prominent preacher at Winchester.

[1] The punctuation should probably be so arranged as to carry the phrase
respecting Plymouth Plantation into connection with the name of Chauncy
rather than Eaton.

to be minded the reverend Mr. Chancie, a very able Preacher,
both learned and judicious; as also the reverend, able, and
pious M. Huet, who came over this year, or rather, as I suppose, the yeare before, who did spend his time and labour
with a people that came over with him; at length the greatest
part of them they settled downe in the Government of Canec-
ticoe, where they planted the Towne of Windsor, and Church
of Christ there, where this gracious servant of Christ continued in his labours, till the Lord laid him in his bed of rest:
somewhat before this time came over the reverend Mr. Smith,
being another of that name, beside the former,[1] he laboured
in the Word and Doctrine with a people at Withersfield in
those parts also; Mr. Henry Whitefield, another Minister of
the Gospel of Christ, of reverend respect, who being returned
for England, the latter of his labours, the Lord assisting, will
sufficiently testifie his sincerity, for the truth and labours of
love in the Lord: here may also be named the reverend Mr.
Peck, Mr. Saxton, and Mr. Lenten [Denton], the residue will
be spoken of in the ensuing story to those that yet remaine.
Of these persons named the Author doth tender this following Meetre.

When reasons Scepter first 'gan sway your hearts,
  Through troublous Seas, this Western world to enter
Among Christs Souldiers, here to act your parts,
  Did not Christs love on [of?] you cause him to center
All those strait lines of your inflam'd desire
  Unto his truths, 'cause him in them you finde?
From wildernesse, not from his truths retire;
  But unto death this wonderous work you'l minde;
No place can claime peculiar interest in
  Christs worship, for all nations are his own;
The day's at hand down falls that man of sin,
  And Christs pure Gospel through the world is blown;
Harvest is come, bid ease and sleep adieu,
  What, trifle time when Christ takes in his Crop?
A Harvest large of Gentil and of Jew
  (You fil'd of Christ), let his sweet Doctrine drop.

[1] The intention is probably to distinguish Henry Smith from Ralph Smith,
pastor of the Plymouth church from 1629 to 1636.

Chap. XVII.

*Of the planting of Long-Island. And of the planting the nine-
teenth Church in the Mattachusets government, called
Sudbury.*

This yeare came over divers godly and sincere servants
of Christ, as I suppose, among whom came over the reverend
godly M. Peirson: This people finding no place in any of the
former erected Colonies to settle in, to their present content,
repaired to an Island, severed from the Continent of New-
haven, with about 16. miles off the salt Sea, and called Long-
Island, being about 120. miles in length, and yet but narrow:
here this people erected a Town, and called it South Hampton.[1]
There are many Indians on the greatest part of this Island,
who at first settling of the English there, did much annoy
their Cattel with the multitude of Doggs they kept, which
ordinarily are young wolves brought up tame, continuing of
a very ravening nature. This people gathered into a Church,
and called to office Mr. Peirson, who continued with them
about 7, or 8. yeares, and then he, with the greatest number
of the people, removed farther into the Island; the other
part that remained invited Mr. Foordum,[2] and a people that
were with him, to come and joyne with them, who accordingly
did, being wandered as far as the Dutch plantation, and there
unsettled, although he came into the Country before them.

This yeare the Town and Church of Christ at Sudbury
began to have the first foundation stones laid, taking up her
station in the Inland Country, as her elder Sister Concord
had formerly done, lying farther up the same River, being
furnished with great plenty of fresh marsh, but it lying very
low is much indammaged with land-flouds, insomuch that
when the summer proves wet, they lose part of their hay; yet

[1] A body of men from Lynn, Mass., having a patent from James Farrett as
representative of Lord Stirling, first settled at Oyster Bay. Driven away by the
Dutch, they established themselves at Southampton, at the other end of the island,
and before long placed themselves under the jurisdiction of Connecticut. Abraham Pierson, their minister, removed to Branford and to Newark, New Jersey.

[2] Rev. Robert Fordham, who in 1644 under a Dutch grant from the director-
general of New Netherland had founded Hempstead, L. I.

are they so sufficiently provided, that they take in Cattell of other Townes to winter. These people not neglecting the chief work, for the which they entred this wildernesse, namely, to worship the Lord in the purity of his Ordinances, and according to the rule of his Word, entred into covenant with him, and one with another, professedly to walk together in Church-fellowship; and according to the same rule they called to the office of a Pastor the Reverend, godly, and able Minister of the Word, Mr. Edmond Brown, whose labours in the Doctrine of Christ Jesus hath hitherto abounded, wading through this wildernesse-work with much cheerfulnesse of spirit, of whom as followeth:

> Both night and day Brown ceaseth not to watch
>   Christs little flock, in pastures fresh them feed;
> The worrying wolves shall not thy weak lambs catch;
>   Well dost thou minde in wildernesse their breed;
> Edmond, thy age is not so great but thou
>   Maist yet behold the Beast brought to her fall; [1]
> Earth's tottering Kingdome shew her legs gin bow;
>   Thou 'mongst Christs Saints with prayers maist her mawle;
> What signes wouldst have faith's courage for to rouse?
>   See, Christ triumphant hath his armies led,
> In wildernesse prepar'd his lovely Spouse,
>   Caus'd Kings and Kingdomes his high hand to dread;
> Thou seest his Churches daily are encreasing,
>   And thou thy selfe amongst his worthyes warring,
> Hold up thy hands, the battel's now increasing,
>   Christ's Kingdom's ay, it's past all mortall's marring.

This Towne is very well watered, and hath store of plow-land, but by reason of the oaken roots, they have little broke up, considering the many Acres the place affords; but this kinde of land requires great strength to break up, yet brings very good crops, and lasts long without mending. The people are industrious, and have encreased in their estates, some of them, yet the great distance it lyes from the Mart Towns maketh it burdensome to the Inhabitants, to bring their corne so far by land. Some Gentlemen have here laid out part of their estates in procuring farmes, by reason of the

[1] Revelation xvii. 8.

store of medow. This Church hath hitherto been blessed
with blessings of the right hand, even godly peace and unity:
they are not above 50. or 60. families, and about 80. souls in
Church-fellowship, their Neat-heard about 300.

Chap. XVIII.

*Of the planting of the twentieth Church of Christ at a Towne
called Braintree.*

About this time there was a Town and Church planted
at Mount Wollestone, and named Braintree, it was occasioned by some old planters and certain Farmers belonging to
the great Town of Boston; they had formerly one Mr. Whele-
wright [1] to preach unto them, (till this Government could no
longer contain them) they many of them in the mean time
belonging to the Church of Christ at Boston, but after his
departure they gathered into a Church themselves; [2] having
some inlargement of Land, they began to be well peopled,
calling to office among them, the reverend and godly Mr.
William Tompson, and Mr. Henry Flint, the one to the office
of a Pastor, the other of a Teacher; the people are purged
by their industry from the sowre leven of those sinful opinions
that began to spread, and if any remain among them it is
very covert, yet the manner of these Erronists that remain
in any place, is to countenance all sorts of sinful opinions, as
occasions serves, both in Church and Commonwealth, under
pretence of Liberty of Conscience, (as well their own opinion
as others). By this Symbol they may be known in Court
and Country. This Town hath great store of Land in tillage,
and is at present in a very thriving condition for outward
things, although some of Boston retain their Farms from
being of their Town, yet do they lye within their bounds; [3]
and, how it comes to pass I know not, their officers have

----

[1] The Antinomian minister, Mrs. Hutchinson's brother-in-law.

[2] In the part of old Braintree now known as Quincy. This church was
really gathered before those of Rowley, Salisbury, and Sudbury; Johnson's
numbering is inexact throughout.

[3] *I. e.*, some Boston men keep their farms from being part of Braintree,
though those farms lie within its borders. Such *enclaves* of town territory were
not uncommon in early New England.

somewhat short allowance. They are well stored with cattel
and corn, and as a people receives, so should they give: And
Reader, I cannot but mind thee of the admirable providence
of Christ for his people in this, where they have been in a low
condition, by their liberality they have been raised to much
in a very little time: And again, in withdrawing their hands
have had their plenty blasted. The reverend Mr. Tompson
is a man abounding in zeal for the propagation of the Gospel,
and of an ardent affection, insomuch that he is apt to forget
himself in things that concern his own good; [1] both him, and
the like gracious M. Flint is here remembred.

> With twofold cord doth Flint and Tompson draw
>   In Christ's yoke, his fallow ground to break,
> Wounding mens hearts with his most righteous Law,
>   Cordials apply to weary souls and weak.
> Tompson thou hast Christ's folk incouraged
>   To war their warfare, putting them in mind
> That Christ their King will make his sons the dread;
>   The day's at hand when they shall mastery find.
> Flint be a second to this Champion stout,
>   In Christ's your strength, while you for him do war,
> When first doth faint, a second helps him out,
>   Till Christ renew with greater strength by far.
> From East to West your labours lasted have,
>   The more you toil, the more your strength encreaseth,
> Your works will bide, when you are laid in grave,
>   His truth advance, whose Kingdom never ceaseth.

CHAP. XIX.

*Of the first promotion of learning in New-England, and the
extraordinary providences that the Lord was pleased to
send for furthering of the same.*

Toward the latter end of this Summer came over the
learned reverend, and judicious Mr. Henry Dunster, [2] before

---

[1] According to Winthrop he was confessedly "a very melancholic man and
of a crazy body." His last years were spent mostly in a state of melancholia.

[2] Dunster, M.A. of Emmanuel College, came to New England in 1640, and
was president of Harvard College from that time to 1654, when he was forced to
resign because of holding Antipædobaptist opinions.

whose coming the Lord was pleased to provide a Patron for erecting a Colledg, as you have formerly heard, his provident hand, being now no less powerful in pointing out with his unerring finger a president, abundantly fitted this his servant, and sent him over for to manage the work; and as in all the other passages of this history, the Wonder-working Providence of Sions Saviour hath appeared, so more especially in this work, the Fountains of learning being in a great measure stopped in our Native Country at this time, so that the sweet waters of Shilo's streams must ordinarily pass into the Churches through the stinking channel of prelatical pride, beside all the filth that the fountains themselves were daily incumbred withall, insomuch that the Lord turned aside often from them, and refused the breathings of his blessed Spirit among them, which caused Satan (in these latter daies of his transformation into an Angel of light) to make it a means to perswade people from the use of learning altogether, that so in the next generation they might be destitute of such helps, as the Lord hath been pleased hitherto to make use of, as chief means for the conversion of his people, and building them up in the holy faith, as also for breaking downe the Kingdom of Antichrist; and verily had not the Lord been pleased to furnish N. E. with means for the attainment of learning, the work would have been carried on very heavily, and the hearts of godly parents would have vanish'd away with heaviness for their poor children, whom they must have left in a desolate wilderness, destitute of the meanes of grace.

It being a work (in the apprehension of all, whose capacity could reach to the great sums of money, the edifice of a mean Colledg would cost) past the reach of a poor Pilgrim people,[1] who had expended the greatest part of their estates on a long voyage, travelling into Forraign Countryes being unprofitable to any that have undertaken it, although it were but with their necessary attendance, whereas this people were forced to travel with wifes, children, and servants; besides they considered the treble charge of building in this new populated

---

[1] The word is of course used in its general sense. "Pilgrim," according to Mr. Albert Matthews, appears not to have been specifically applied to the early settlers of Plymouth until 1798, nor "Pilgrim Fathers" until 1799. In this use the term is derived from a well-known passage in Bradford.

desart, in regard of all kind of workmanship,[1] knowing likewise, that young Students could make but a poor progress
in learning, by looking on the bare walls of their chambers,
and that Diogenes would have the better of them by far, in
making use of a Tun to lodg in, not being ignorant also, that
many people in this age are out of conceit with learning, and
that although they were not among a people who counted
ignorance the mother of devotion, yet were the greater part
of the people wholly devoted to the Plow, (but to speak
uprightly, hunger is sharp, and the head will retain little
learning, if the heart be not refreshed in some competent
measure with food, although the gross vapors of a glutted
stomack are the bane of a bright understanding, and brings
barrenness to the brain) but how to have both go on together,
as yet they know not; amidst all these difficulties, it was
thought meet learning should plead for it self, and (as many
other men of good rank and quality in this barren desart)
plod out a way to live: Hereupon all those who had tasted
the sweet wine of Wisdoms drawing, and fed on the dainties
of knowledg, began to set their wits a work, and verily as the
whole progress of this work had a farther dependency then on
the present eyed means, so at this time chiefly the end being
firmly fixed on a sure foundation, namely, the glory of God,
and good of all his elect people, the world throughout, in vin-
dicating the truths of Christ, and promoting his glorious
Kingdom, who is now taking the heathen for his inheritance,
and the utmost ends of the earth for his possession, means
they know there are, many thousands uneyed of mortal
man, which every daies Providence brings forth; upon these
resolutions, to work they go, and with thankful acknowledgment, readily take up all lawful means as they come to hand;
for place they fix their eye upon New-Town, which to tell
their Posterity whence they came, is now named Cambridg,[2]
and withal to make the whole world understand, that spiritual
learning was the thing they chiefly desired, to sanctifie the

---

[1] Wages were high, as they always are when free or cheap land is drawing
the laborer away from wage-service. Thus we find the General Court passing
laws to restrict excessive wages.

[2] Most of the early ministers were Cambridge men, Oxford being much less
productive of Puritans.

other, and make the whole lump holy, and that learning being
set upon its right object, might not contend for error instead
of truth; they chose this place, being then under the Orthodox, and soul-flourishing Ministery of Mr. Thomas Shepheard,
of whom it may be said, without any wrong to others, the
Lord by his Ministery hath saved many a hundred soul. The
scituation of this Colledg is very pleasant, at the end of a
spacious plain, more like a bowling green then a Wilderness,
neer a fair navigable river, environed with many Neighbouring Towns of note, being so neer, that their houses joyn with
her Suburbs; the building thought by some to be too gor-
geous for a Wilderness, and yet too mean in others apprehensions for a Colledg,[1] it is at present inlarging by purchase
of the neighbour houses; it hath the conveniencies of a fair
Hall, comfortable Studies, and a good Library,[2] given by the
liberal hand of some Magistrates and Ministers, with others:
The chief gift towards the founding of this Colledg, was by
Mr. John Harnes,[3] a reverend Minister; the Country being
very weak in their publike Treasury, expended about 500. *l.*
towards it, and for the maintenance thereof, gave the yearly
revenue of a Ferry passage between Boston and Charles Town,
the which amounts to about 40. or 50. *l. per annum.* The
Commissioners of the four united Colonies also taking into
consideration, of what common concernment this work would
be, (not only to the whole plantations in general, but also to
all our English Nation) they endeavoured to stir up all the
people in the several Colonies to make a yearly contribution
toward it, which by some is observed, but by the most very
much neglected; the Government hath endeavoured to grant
them all the priviledges fit for a Colledg, and accordingly the
Governour and Magistrates, together with the President of
the Colledg, for the time being, have a continual care of ordering all matters for the good of the whole. This Colledg hath
brought forth, and nurst up very hopeful plants, to the sup-

---

[1] Yet in 1655 the corporation and overseers declare that the building is "in
a very ruinous condition . . . not fit for scholars to abide in as it is."

[2] John Harvard's library, which he bequeathed entire to the college, consisted of 260 volumes. Its catalogue, still existing, shows it to have been a good
foundation.

[3] Misprint for Harvard.

plying some Churches here,[1] as the gracious and godly Mr.
Wilson, son to the grave and zealous servant of Christ Mr.
John Wilson, this young man is Pastor to the Church of Christ
at Dorchester; as also Mr. Buckly, son to the reverend M.
Buckly of Concord; as also a second son of his, whom our
Native Country hath now at present help in the Ministery,
and the other is over a people of Christ in one of these Col-
onies, and if I mistake not, England hath I hope not only
this young man of N. E. nurturing up in learning, but many
more, as M. Sam. and Nathanael Mathers, Mr. Wells, Mr.
Downing, Mr. Barnard, Mr. Allin, Mr. Bruster, Mr. William
Ames.   Mr. Jones, Another of the first fruits of this Colledg,
is imployed in these Western parts in Mevis, one of the summer
Islands; beside these named, some help hath been had from
hence in the study of Physick, as also the godly Mr. Sam.
Danforth, who hath not only studied Divinity, but also
Astronomy; he put forth many Almanacks, and is now called
to the office of a teaching Elder in the Church of Christ at
Roxbury, who was one of the fellows of this Colledg.   The
number of Students is much encreased of late, so that the
present year 1651. on the twelfth of the sixth moneth, ten of
them took the degree of Batchelors of Art, among whom the
Sea-born son of Mr. John Cotton was one; some Gentlemen
have sent their sons hither from England, who are to be commended for their care of them, as the judicious and godly
Doctor Ames, and divers others.   This hath been a place
certainly more free from temptations to lewdness then ordinarily England hath been, yet if men shall presume upon this
to send their most exorbitant children intending them more
especially for Gods service, the Justice of God doth sometimes

[1] The hopeful plants mentioned below are: John Wilson of the class of 1642;
John Bulkley, 1642; and Edward Bulkley (see p. 110, note 2); Samuel and
Nathaniel Mather, 1643 and 1647, sons of Rev. Richard, and preachers in Dublin
and London, respectively; Edmund Weld, 1650, preacher in Ireland; George
Downing, 1642, the most famous of them all, scout-master-general under Cromwell and ambassador under him and Charles II.; Tobias Barnard, 1642; John
Allin, 1643; Nathaniel Brewster, 1643; William Ames, 1645, son of the celebrated minister at Rotterdam (of these four Brewster preached in Ireland, the
other three in England); John Jones, 1643, who preached at Mevis or Nevis in
the West Indies (not Bermudas or Somers Islands); Samuel Danforth, 1643,
colleague of Eliot; and Seaborn Cotton (see p. 63).

meet with them, and the means doth more harden them in their way, for of late the godly Governors of this Colledg have been forced to expell some, for fear of corrupting the Fountain, wherefore the Author would ye should mind this following verse.

You that have seen these wondrous works by Sions Savior don,
  Expect not miracle, lest means thereby you over-run;
The noble Acts Jehovah wrought, his Israel to redeem,
  Surely this second work of his shall far more glorious seem;
Not only Egypt, but all Lands, where Antichrist doth raign,
  Shall from Jehovahs heavy hand ten times ten plagues sustain:
Bright shining shall this Gospel come, Oh glorious King of Saints,
  Thy blessed breath confounds thy foes, all mortal power faints,
The ratling bones together run with self-same breath that blows,
  Of Israels sons long dead and dry, each joynt their sinew grows,
Fair flesh doth cover them, and veins (lifes fountain) takes there place.
    Smooth seamless coats doth cloath their flesh, and all their structure
      grace.
The breath of Life is added, they no Antinomians are,
  But loving him who gives them life, more zealous are by far,
To keep his Law, then formerly when righteousnesse they sought
  In keeping that they could not keep, which then their downfal
    brought.
Their ceremonies vanisht are, on Christ's all their desires,
  Their zeal all Nations doth provoke, inkindled are loves fires:
With hast on horseback, bringing home their sons and daughters, they
  Rejoyce to see this glorious sight, like Resurrections day;
Up and be doing, you young plants, Christ calls his work unto.
  Polluted lips, touch'd with heav'ns fire, about this work shall go.
Prostrate in prayer, parents and you young ones, on Christ call,
  Suppose of you he will make use, whereby that beast shall fall:
So be it, Lord, thy servants say, who are at thy disposing,
  With outward word work inward grace, by heavenly truths dis-
    closing.
Awake, stand up from death to life, in Christ your studies enter,[1]
  The Scriptures search, bright light bring forth, upon this hardship
    venter.
Sound doctrine shall your lips preach out, all errors to confound
  And rid Christ's Temple from this smoke, his glory shall abound;
Precipitant doth Dagon fall, his triple head off cut,
  The Beast that all the world admires, by you to death is put:

[1] Center?

Put hand to mouth, with vehement blast your silver Trumpets sound,
   Christ calls to mind his peoples wrongs, their foes hee'l now con-
      found:
Be strong in God and his great might, his wondrous works do tell,
   You raised are unwonted ways, observe his workings well.
As Jordans streams congeal'd in heaps, and Jerico's high walls
   With Rams horns blast, and Midians Host, with pitcher breaking
      falls;
Like works, your faith for to confirm in these great works to come,
   That nothing now too hard may seem, Jehovah would have don.
The rage of Seas, and hunger sharp, wants of a desart Land,
   Your noble hearts have overcom, what shall this work withstand?
Not persecutors pride and rage, strong multitudes do fall
   By little handfuls of least dust, your Christ confounds them all;
Not Satan and his subtil train with seeming shew reforming,
   Another Gospel to bring forth, brings damned errors swarming:
Your selves have seen his paint washt off, his hidden poysons found,
   Christ you provides with Antidotes, to keep his people sound:
There's nought remains but conquest now, through Christ's continued
      power,
   His hardest works have honors most attend them every hour.
What greater honor then on earth, Christ's Legat for to be,
   Attended with his glorious Saints in Church fraternity.
Christ to behold adorning now his Bride in bright array,
   And you his friends him to attend upon his Nuptial day,
With crowned heads, as Conquerors triumphant by his side;
   In's presence is your lasting joy, and pleasures ever bide.

   Mr. Henry Dunstar is now President of this Colledg, fitted
from the Lord for the work, and by those that have skill that
way, reported to be an able Proficient, in both Hebrew, Greek,
and Latine languages, an Orthodox Preacher of the truths of
Christ, very powerful through his blessing to move the affection; and besides he having a good inspection into the well-
ordering of things for the Students maintenance (whose commons hath been very short hitherto) by his frugal providence
hath continued them longer at their Studies then otherwise
they could have done;[1] and verily it's great pity such ripe

---

[1] In September, 1653, Johnson was placed on a committee of the General
Court "to examine the state of the College in all respects," the commons being
particularly mentioned. For a most amusing account of the short commons
before President Dunster's time, see the landlady's testimony in Savage's edition
of Winthrop, I. 310, 311.

heads as many of them be, should want means to further
them in learning: But seeing the Lord hath been pleased to
raise up so worthy an instrument for their good, he shall not
want for incouragement to go on with the work, so far as a
rustical rime will reach.

> Could man presage prodigious works at hand,
>   Provide he would for's good and ill prevent,
> But God both time and means hath at's command,
>   Dunster in time to his N. E. hath sent.
> When England 'gan to keep at home their guides,
>   N. E. began to pay their borrowed back,
> Industrious Dunster, providence provides,
>   Our friends supply, and yet our selves no lack:
> With restless labour thou dost delve and dung,
>   Surculus[1] set in garden duly tended,
> That in Christs Orchard they, with fruit full hung,
>   May bless the Lord, thy toil gone, them expended,
> Thy constant course proves retrograde in this,
>   From West to East thy toil returns again,
> Thy husbandry by Christ so honored is,
>   That all the world partaketh of thy pains.

Chap. XX.

*Of the planting of the one and twentieth Church of Christ at a
Town called Glocester, and of the Church and Town of
Dover, and of the hardships that befel a certain people,
who thirsted after large liberty in a warm Country.*

For the Government of this little Commonwealth, this
year was chosen for Governour Richard Belingham, Esquire,
and John Endicut Esquire for Governors [Deputy Governor];
the number of Freemen added this year, were about 503.[2]

There was another Town and Church of Christ erected in
the Mattachuset Government, upon the Northern-Cape of
the Bay, called Cape Ann, a place of fishing, being peopled
with Fishermen, till the reverend Mr. Richard Blindman

[1] Scion.
[2] The real number was 126.

came from a place in Plimouth Patten, called Green-Harbor,[1] with some few people of his acquaintance, and setled down with them, named the Town Glocester, and gathered into a Church, being but a small number, about fifty persons, they called to office this godly reverend man, whose gifts and abilities to handle the word is not inferiour to many others, labouring much against the errors of the times, of a sweet, humble, heavenly carriage. This Town lying out toward the point of the Cape, the access thereunto by Land becomes uneasie, which was the chief cause it was no more populated. Their fishing trade would be very beneficial, had they men of estates to mannage it; yet are they not without other means of maintenance, having good timber for shipping, and a very sufficient builder, but that these times of combustion the Seas throughout hath hindered much that work, yet have there been Vessels built here at this Town of late. Their reverend Elder is here remembred.

> Thou hast thy prime and middle age here spent,
>   The best is not too good for him that gave it,
> When thou did'st first this Wilderness frequent,
>   For Sions sake it was, that Christ might save it.
> Blinman be blith in him, who thee hath taken
>   To feed his Flock, a few poor scattered sheep,
> Why should they be of thee at all forsaken?
>   Thy honor's high, that any thou may'st keep.
> Wait patiently thy Masters coming, thou
>   Hast hitherto his peoples portions dealt,
> It matters not for high preferment; now
>   Thy crown's to come, with joyes immortal felt.

About this time the people inhabiting the Town of Dover, although they lay out of any of these Colonies mentioned (yet hearing and seeing with what sweet harmony, both in Churches and civil Government, the Mattachusets peopled patten was carried on prosperously) desired greatly to submit unto the same, by putting themselves under their protection; and for that end they petitioned their General Cort to admit of them, and administer Justice as occasion served, by the

---

[1] Now Marshfield, whence Rev. Richard Blinman and his associates removed because of an irreconcilable dispute in the church.

hands of their godly Magistrates, which accordingly was granted,[1] and they have been partakers of the benefit hitherto, having also the benefit of some one Minister to preach unto them, till it pleased God to fit stones by the continual hewing of his word for his Temple-work, and they gather a Church according to the rule of the word, and called to office of a Pastor one M. Maude, both godly and diligent in the work. This Town is scituate upon Puscataque river, lying to the Northeast of Boston, which river, although it be not nigh so broad as Merrinaeck river, yet is it navigable, being very deep, and her banks in many places fil'd with stately timber, which hath caused one or two Saw-Mills to be continued; there they have a good quantity of Meddow Land, and good ground for India corn. To end this year 1641. the Lord was pleased to send a very sharp Winter, insomuch that the Harbor where Ships ordinarily Anchor, was frozen over of such a thickness, that it became passeable, both for horse, carts, and oxen, for the space of five weeks. And here the Reader must be minded of the wonder-working providence of Christ for his poor Churches, in altering the very season for their comfort, to the wonder of English and Indians, the Winter and Summer proving more moderate, both for heat and cold, unmasking many by this means, it being a frequent thing with some, that after the novelties of a new land began to be stale with them, and the sweet nourishment of the soul by the presence of Christ in the preaching of his Word, began to dry up through the hot heady conceit of some new conceived opinion, Then they wanted a warmer country, and every Northwest wind that blew, they crept into some odd chimney-corner or other, to discourse of the diversity of Climates in the Southerne parts, but chiefly of a thing very sweet to the pallate of the flesh, called liberty, which they supposed might be very easily attain'd, could they but once come into a place where all men were chosen to the office of a Magistrate, and

---

[1] There was a settlement at Dover, N. H., as early as 1628, perhaps as early as 1623. In 1641, after violent contests between an Anglican and a Puritan party, the holders of both the Hilton patent and the Piscataqua patent gave over their rights of jurisdiction to Massachusetts, which proceeded to extend its authority over Dover and the rest of New Hampshire. Rev. Daniel Maude, minister of Dover, was M.A. of Emmanuel College, and had been schoolmaster in Boston.

all were preachers of the Word, and no hearers, then it would be all Summer and no Winter. This consultation was to be put in practice speedily, as all headstrong motions are, but the issue proved very sad, both to these and others also; for thus it befell, when the time of the year was come that a sea-voyage might be undertaken, they having made sale of a better accommodation then any they could afterward attain unto, prepare for the voyage with their wifes and children, intending to land them in one of the Summer Islands, called the Isle of Providence,[1] and having wind and seas favouring them, as they supposed, or to speak more proper, the provident hand of the most high God directing it, they were brought so neer the shore for convenient landing, that they might have heaved a Bisket cake on land; their Pilate wondring he could not see the English colours on the Fort, he began to mistrust the Island was taken, and more especially, because they saw not the people appear upon the shores as they usually did when any Vessel was a coming in, but now and then they saw some people a far off wafting to them to come in, till they were even come to an Anchor, and then by the hoising up and down the heads of those on shore, they were fully confirmed in it, that the Island was taken, as indeed it was by the Spaniards, who as soone as they tackt about to be gone, made shot at them, and being in great fear they made all the sail they could, but before they could get out of shot, the Master of the Vessel was slain, the main sail shot through, and the Barque also; the people some of them returned back again for New-England, being sore abashed at this providence that befel them, that they would never seek to be governed by liberty again to this very day; yet others there are were so strongly bent for the heat of liberty, that they indured much pinching penury upon an uninhabited Island, til at length meeting some others like-minded with themselves, they made a voyage to another Island. The chiefest part of their Charter of Freedom was this, That

---

[1] Not one of the Somers Islands or Bermudas, but an island in the Caribbean Sea, off the coast of Nicaragua. Charles I. granted it in 1630, by a patent similar to that of Massachusetts, to a company, mostly Puritans, who held it till 1641, when the Spaniards captured it. In the summer of that year the emigrants from Massachusetts went there, as described above and in Winthrop, I. 333; II. 11–12, 33–35.

no man upon pain of death should speak against anothers
Religion; where they continued, till some of them were fam-
ished, and others even forced to feed on Rats, and any other
thing they could find to sustain nature, till the provident
hand of God brought a Ship to the place, which took them off
the Island, and saved their lives: But upon this the Winters
discourse ceased, and projects for a warmer Country were
husht and done.

CHAP. XXI.

*Of the suddain and unexpected fall of Cattel, and the great bless-
ing of God in giving plenty of provision.*

For this year 1642. John Winthrope Esquire was chosen
Governour, and John Endicut Esquire Deputy Governor:
The number of Freemen added were about 1232.[1] This
Spring Cowes and Cattle of that kind (having continued at
an excessive price so long as any came over with estates to
purchase them) fell of a suddain in one week from 22 *l.* the
Cow, to 6. 7. or 8. *l.* the Cow at most, insomuch that it made
all men admire how it came to pass,[2] it being the common
practice of those that had any store of Cattel, to sell every
year a Cow or two, which cloath'd their backs, fil'd their
bellies with more varieties then the Country of it self afforded,
and put gold and silver in their purses beside. Here the
Reader is desired to take notice of the wonderful providence
of the most high God toward these his new-planted Churches,
such as was never heard of, since that Jacobs sons ceased to
be a people, that in ten or twelve years planting, there should
be such wonderful alteration, a Nation to be born in a day,
a Commonwealth orderly brought forth from a few Fugitives.
All the Forraign plantations that are of forty, fifty, or a hundred years standing, cannot really report the like, although
they have had the greatest incouragements earth could afford,
Kings to countenance them, staple commodities to provoke
all manner of Merchants to resort unto them, silver, gold,

---

[1] True figure, 138.

[2] Probably the main explanation lay in the stopping of emigration by the
changed conditions in England since the summons of the Long Parliament.

precious stones, or whatever might intice the eye or ear to incline the motion of man toward them. [T]his remote, rocky, barren, bushy, wild-woody wilderness, a receptacle for Lions, Wolves, Bears, Foxes, Rockoones, Bags, Bevers, Otters, and all kind of wild creatures, a place that never afforded the Natives better then the flesh of a few wild creatures and parch't Indian corn incht out with Chesnuts and bitter Acorns, now through the mercy of Christ becom a second England for fertilness in so short a space, that it is indeed the wonder of the world; but being already forgotten of the very persons that tast of it at present, although some there be that keep in memory his mercies multitude, and declare it to their childrens children.

First to begin with the encrease of food, you have heard in what extream penury these people were in at first planting. For want of food, gold, silver, rayment, or whatsoever was precious in their eyes they parted with (when ships came in). For this, their beast that died, some would stick before they were cold, and sell their poor pined flesh for food, at 6. *d. per* pound, Indian Beans at 16. *s. per* bushel. When Ships came in, it grieved some Master[s] to see the urging of them by people of good rank and quality to sell bread unto them. But now take notice how the right hand of the most high hath altered all, and men of the meaner rank are urging them to buy bread of them, and now good white and wheaten bread is no dainty, but even ordinary man hath his choice, if gay cloathing, and a liquerish tooth after sack, sugar, and plums lick not away his bread too fast, all which are but ordinary among those that were not able to bring their owne persons over at their first coming; there are not many Towns in the Country, but the poorest person in them hath a house and land of his own, and bread of his own growing, if not some cattel: beside, flesh is now no rare food, beef, pork, and mutton being frequent in many houses, so that this poor Wilderness hath not onely equalized England in food, but goes beyond it in some places for the great plenty of wine and sugar, which is ordinarily spent, apples, pears, and quince tarts instead of their former Pumpkin Pies. Poultry they have plenty, and great rarity, and in their feasts have not forgotten the English fashion of stirring up their appetites with variety of cooking their food;

and notwithstanding all this great and almost miraculous work of the Lord, in providing for his people in this barren desart, yet are there here (as in other places) some that use these good creatures of God to excess, and others, to hoard up in a wretched and miserable manner, pinch themselves and their children with food, and will not tast of the good creatures God hath given for that end, but cut Church and Commonwealth as short also: Let not such think to escape the Lords hand with as little a stroke, as the like do in other places.

Secondly, For rayment, our cloth hath not been cut short, as but of late years the traders that way have encreased to such a number, that their shops have continued full all the year long, all one England;[1] besides the Lord hath been pleased to encrease sheep extraordinarily of late, hemp and flax here is great plenty, hides here are more for the number of persons then in England; and for cloth, here is and would be materials enough to make it; but the Farmers deem it better for their profit to put away their cattel and corn for cloathing, then to set upon making of cloth; if the Merchants trade be not kept on foot, they fear greatly their corne and cattel will lye in their hands: assuredly the plenty of cloathing hath caused much excess of late in those persons, who have clambered with excess in wages for their work, but seeing it will be the theam of our next discourse, after the birds are setled, it may be here omitted.

Further, the Lord hath been pleased to turn all the wigwams, huts, and hovels the English dwelt in at their first coming, into orderly, fair, and well-built houses, well furnished many of them, together with Orchards filled with goodly fruit trees, and gardens with variety of flowers: There are supposed to be in the Mattachusets Government at this day, neer a thousand acres of land planted for Orchards and Gardens, besides their fields are filled with garden fruit, there being, as is supposed in this Colony, about fifteen thousand acres in tillage, and of cattel about twelve thousand neat, and about three thousand sheep. Thus hath the Lord incouraged his people with the encrease of the general, although

---

[1] The same as in England.

many particulars are outed,[1] hundreds of pounds, and some thousands, yet are there many hundreds of labouring men, who had not enough to bring them over, yet now worth scores, and some hundreds of pounds; to be sure the Lord takes notice of all his talents, and will call to accompt in time: This brief survey of things will be of good use when time serves, in mean time you shall understand,

Chap. XXII.

Of the manner of planting Towns and Churches in N. E. and in particular of the Church and Town at Wooburn, being the three and twentieth Church of Christ in the Matta-chusets Government.[2]

There was a Town and Church erected called Wooburn,[3] this present year, but because all the action of this wandering people meet with great variety of censures, the Author will in this Town and Church set down the manner how this people have populated their Towns, and gathered their Churches, that the reverend Mr. Rathbone may be better informed, then when he wrote his book concerning the Churches of N. E.[4] and all others that are experienced in the holy Scriptures, may lay the actions of N. E. to the Rule, and try them

[1] Many individuals have lost, are out of pocket.

[2] This chapter is in its way a *locus classicus* for the genesis of the Massachusetts towns and churches, or at least for the procedure followed after the General Court and the people had settled down to a regular course of action. The earliest towns—Salem, Dorchester, Charlestown, Watertown, Boston—did not owe their foundation as settlements to definite acts of the General Court, but came into existence by less formal processes. Woburn's case is, however, typical of the greater number. The fulness with which it is narrated is, of course, owing to the prominent part which the author had in the beginnings of town and church there. See the Introduction.

[3] The name Woburn was given in compliment to Captain Robert Sedgwick of Charlestown, a neighbor of Johnson's and a member of Charlestown's committee for the survey, who was born at Woburn in Bedfordshire. Later, Sedgwick was sergeant-major of the Essex regiment (see p. 229, *post*), then an officer and finally a major-general under Cromwell. He died in 1656 in Jamaica, having been appointed by the Protector one of the commissioners for governing that island after the capture by Penn and Venables.

[4] See p. 137, note 1.

A pritty Ryttle to Rockyng that went too

Coo nusss ... vnconto then the ryst

first houses finish thus the Ryttle you first

He Rare to for how this poort towns ... rya

By wigkly means two whyle in first ass eys

And Just it is that insttttes Clees Eggtraction

Hel never shays in this poort towns Ergtion

Without which insttll and ... sum fresh frebs

Patorns Conclu the never ayy wott ryt

If Ever the mayst Rays have a: ptatron

ty has from paysntee not his Eucation

Doen Conclu the Eds own hao though

that will with means ... bing this nargh to pass

Not only towns but Sistr church to his

... out of ... and Affy now is ...

Non all forhatit ... towns thy ntak

The Lod not means J ... one ...

by the balance of the Sanctuary, for assuredly they greatly
desire they may be brought to the light, for great is the truth,
and will prevail, yet have they their errings as well as others,
but yet their imperfections may not blemish the truths of
Christ; let them be glorified, and these his people will willingly take shame to themselves, wherein they have miscarried:
But to begin, this Town, as all others, had its bounds fixed by
the General Court, to the contenese [contents] of four miles
square, (beginning at the end of Charles Town bounds).
The grant is to seven men of good and honest report,[1] upon
condition, that within two year they erect houses for habitation thereon, and so go on to make a Town thereof, upon the
Act of Court; these seven men have power to give and grant
out lands unto any persons who are willing to take up their
dwellings within the said precinct, and to be admitted to al
common priviledges of the said Town, giving them such an
ample portion, both of Medow and Upland, as their present
and future stock of cattel and hands were like to improve,
with eye had to others that might after come to populate the
said Town; this they did without any respect of persons, yet
such as were exorbitant, and of a turbulent spirit, unfit for a
civil society, they would reject, till they come to mend their
manners; such came not to enjoy any freehold. These seven
men ordered and disposed of the streets of the Town, as might
be best for improvement of the Land, and yet civil and religious society maintained; to which end those that had
land neerest the place for Sabbath Assembly, had a lesser
quantity at home, and more farther off to improve for corn,
of all kinds; they refused not men for their poverty, but according to their ability were helpful to the poorest sort, in
building their houses, and distributed to them land accordingly; the poorest had six or seven acres of Medow, and
twenty five of Upland, or thereabouts. Thus was this Town

[1] In the case of Woburn it was, by exception, the Charlestown church that
in November, 1640, appointed the seven men who supervised the new settlement.
Johnson was one of them, and was at once chosen their recorder or town clerk.
The town records (after a preliminary piece of characteristic verse, reproduced
in fac-simile on the opposite page) open with a minute and interesting narrative
of the surveys and other preliminaries, written by Johnson. Building probably
began in 1641.

populated, to the number of sixty families, or thereabout, and after this manner are the Towns of New England peopled. The scituation of this Town is in the highest part of the yet peopled land, neere upon the head-springs of many considerable rivers, or their branches, as the first rise of Ipswitch river, and the rise of Shashin [1] river, one of the most considerable branches of Merrimeck, as also the first rise of Mistick river and ponds, it is very full of pleasant springs, and great variety of very good water, which the Summers heat causeth to be more cooler, and the Winters cold maketh more warmer; their Medows are not large, but lye in divers places to particular dwellings, the like doth their Springs; their Land is very fruitful in many places, although they have no great quantity of plain land in any one place, yet doth their Rocks and Swamps yeeld very good food for cattel; as also they have Mast and Tar for shipping, but the distance of place by land causeth them as yet to be unprofitable; they have great store of iron ore; their meeting-house stands in a small Plain, where four streets meet; the people are very laborious, if not exceeding some of them.

Now to declare how this people proceeded in religious matters, and so consequently all the Churches of Christ planted in New-England, when they came once to hopes of being such a competent number of people, as might be able to maintain a Minister, they then surely seated themselves, and not before, it being as unnatural for a right N. E. man to live without an able Ministery, as for a Smith to work his iron without a fire; therefore this people that went about placing down a Town, began the foundation-stone, with earnest seeking of the Lords assistance, by humbling of their souls before him in daies of prayer, and imploring his aid in so weighty a work, then they address themselves to attend counsel of the most Orthodox and ablest Christians, and more especially of such as the Lord had already placed in the Ministery, not rashly running together themselves into a Church, before they had hopes of attaining an Officer to preach the Word, and administer the Seals unto them, chosing rather to continue in fellowship with some other Church for their

---

[1] Shawshin or Shawsheen.

Christian watch over them, till the Lord would be pleased to provide: They after some search meet with a young man named Mr. Thomas Carter, then belonging to the Church of Christ at Water-Town, a reverend godly man, apt to teach the sound and wholesome truths of Christ; having attained their desires, in hopes of his coming unto them, were they once joyned in Church-estate, he exercising his gifts of preaching and prayer among them in the mean time, and more especially in a day of fasting and prayer.[1] Thus these godly people interest their affections one with the other, both Minister and people: After this they make ready for the work, and the 24. of the 6. moneth[2] 1642. they assemble together in the morning about eight of the clock; After the reverend Mr. Syms had continued in preaching and prayer about the space of four or five houres, the persons that were to joyn in Covenant, openly and professedly before the Congregation, and messengers of divers Neighbour Churches—among whom the reverend Elder of Boston, Mr. Cotton, Mr. Wilson, Mr. Allen of Charles-Town, Mr. Shepheard of Cambridg, Mr. Dunster of Water-Town, Mr. Knowles of Deadham, Mr. Allen of Roxbury, Mr. Eliot of Dorchester, Mr. Mather: As also it is the duty of the Magistrates (in regard of the good and peace of the civil Government) to be present, at least some one of them (not only to prevent the disturbance might follow in the Commonwealth by any, who under pretence of Church-Covenant, might bring in again those cursed opinions that caused such commotion in this and the other Colony, to the great dammage of the people) but also to countenance the people of God in so pious a work, that under them they may live a quiet and peaceable life, in all godliness and honesty; for this cause was present the honored Mr. Increase Nowel—the persons stood forth and first confessed what the Lord had done for their poor souls, by the work of his Spirit in the preaching of his Word, and Providences, one by one; and that all might know their faith in Christ was bottomed

[1] In April, 1642.   They had first tried to engage Rev. Jonathan Burr (p. 192) as pastor, then Rev. John Miller.   Thomas Carter, M.A. of St. John's College, Cambridge, 1633, came to New England in 1635.   He was pastor of the Woburn church forty-two years.

[2] *I. e.*, August 24.   But the Woburn town records give the date as August 14.

upon him, as he is revealed in his Word, and that from their own knowledg, they also declare the same, according to that measure of understanding the Lord had given them; the Elders, or any other messengers there present question with them, for the better understanding of them in any points they doubt of, which being done, and all satisfied, they in the name of the Churches to which they do belong, hold out the right hand of fellowship unto them, they declaring their Covenant, in words expressed in writing to this purpose.

The Church-Covenant.

We that do assemble our selves this day before God and his people, in an unfeigned desire to be accepted of him as a Church of the Lord Jesus Christ, according to the Rule of the New-Testament, do acknowledg our selves to be the most unworthy of all others, that we should attain such a high grace, and the most unable of our selves to the performance of any thing that is good, abhorring our selves for all our former defilements in the worship of God, and other wayes, and resting only upon the Lord Jesus Christ for attonement, and upon the power of his grace for the guidance of our whole after course, do here in the name of Christ Jesus, as in the presence of the Lord, from the bottom of our hearts agree together through his grace to give up our selves, first unto the Lord Jesus as our only King, Priest and Prophet, wholly to be subject unto him in all thing, and therewith one unto another, as in a Church-Body to walk together in all the Ordinances of the Gospel, and in all such mutual love and offices thereof, as toward one another in the Lord; and all this, both according to the present light that the Lord hath given us, as also according to all further light, which he shall be pleased at any time to reach out unto us out of the Word by the goodness of his grace, renouncing also in the same Covenant all errors and Schismes, and whatsoever by-wayes that are contrary to the blessed rules revealed in the Gospel, and in particular the inordinate love and seeking after the things of the world.

Every Church hath not the same for words, for they are not for a form of words.

The 22. of the 9. moneth[1] following Mr. Thomas **Carter** was ordained Pastor, in presence of the like Assembly. After he had exercised in preaching and prayer the greater part of the day, two persons in the name of the Church laid their hands upon his head, and said, We ordain thee Thomas Carter to be Pastor unto this Church of Christ; then one of the Elders Priest [Present], being desired of the Church, continued in prayer unto the Lord for his more especial assistance of this his servant in his work, being a charge of such weighty importance, as is the glory of God and salvation of souls, that the very thought would make a man to tremble in the sense of his own inability to the work. The people having provided a dwelling house, built at the charge of the Town in general, welcomed him unto them with joy, that the Lord was pleased to give them such a blessing, that their eyes may see their Teachers. After this there were divers added to the Church daily after this manner: the person desirous to joyn with the Church, cometh to the Pastor, and makes him acquainted therewith, declaring how the Lord hath been pleased to work his conversion, who discerning hopes of the persons faith in Christ, although weak, yet if any appear, he is propounded to the Church in general for their approbation, touching his godly life and conversation, and then by the Pastor and some brethren heard again, who make report to the Church of their charitable approving of the person; but before they come to joyn with the Church, all persons within the Towne have publike notice of it, then publikely he declares the manner of his conversion, and how the Lord hath been pleased by the hearing of his Word preached, and the work of his Spirit in the inward parts of his soul, to bring him out of that natural darkness, which all men are by nature in and under, as also the measure of knowledg the Lord hath been pleased to indue him withal. And because some men cannot speak publikely to edification through bashfulness, the less is required of such, and women speak not publikely at all, for all that is desired, is to prevent the polluting the blessed

---

[1] November 22. The ordination of Carter was famous, and by Winthrop (II. 88) was censured because its central ceremony, the imposition of hands, was performed by lay members of the church (one of them doubtless Johnson himself), Congregational custom requiring that this should be performed by some of the elders or ministers present.

Ordinances of Christ by such as walk scandalously, and that men and women do not eat and drink their own condemnation, in not discerning the Lords body. After this manner were many added to this Church of Christ, and those 7. that joyned in Church-fellowship at first, are now encreased to 74. persons, or therabout; of which, according to their own confession, as is supposed, the greater part having been converted by the preaching of the Word in N. E. by which may appear the powerful efficacy of the word of Christ in the mouth of his Ministers, and that this way of Christ in joyning together in Church-Covenant, is not only for building up of souls in Christ, but also for converting of sinners, and bringing them out of the natural condition to be ingrafted into Christ, for if this one Church have so many, then assuredly there must be a great number comparatively throughout all the Churches in the Country. After this manner have the Churches of Christ had their beginning and progress hitherto; the Lord continue and encrease them the world throughout. The Pastor of this Church hath much encreased with the encreasings of Christ Jesus, of whose labours in the Lord as followeth.

> Carter, Christ hath his wayes thee taught, and them [thou]
>   Hast not with-held his Word, but unto all
> With's word of power dost cause stout souls to bow,
>   And meek as Lambs before thy Christ to fall:
> The antient truths, plain paths, they fit thee best,
>   Thy humble heart all haughty acts puts by,
> The lowly heart, Christ learns his lovely hest,
>   Thy meekness shews thy Christ to thee is nigh;
> Yet must thou shew Christ makes his bold to be
>   As Lions, that none may his truths tread down,
> Pastoral power he hath invested thee
>   With, it maintain, least he on thee do frown:
> Thy youth thou hast in this New-England spent,
>   Full sixteen years to water, plant, and prune
> Trees taken up, and for that end here sent;
>   Thy end's with Christ, with's Saints his praises tune.

This year the General Court made an order about preparing houses for Salt-peter, that there might be powder made in the Country, but as yet it hath not gone on.

Chap. XXIII.

Of the uniting of the four English Colonies in N. E. and the battel fought between the Narragansets, and Mawhiggins.

The yeare 1643, the honored John Winthrop Esquire was chosen Governor again, and John Endicut Esquire Deputy Governour; the freemen added were about 87.[1] this year. The four Colonies, the Mattachusets, Plimoth, Canectico, and New-haven, taking into consideration the many Nations of Dutch, Zewes,[2] and French, that were on either side of them; as also how apt they were to lay claim to lands they never had any right unto, but only a paper possession of their own framing; and further, that the inhumane and barbarous Indians would be continually quarrelling and contending, could they see any hopes of prevailing, together with the contestion begun in our Native country, and withal, that although providence had cast them into four several Colonies, yet Religion had already united them, coming over all for one and the same end. Hereupon by Commissioners sent from the several colonies, they concluded a firm confederation to assist each other in all just and lawful war, bearing an equal proportion in the charge, according to the number of persons inhabiting each colony; but herein the Mattachuset had the worst end of the staff, in bearing as much, or more charge, then all the other three, and yet no greater number of Commissioners to negotiate and judg in transacting of affairs concerning peace and war, then the least of the other, and any one of the other as likely to involve them in a chargeable war with the naked Natives, that have neither plunder nor cash to bear the charge of it, nay hitherto the most hath risen from the lesser colonies, yet are the Mattachusets far from deserting them, esteeming them highly, so long as their Governments maintain the same purity in Religion with themselves, for indeed this is that they have spent their whole travel for, and therefore if Plimoth, or any of the other shall

[1] Read 78.

[2] Read Swedes. For the text of the famous New England Confederation of 1643, see Bradford, in this series, pp. 382–388, or Winthrop. II. 100–105

draw back herein, the chiefest end of their confederacy would be lost; for should it come to pass that (in venturing their persons and estates so far for purity in the Ordinances and Discipline of Christ) they should lose the purity in doctrine, all their cost and labour were lost. This confederacy being finished, there came in certain Indian Sachims, and submitted to the English Government, as Pomham, and Soccananocoh to the Mattachusets; also Miantonemo and Uncas; but between these two latter Princes arose a very hot quarrel, the English seeking by all means to quench it, but could not, it being, as is supposed, fomented by a small company of vacabond English, who were then for their crimes banished from their own complices at Rhode Island, the Ringleader of them being one Samuel Gorton, by whose mean they were drawn into damnable errors.[1] These Gortonists, as is said, lent Miantonenemo a Corslet for safeguard of his own person in the following fight, and he promised each of them a Mawchiggin [2] papoose, which was the people Uncas was Prince of. For although Miantonemo were the more potent Prince by far, and a very austere man, yet did he chuse rather to take Uncasses life away by treachery if he could; and to that end hired a young man of the Pegod Nation to murther him, as is supposed, for in an evening, when it was very neer dark, this Sachim passing without any of his Retinue from one wigwam to another, was suddainly shot through the arm with an arrow, seeing not whence it came; but yet recovering the Palace he was passing unto, without receiving any more shot, he had the arrow drawn forth, and the wound cured in a short time after; the young man, who was suspected to have done the fact, having great store of Wampumpeage about this time, being questioned how he came by it, could give no good accompt, which encreased the suspition the more, that he had received it as hire from Miantonemo for this fact;

[1] Samuel Gorton had come to Plymouth in 1636, to Aquidneck in 1639, to Providence (Pawtuxet) in 1641, everywhere becoming involved in controversy, and in 1643 to Shawomet (now Warwick, R. I.), where, on land bought from Miantonomoh, he and his followers made their final settlement. Heretical in religion, insubordinate and contentious in disposition, they were a thorn in the side of Massachusetts, and were finally suppressed in the high-handed manner described in the next chapter.

[2] Mohegan.

and hereupon the young man fled unto him, which caused Uncas to complain to the English, who having the hearing of the case at a General Court holden at Boston, at the same time Miantonemo coming thither with his attendance, and sending one of his Councellors to follow the matter in hand, the young man was examined in presence of Miantonemo; being, as is supposed, tutored by him, he told this tale, that while he was in Uncasses Court, on a day travelling alone by a thick swamp, Uncas call'd him out of the swamp, charging him to be true to him, in declaring to the English what he required to him, which was, that he should say he had been hired of Miantonemo to kill him, and to make his matter good, quoth the young man, he then cut his arm on the top and underneath with the flint of his Gun, to make men think he had beene shot through with an arrow. This tale made the English more to suspect Miantonemo then before; and therefore desired to examine the young man alone, which he was very unwilling they should do; but upon further examination alone, they did verily believe this young man had done the fact, yet for present they let him depart with Miantonemo, advising him to send him home to Uncas, but by the way he, instead of returning him home, cut off his head, and forthwith gathered an army of about a thousand men to fight with Uncas, who feared not to meet him in the field with half the number; the battel being come within shot one of another, with a great hubbub they let their long shafts fly one at another, and after came to a close with other weapons, till the Narrowgansets multitude being sorely distressed by the Mawhiggins valour, they began to cry out Wammeck,[1] which is to say, enough. Uncas like a stout commander, with others of his bloud-royal that were about him, sought to perfect his victory, by possessing himself with the person of their Prince, which he effected, by putting his Life-guard to flight, and taking hold on the Sachim himself, carried him victoriously away to the Town of Hartford, neer the which he kept his residence at this time, and then made the English acquainted there with his noble design, and desired to have the advise of the united colonies what to do with his prisoner; the Nar-

---

[1] Wood gives the word as *wawmott*.

rowgansets sought to ransom him home, being much abashed,
that so mean a Prince as Uncas was should scape scotfree
with such a victory; but the honored Commissioners have
had proof of Miantonemo's treachery, both toward this
Prince that had him in possession, and toward the English
in falsifying his promise with them; they advised Uncas to
put him to death, but withall, that he should forbear to exercise any barbarous cruelty toward him, as their manner is,
and by this means the English prevented another war, both
with English and Indians, which was very neer joyning
in battel.   Not many years after,[1] the Indian Sachim upon
this advise, caused Miantonemo to be led forth, as if he would
remove him to a more safer place of custody, and by the way
caused him to be executed; the Indians, his kindred and subjects, were much grieved at his death, yet took it quietly at
present, but the lesser Princes, his Neighbours, rather rejoyced, he having tyrannized over them, and enforced them
to subject to his will, right or wrong.

Chap. XXIV.

*Of the proceeding of certain persons called Gortonists, against
the united Colonies, and more especially against the Mattachusets, and of the blasphemous doctrines broached by Gorton, deluding a company of poor ignorant people therewith.*[2]

For not long before, those persons that we spake of, who
incouraged Miantonemo to this war, and with the help of
him enforced Pomham and Socananocho to set their hands
to a writing which these Gortonists had framed, to take their
land from them; but the poor Sachems, when they saw they

[1] Only a few weeks after. The sachem of the Narragansetts was one of
the nobler sort of savages, and his fate has commanded frequent sympathy.

[2] One would not learn from Johnson that the "harrying of the Gortonists"
was one of the most discreditable episodes of early Massachusetts history.   Pum-
ham and Socananoco were savages of the baser sort, and the English neighbors
of Gorton mentioned below were selfish schemers trying to get his lands, but the
government of Massachusetts lent itself to their machinations, and, extending
its jurisdiction unwarrantably over the Shawomet region, drove out the heretics
with great harshness and illegal cruelty.

were thus gull'd of their land, would take no pay for it, but complained to the Mattachusets Government, to whom they had subjected themselves and their lands: As also at this time certain English inhabiting those parts, with the Indians good leave and liking, desired to have the benefit of the Mattachusets Government, as Dover formerly had done, to whom this Government condescended, in hope they might encrease to such a competent number of godly Christians, as that there might be a Church of Christ planted, the place being capable to entertain them in a comfortable measure for outward accommodation, but hitherto it hath been hindred by these Gortonists, and one of Plimoth who forbad our people to plant there: These person[s] thus submitting, came at this time also to complain of certain wrongs done them by these Gortonists, who had thus incroached, and began to build on the Indians land; upon these complaints, the Governor and the honored Mr. Dudly issue forth their Warrant, to summon them to appear, they being then about five or six persons, without any means for instructing them in the wayes of God, and without any civil Government to keep them in civility or humanity, which made them to cast off most proudly and disdainfully any giving accompt to man of their actions, no not to the chiefest in authority, but returned back most insolent, scornful, scurrilous speeches. After this, the Government of the Mattachusets sent two messengers on purpose to perswade them to come and have their cause heard, assuring them like justice in their cause with any other; but Samuel Gorton being the ring-leader of the rout, was so full gorged with dreadful and damnable errors, (the which he had newly insnared these poor souls with) that soon after the departure of the messenger, he layes aside all civil justice, and instead of returning answer to the matter in hand, he vomits up a whole paper[1] full of beastly stuff, one while scoffing and deriding the ignorance of all beside himself, that think Abraham, Isaac, etc., could be saved by Christ Jesus, who was after born of the Virgin Mary, another while mocking at the Sacraments of Baptism and the Lords Supper, in an opprobrious manner, deriding at the Elements Christ was pleased to in-

[1] The paper is preserved in Gorton's strange book entitled *Simplicities Defence against Seven-Headed Policie* (London, 1646).

stitute them in, and calling them Negromancers that administer them at all; and in a word, all the Ordinances of the Gospel abominable Idolatry he called, and likened them to Molock, and the Star of the Idol Rempham; [1] his paper was thrust full of such filthiness, that no Christian ear could hear them without indignation against them, and all was done by him in a very scornful and deriding manner, upbraiding all that use them; in the mean time magnifying his own glorious light, that could see himself to be personally Christ, God-Man, and so all others that would believe as he did. This paper he got to be subscribed, with about twelve or thirteen hands, his number of Disciples being encreased, for assuredly the man had a very glosing tongue, but yet very deceitful, for when he had but a few with him, then he cried out against all such as would rule over their own species, affirming, that the Scripture termeth such to be Gods of the world, or divels; but after his return from England, having received some incouragement from such as could not look into the depth of his deceits, being done at so large a distance, he getting into favour again with those, who had formerly whipt him out of their company, turns divel himself. The godly Governors of the Mattachusets seeing this blasphemous Bull of his, resolved to send forty persons [2] well-appointed with weapons of war for apprehending of him, who accordingly, with some waiting, did apprehend him and the rest of his company, except two or three which ran away, without any hurt to any person, although he gave out very big words, threatning them with bloud and death so soon as they set foot on the ground, and yet this brazenfac'd deceiver published in print the great fear their women were put unto by the souldiers, whereas they came among them day by day, and had it not been that they intended peaceably to take them, they would never have waited so long upon their worships as they did, but being apprehended, and standing to that they had written (yet would they willingly have covered it with some shifts if they could) the greatest punishment they had, was to be confin'd to certain Towns for a few moneths, and afterward ban-

---

[1] Acts vii. 43.

[2] Three commissioners were at the head of the party, and our author was one of the three. They carried out their instructions with great severity.

ished; but to be sure there be them in N. E. that have Christ Jesus and his blessed Ordinances in such esteem, that the Lord assisting, they had rather lose their lives, then suffer them to be thus blasphemed if they can help it; and whereas some have favoured them, and endeavoured to bring under blame such as have been zealous against their abominable doctrines, the good God be favourable unto them, and prevent them from coming under the like blame with Ahab, yet they remain in their old way, and there's somewhat to be considered in it to be sure, that in these daies, when all look for the fall of Antichrist, such detestable doctrines should be upheld, and persons suffered, that exceed the Beast himself for blasphemy, and this to be done by those that would be counted Reformers, and such as seek the utter subversion of Antichrist.

To end this year, or rather at the beginning of it, the Lord caused another Earthquake, much less then the former, it was on the fifth of the first moneth called March[1] in the morning.

CHAP. XXV.

Of the planting the twenty fourth Church of Christ at the Town of Readding, and the twenty fifth Church of Christ in the Mattachusets Government, called Wenham.

This year was chosen to the place of Governor John Endicut Esquire, and John Winthrope Esquire Deputy Governour; the number of freemen added about 145. this year.[2]

The Town of Readding had her foundation stone laid about this time.[3] This and the Town of Wooburn were like the twins in the womb of Tamar, Readding thrusting forth the hand first, but Wooburn came first to the birth.[4] This Town is well watered, and scituate about a great pond, besides it hath two mills, the one a Saw-mill, the other a Cornmill, which stand on two several streams; it hath not been so fruitful for children as her Sister hath, her habitation is fallen in the very center of the country; they are well stocked

---

[1] *I. e.*, March 5, 1644.   [2] In fact, 46.
[3] Really, in 1645.   [4] Genesis xxxviii. 28–30.

with cattel, for the number of people they have. They gathered into a church, and ordained a Pastor from among themselves at the same time, a young man of good abilities to preach the Word, and of a very humble behaviour, named Mr. Green. He having finished his course, departed this life not long after, whose labours are with the Lord; after him succeeded in the place one Mr. Hoph, a young man, one of the first fruits of N. E. a man studious to promote the truths of Christ; they are both remembred in this following verse.[1]

> On earths bed thou at noon hast laid thy head;
>   You for that [that for] Christ (as Green) here toyl have taken,
> When nature fails, then rest it in earths dead,
>   Till Christ by's word with glory thee awaken.
> Young Hoph thou must be second to this man,
>   In field incounter, with Christ's foes shalt thou
> Stand up, and take his bright sword in thy hand,
>   Error cut down, and make stout stomacks bow;
> Green's gone before, thy warfare's now begun,
>   And last it may to see Romes Babel fall;
> By weakest means Christ mighty works hath done,
>   Keep footing fast, till Christ thee hence do call.

The next Town and church of Christ planted in this colony, was between Salem and Ipswitch. Salem the eldest of all the Sisters was very helpful to this her little Sister, nourishing her up in her own bosom, till she came of age, being beneficial to her besides, in giving her a good portion of Land; this Town is called Wenham, and is very well watered, as most in-land Towns are. The people live altogether upon husbandry, New England having train'd up great store to this occupation; they are encreased in cattel, and most of them live very well, yet are they no great company; they were some good space of time there before they gathered into a Church-body. The godly and reverend Mr. John Fisk went thither with them, at first setting down as a planter among them, yet withal he became helpful in preaching the Word unto them, when they were but a few in number;

----

[1] The Reading church was organized in 1645. Henry Green died in 1648, and was succeeded by Samuel Hough, who, as Johnson's phrase implies, was one of the earliest students at Harvard College, but was not graduated.

they afterward call'd him to the office of a Pastor, with whom he now remains, labouring in the Word and Doctrine, with great industry,[1] of whom it may be thus said:

> To wade through toyl of Wilderness, thou hast
>   Doubled thy work, thy wages treble are;
> Christ hath thee call'd and in his vineyard plac't,
>   He'l bear thee up above all fainting far.
> Sions strong Mount must now again be built,
>   Thy faith, oh Fisk, the Lord hath holpen much;
> With dreadful sighs the Prelats power hath split,
>   All pride he'l stain by his almighty touch.
> His truths unstain'd by liberty keep thou,
>   To please the most, authority must fall,
> What Christ hath given, it safely keep with you,
>   Till he to thee for thine accompt do call.

CHAP. XXVI.

Of the military affairs, the forts of Boston, and Charles[town], the Castle erected anew by the six neerest Towns, with the manner of putting the Country in a posture of war, to be ready upon all occasions.

These souldiers of Christ Jesus, having made a fair retreat from their Native country hither, and now being come to a convenient station, resolved to stand it out (the Lord assisting) against all such as should come to rob them of their priviledges, which the Lord Christ had purchased for them at a very high rate, and now out of the riches of his grace was minded to give them, yet would he have them follow him into this Wilderness for it: although the chiefest work of these select bands of Christ, was to mind their spiritual warfare, yet they knew right well the Temple was surrounded with walls and bulworks, and the people of God in re-edifying the same, did prepare to resist their enemies with weapons of war, even while they continued building. This people no less diligent to make use of such means as the Lord afforded them,

---

[1] Rev. John Fiske and most of the Wenham church removed bodily to Chelmsford in 1655.

ordered and decreed, That all the souldiers belonging to the 26. bands in the Mattachusets Government, should be exercised and drill'd eight daies in a yeare, and whosoever should absent himself, except it were upon unavoidable occasion, should pay 5 s. for every daies neglect; there are none exempt, unless it be a few timerous persons that are apt to plead infirmity, if the Church chuse them not for Deacons, or they cannot get to serve some Magistrate or Minister; [1] but assuredly the generality of this people are very forward for feats of war, and many have spent their time and estates to further this work; the Town of Boston hath afforded many active, Charles-Town hath not been inferiour, unless it be in number. This year the Court appointed certain persons to spend their skill in putting the people possessing this desolate desart in a ready posture of drawing their forces together, upon any suddain accident that might befall them, to mannage, guide, order, and direct all things, as may be best for the good of the whole, they being a poor and mean people, laboured to avoid high titles, yet order they knew was necessary, therefore ordained they only one General Officer in time of war, under the name of Major General; [2] the Governor and Magistrates for the time being are the standing Councel for peace or war, and either they or the General Court may appoint any to the office of a General; the first Major-General was the much honored Tho. Dudly Esquire, whose faithfulness and great zeal and love to the truths of Christ, caused the people to chuse him to this office, although he were far stricken

[1] Act of November, 1647, decreeing eight days for training. "All majestrates, deputies, officers of Court, elders and deacons, the president, ffellowes, students, and officers of Harvard Colledge, and all proffessed schoole masters allowed by any two majestrates, the treasurer, auditor gene[ll], surveior gennerall of the armes, publick notaries, phisitions, chirurgeons allowed by any two majestrates, masters of shipps, and other vessells above twenty tunns, millers and constant heardsmen, and such other as shall by any Court be dischardged, either for bodily infirmity or other reasonable cause, shall be exempt from ordinary traynings, watchings, and wardings, but not their sonns or servants, save one servant of every majestrate allowed exemption." Johnson glances humorously at the easiest means of escape.

[2] "Avoiding high titles," they called the commander of each of their regiments not colonel but sergeant-major, and then gave to their commander-in-chief the title of sergeant-major-general (i. e., general sergeant-major), whence major-general.

in years;[1] the Government is divided into four Counties, which to shew, they would their posterity should mind whence they came, they have named, Suffolk, Middlesex, Essex, and Northfolk, each containing a Regiment, over whom the chief Commander is only a Serjeant-Major; the first chosen to this office over the Regiment of Suffolk, was Major Edw. Gibbons, who hath now the office of Major-General also, he is a man of a resolute spirit, bold as a Lion, being wholly tutor'd up in N. E. Discipline, very generous, and forward to promote all military matters; his Forts are well contrived, and batteries strong, and in good repair, his great Artillery well mounted, and cleanly kept, half Canon, Culverins and Sakers,[2] as also field-pieces of brass very ready for service, his own company[3] led by Capt. Lieutenant Sarag, are very compleat in their arms, and many of them disciplin'd in the military garden[4] beside their ordinary trainings; the Captains under him, are Capt. Humphry Atherton, of the Band of Dorchester; a very lively couragious man, with his stout and valiant Lieutenant Clapes, strong for the truth; of the Band of Roxbury, Capt. Prichard, and Ensign Johnson; of the Band of Waymoth, Capt. Perkins, and his proper and active Lieutenant Torry; of the Band of Hingham, Capt. Bozoan Allen; of the Band of Deadham, Capt. Eliazer Lusher, one of a nimble and active spirit, strongly affected to the ways of truth; of the Band of Braintree, Capt. William Tinge, these belong to the Regiment of Suffolk; the first Serjeant-Major chosen to order the Regi-

[1] The office of sergeant-major-general was provided for in 1643; Dudley was elected to it in 1644, being then sixty-seven years of age. Of the names which follow, several have already appeared in Johnson's enumeration of conspicuous deputies, in bk. I., ch. XLV. Comment on them is in most cases not requisite, except to correct misspellings: read Savage for Sarag, Clap for Clapes, Jennison for Jenings, Gookin for Goggin, Greenleaf for Greenlife. Of the three sergeants-major, Gibbons (see p. 64, note 2) became major-general in 1649; for Sedgwick, see p. 212, note 3; Denison was major-general after Atherton, 1661–1682.

[2] Culverins were about equivalent to fifteen or eighteen-pounders; sakers to five or six-pounders.

[3] In the military organization of the seventeenth century, the theory was that the colonel, or sergeant-major, commanding a regiment was also captain of its senior company. Hence the officer who actually led that company was, by title, only captain-lieutenant of it.

[4] Garden in the sense of training-ground. So in "Artillery garden," below.

ment of Essex,[1] was Major Robert Sedgwick, stout and active
in all feats of war, nurst up in Londons Artillery garden,
and furthered with fifteen years experience in N. E. exact
theory, besides the help of a very good head-piece, being a
frequent instructor of the most martial troops of our Artillery
men; and although Charles Town, (which is the place of his
own companies residence) do not advantage such o're-topping
batteries as Boston doth, yet hath he erected his to very good
purpose, insomuch that all shipping that comes in, either to
Boston or Charles-Town, must needs face it all the time of
their coming in; the cost he hath been at, in helping on the
Discipline of his Regiment hath profited much; his own company are led by the faithful Capt. Lieutenant Francis Norton,
(a man of a bold and cheerful spirit) being well disciplin'd and
an able man; the companies under his service have not all
Captains at present, Water-Town Band was led by Capt.
Jenings, who is supposed to be now in England, his Lieutenant
remains Hugh Mason; the band of Cambridg led by Capt.
George Cook, now Colonel Cook in the wars of Ireland, but
now led by Capt. Daniel Gookin, a very forward man to advance Marshal discipline, and withal the truths of Christ;
the Band of Concord led by Capt. Simon Willard, being a
Kentish souldier, as is Capt. Goggin; the Band of Sudbury
lately led by Capt. Pelham, who is in England at present, his
Lieutenant remains, Edm. Goodinow; the band of Wooburn
led by another Kentish Captain;[2] the Band of Reading led
by Lieutenant Walker; the Band of Malden, being as yet a
young Town, who have not chosen their Officers, are led by
Mr. Joseph Hill. These belong to the Regiment of Middlesex;
the two Counties of Essex and Northfolk are for present joyned
in one Regiment, their first Major, who now commandeth this
Regiment, is the proper and valiant Major Daniel Denison, a
good souldier, and of a quick capacity, not inferiour to any
other of these chief Officers; his own company are well instructed in feats of warlike activity, his Capt. Lieutenant
departed this life some few years since, a godly and faithful
man, which is indeed the fountain of true validity, named
Mr. Whiting[h]am; the Band of Salem led by the bold and

---

[1] Middlesex.   [2] Johnson himself.

worthy Capt. William Hauthorn, a man of an undaunted courage, with his Lieutenant Lothrope; the Band of Lyn led by the honored and much respected Capt. Robert Bridges, who is also a Magistrate, being endued with able parts, and forward to improve them [1] for the glory of God and his peoples good; the Band of Nuberry led by Capt. Gerish, with his antient and experienced Lieutenant Greenlife; the Band of Rowly led by Capt. Brigham; the Bands of Glocester, Wenham and Andover, have not yet made choice of Superiour Officers, being in their minority; these are the Bands of the Regiment of Essex, to the which are joyned the three Bands of the County of Northfolk, Salsbury, Hampton, and Haverhil. There are none chosen to office in any of these Bands, but such as are freemen supposed to be men indued with faith in Christ Jesus, wherefore let all that truly love the Lord Christ say with Deborah, My heart is toward the Governors of Israel, that offered themselves willingly among the people.[2] Their Officers are chosen by the major Vote of the souldiers, being installed into their place by the Major of their Regiment. There are of late a very gallant horse-troop listed, it being a frequent thing with the Officers of the foot companies, to turn Troopers (when their own Regiment is not in exercise) for incouragement of others. The Regiments are exercised once a year by turnes; they are also very observant to keep their armes in good order; each souldier is to keep constantly by him powder, bullet, and match, besides every Town is injoyned to have a common stock in like manner, as also the country have their ammunition exactly looked unto, by Surveyor General Johnson,[3] one very well qualified for the work, ready at all times to put the General Court in mind of keeping their store renued by fresh supply, and to say right, some particular persons may be penurious in laying out their estates upon ammunition, but the general of Officers and souldiers are very generous that way; the reverend Doctor Wilson gave bountifully for the furthering this Wilderness-work, the which was

---

[1] *I. e.*, to make use of them.   [2] Judges v. 9.

[3] John Johnson of Roxbury, at whose death in 1659 our Captain Edward Johnson was appointed his successor; they are not known to have been related. The duty of the office was to care for the arms, ordnance, ammunition, and military stores of the colony.

expended upon great Artillery, his gift being a thousand pound. Beside, many persons that came over, the Lord was pleased to indow with a large portion of the things of this life, who were not backward liberally to dispose of it, to procure means of defence, and to that end there was a castle built on an Island, upon the passage into the Mattachu[setts] Bay, wholly built at first by the country in general, but by reason the country affords no Lime, but what is burnt of Oyster-shels, it fell to decay in a few years after, which made many of the Towns that lay out of the defence thereof to desert it, although their safety (under God) was much involved in the constant repair and well-mannaging thereof; hereupon the next six Towns take upon them to rebuild it at their proper cost and charges, the rest of the country upon the finishing thereof gave them a small matter toward it;[1] upon this there was a Captain ordained, and put in possession thereof by the country, having a yearly Stipend allowed him for himself and his souldiers, which he is to keep in a constant readiness upon the Island, being about eight acres of ground; the Castle is built on the North-East of the Island, upon a rising hill, very advantageous to make many shot at such ships as shall offer to enter the Harbor without their good leave and liking. The Commander of it is one Captain Davenport, a man approved for his faithfulness, courage and skill, the Master Canoneer is an active Ingineer also; this Castle hath cost about four thousand pounds, yet are not this poor pilgrim people weary of maintaining it in good repair; it is of very good use to awe any insolent persons, that putting confidence in their ship and sails, shall offer any injury to the people, or contemn the Government. They have certain signals of alarums, which suddainly spread through the whole country; were there but one Town more erected in this Government, which were one and thirty, it would joyn all the Towns in the same neighbourly together, excepting Springfield. Thus are these people with great diligence provided for these daies of war, hoping the day is at hand wherein the Lord will give Antichrist the double of all her doings, and therefore they have nursed up in their Artillery garden some

---

[1] The first fortifying of Castle Island was begun in 1634, the ordnance removed in 1638, the second fortifying, by the six towns, begun in 1643.

who have since been used, as instruments to begin the work; but that which gives the greatest hope concerning this particular, is this, that these times afford more souldiers depending on the Lord Christ through faith for deliverance and true valour, then any age since Antichrist began to fall, without which, all these preparations were but as so many traps and snares to catch a people in, and to the which these Commanders and souldiers are daily exhorted, and therefore let all people know that desire the downfal of New-England, they are not to war against a people only exercised in feats of war, but men who are experienced in the deliverances of the Lord from the mouth of the Lion, and the paw of the Bear, and now woe be to you, when the same God that directed the stone to the forehead of the Philistine, guides every bullet that is shot at you, it matters not for the whole rabble of Antichrist on your side, the God of Armies is for us a refuge high. *Shela.*

WONDER–WORKING PROVIDENCE OF SIONS SAVIOUR IN NEW-ENGLAND.

Book III.

CONTAINING THE PASSAGES OF GODS PROVIDENCE TOWARD THIS WANDERING RACE OF JAACOBITES IN THESE LATTER SEVEN YEARS, FROM THE YEAR 1645. TILL TOWARD THE LATTER END OF 51.

CHAP. I.

Of planting the twenty sixth Church of Christ at the Town of Haverhil, and of preparation for a second war with the Indians.

THIS year that antient, honored and trusty souldier of the truth, Thom. Dudly Esquire was chosen Governor, and the honored John Winthrop Esquire was chosen Deputy Governor, John Endicut Esquire to the office of Major-General. You have heard in the former book of the fortifying of the Castle, and placing a Captain therein, which was not finished till this year; the number of freemen added was 56.[1] The Town of Haverhil was built much about this time, lying higher up then Salisbury, upon the fair and large river of Merrimeck: the people are wholly bent to improve their labour in tilling the earth, and keeping of cattel, whose yearly encrease incourages them to spend their days in those remote parts. The constant penetrating farther into this Wilderness, hath caused the wild and uncouth woods to be fil'd with frequented wayes, and the large rivers to be over-laid with Bridges passeable, both for horse and foot; this Town is of a large extent, supposed to be ten miles in length, there being an over-weaning desire in most men after Medow land, which

[1] Properly 79.

234

hath caused many towns to grasp more into their hands then
they could afterward possibly hold; the people are laborious
in the gaining the goods of this life, yet are they not unmindful also of the chief end of their coming hither, namely, to be
made partakers of the blessed Ordinances of Christ, that their
souls might be refreshed with the continual income of his rich
grace, to which end they gathered into a Church-body, and
called to office the reverend M. Ward,[1] son to the former named
M. Ward of Ipswitch.

> With mind resolv'd run out thy race at length,
>   Young Ward, begin whereas thy father left,
> Left hath he not, but breaths for further strength,
>   Nor thou, nor he, are yet of hope bereft:
> Fruit of thy labours thou shalt see so much,
>   The righteous shall hear of it and rejoyce;
> When Babel falls by Christ's almighty touch,
>   All's folk shall praise him with a cheerful voice.
> They prosper shall that Sions building mind,
>   Then Ward cease not with toyl her stones to lay,
> For great is he thee to this work assign'd,
>   Whose pleasure is, heavens Crown shall be thy pay.

This year, although divers Indian Sachems not long before
had desired to subject themselves and lands unto this Government, yet the sons of old Canonicus,[2] having not inherited their
fathers prudence with his subjects and land, fell to hot contention with their own neighbours and native inhabitants,
although they were forbidden by the united Colonies, and
prosecuted [3] so, that they would not stick to wage war with
the English also, which the Commissioners perceiving, they
raised an Army of horse and foot out of the Colonies, and
appointed as Commander in chief over them Major-General
Edward Gibbons; the reverend Mr. Tompson, one of the

[1] Rev. John Ward, son of Nathaniel Ward, the "Simple Cobler of Aggawam," was born at Haverhill in England, in which town his grandfather John
Ward was rector, and after which our Haverhill was named, in compliment to
the pastor.   He was of Emmanuel College, Cambridge.

[2] Canonicus did not die till 1647.   The leaders in these machinations of
1645, here spoken of as his sons and heirs, were doubtless his son Mixan or
Mexanino, and his nephew Pessacus, brother of Miantonomoh.

[3] Proceeded.

Elders of the Church at Braintree, was to accompany them, and to preach the Word of God unto them, during the time of the war; but the Indians hearing of this preparation against them, sent a certain number of their chief Nobility to treat with the Commissioners of the united Colonies about a peace, who then sitting at Boston gave them audience. The Indians coming into their presence, could speak no more English, but peace, peace; the English were very desirous of an opportunity to shew them mercy, and yet would they should not despise them, in gaining it upon such easie terms, as might cause them to move war again, and therefore allotted them to pay some part of the charge of the war intended, and therefore appointed them to give four of their sons for hostages till they had wholly paid it; the Indians gladly accepted of the terms, and accordingly brought their children. Here the Reader should be minded of the admirable acts of the Lord Christ in awing these multitudes of Heathens, for they were the most populous of any that are in these parts; but it is reserved for another place in this history, the Indians being slow in their performance, had their hostages returned home before the Wapom [1] was paid, yet their two Princes Pesicus and Mexanimo, did upon the sending certain armed men to demand the remainder, send the sum demanded.

CHAP. II.

Of the planting of the twenty seventh Church of Christ at the Town called Springfield, and of the earnest seeking the Lord by all the Churches of N. E. for his gracious assistance in the work of Reformation.

About this time one Mr. Pinchin, sometime a Magistrate,[2] having out of desire to better his estate, by trading with the Indians, setled himself very remote from all the Churches of Christ in the Mattachusets Government, upon the river of

---

[1] Wampum.

[2] William Pynchon, founder of Roxbury and Springfield, came from Springfield in Essex, England. He was one of those named as the first assistants in the patent of Massachusetts.

Canectico, yet under their Government,[1] he having some
godly persons resorting unto him, they there erected a Town
and Church of Christ, calling it Springfield; it lying upon this
large navigable river, hath the benefit of transporting their
goods by water, and also fitly seated for a Bever trade with the
Indians, till the Merchants encreased so many, that it became
little worth, by reason of their out-buying one another, which
hath caused them to live upon husbandry; this Town is mostly
built along the river side, and upon some little rivelets of the
same. There hath of late been more then one or two in this
Town greatly suspected of witchcraft, yet have they used
much diligence, both for the finding them out, and for the Lords
assisting them against their witchery, yet have they, as is
supposed, bewitched not a few persons, among whom two of
the reverend Elders children.[2] These people inhabiting this
Town having gathered into a Church-body, called to the
office of a Pastor the reverend M. Moxon, who remaineth with
them at this very day, of whom as followeth.

> As thou with strong and able parts art made,
>   Thy person stout with toyl and labour shall
> With help of Christ through difficulties wade;
>   Then spend for him, spare not thy self at all.
> When errors crowd close to thy self and friends,[3]
>   Take up truths sword, trifle not time, for why,
> Christ call'd his people hither for these ends,
>   To tell the world that Babels fall is nigh;
> And that his Churches through the world shall spread,
>   Maugre the might of wicked men and devils,
> Then Moxon thou need'st not at all to dread,
>   But be aveng'd on Satan for his evils,
> Thy Lord Christ will under thy feet him tread.

This year the great troubles in our native country en-
creaseing, and that hearing [hearing that] prophane Esau had

---

[1] At first, 1636–1641, this remote frontier settlement had been regarded as
under the jurisdiction of Connecticut rather than of Massachusetts.

[2] Perhaps the earliest serious manifestation of the witchcraft delusion in
New England.

[3] This is probably a gentle reference to Pynchon's heretical book, *The Meritorious Price of Our Redemption* (London, 1650). It was condemned by the magistrates to be burned by the hangman, and Pynchon and Moxon soon after went
back to England.

mustered up all the Bands he could make to come against his brother Jacob, these wandering race of Jacobites deemed it now high time to implore the Lord for his especial aid in this time of their deepest distress, and the rather being incouraged hereunto from former deliverances and wonderful mercies received, the which they now presented before the Lord with the several branches and inlarged bounties thereof to refresh their frozen affections, and move a melting heart in their barren brests, that began to dry up with a lazy lethargy, and therefore thrusting themselves on to the work by the loving invitation of that godly Government the Lord in his mercy had peaceably placed among them, each Church in their own proper place meeting together in daies of solemn seeking of the Lords pleasing countenance in Christ [1] (the Lord in his mercy helping them) after a serious acknowledgment of their own unworthiness, by reason of their sinful provocations of the Lord to anger against them aggravated, in that they were committed immediately upon the receipt of a multitude of marvellous mercies, they acknowledg unto the Lord in the audience of the great Congregation the manner of his wonderful providence extended toward them, that as Jacob professes, I came over this Jordan with my staff, and now have I gotten two Bands; [2] so they came over this boysterous billow-boyling Ocean, a few poor scattered stones newly raked out of the heaps of rubbish, and thou Lord Christ hast now so far exalted them, as to lay them sure in thy Sion, a building, to be the wonder of the world; orderly are they placed in five and forty [3] several Churches, and that in a Wilderness, where civility scarce ever took place, much less any Religion, and now to the Lord earnestly they cry to be delivered from the cruel hands of those that would destroy both young and old, the bird and her young together, and as Jacobs fear was, the seed of Christs Church in the posterity of Israel should be cut off, and therefore pleaded the promise of the Lord in the multiplying of his seed; so these people at this very time, pleaded not only the Lords promise to Israel, but to his only Son Christ

---

[1] August 28, 1645, was appointed as a day of fasting and humiliation for troubles in Old England and New; other such, with similar reference to the mother country, had also been appointed in 1643 and 1644.

[2] Genesis xxxii. 10.   [3] But see p. 49, note 1.

Jesus; Lord, hast thou not said, *Ask of me, and I will give thee the Heathen for thine inheritance, and the uttermost ends of the earth for thy possession*; and now Lord, are not these the Churches of Christ which thou hast planted for his possession; and that as Rachel and Leah built the house of Israel, so now shall these and the like Sister-churches spread the whole earth, the Lord Christ raigning as King and Lord for ever over them; Then why do the Heathen rage, and the people imagin a vain thing, seeing the time of the Lords arising to have mercy upon Sion is come, yea his appointed time is at hand; and he who walks in the midst of his golden Candlesticks, whose eyes are as a flaming fire, will not suffer his Churches to be trodden under feet of that Antichristian Lordly prelacy any longer, nor yet defiled with any transformed Saint-seeming Angels of light with their painted doctrines. Thus did this poor people plead with the Lord, not only for themselves, but for their dearly beloved brethren in England, I [ay] and all that are Christs chosen people the world throughout; and although they were not unmindful from day to day of them, yet this year 1645. the Lord was pleased to stir up their affections in more then an ordinary manner. What success their prayers have had, let all (that love and long to behold the beauty of Christ shining on and in his beloved Bride) declare the loving kindness of the Lord toward his Churches, and let all the Churches of Christ, though never so remote the one from the other, yet joyned together in one faith and one Christ, be frequent in prayer one for another, congregate together at the Throne of the Lord, be present in spirit though absent in body; these New-England Churches are neer one hundred miles distant one from another, and yet communicate, counsel, care, love, joy, grieve with, and for one another, dismiss some, and commend others (as occasion serves) to the Christian care and watchfulness, from one Church to another, and why may not this be practiced the world throughout, even from Jerusalem, and round about to Illyricum?

Chap. III.

Of the opposition the Government of the Mattachusets Colony met withal, by certain persons, under the name of Petitioners.

In place of Governor was chosen for this year John Winthrop Esquire, and for Deputy Governor Thomas Dudly Esquire, the number of freemen were about 72.[1] At the Court of Election there was a Petition drawn, and presented to the Court by a Doctor of Physick, with seven hands to it, the persons were of a Linsiwolsie [2] disposition, some for Prelacy, some for Presbytery, and some for Plebsbytery, but all joyned together in the thing they would, which was to stir up the people to dislike of the present Government, one while envying [3] against the constitution of the Government as not popular enough, another while against the Laws or orders of this little Commonwealth as two [too] strict, and then to provoke, at least the penurious, they tell them of great expence of the publike Treasury, and intolerable taxations; the matter they petitioned for, was a bottom to build their quarrel upon, under the name of a Presbyterian Government, and this they supposed would suit well with their Bill of complaint, which they intended for England, not that they cared for a Presbyterian Church, for had they so done, they might have found out one in the country before they petitioned, but because they supposed that the Parliament in England would establish that way only, and therefore bore themselves bold upon it, that although their seditious and scandalous words and practices should incur a penalty (as none could deem any other, unless

[1] In fact, 31.

[2] Linsey-woolsey. Dr. Robert Child, William Vassall, Samuel Maverick, and others petitioned the General Court that all members of the Church of England and of the Church of Scotland might be admitted to the communion of the New England churches, and that those debarred from the suffrage and from civil office because of not belonging to those churches (doubtless the greater number of the male inhabitants were so debarred) might be enfranchised; and they threatened an appeal to Parliament, then mostly Presbyterian in sentiment, if their demands were not granted. The incident raised grave questions as to the status of the colonial government, the charter, and the rights of Parliament.

[3] Inveighing.

it be such as are all for liberty, and nothing for Government) yet they might bear men in hand, it was for petitioning for a Presbyterian Church-Government, according to this tenor; the Court being somewhat slow in censuring them, they prepared a plot, wrapping in some few persons more with them, laying very gross matters to the charge of this Government in their Bill of complaint, but being suspected by the honoured Magistrates of this Government, their plot was found out, and writing publikely read unto them, for all which they had a small penalty laid upon them,[1] hardly countervail the charge they put the country unto; but assuredly it was the Lords gracious goodness to quell their malice against his people, and indeed the proud Bishops sped no better, or not so well, especially some of them, nor have any other hitherto prospered, who have maligned these poor Churches of Christ, yet because the Gortonist painted over a far worser cause, that those honorable personages in England who had the hearing thereof could not discern, the Government thought meet to send over this year the honored M. Winslow to manifest and declare the naked truth of things, having full power and commission from this Government to deal for them in all matters wherein they may be concerned; and verily the chief Gortonian might have returned from England hither, to have triumphed in his blasphemies over the Churches of Christ and all the united colonies, had not the divel shewed his horns in that book he printed, wherein he takes upon him a monstrous interpretation of the words of our Lord Christ in John, *Except ye eat my flesh, and drink my bloud, etc.* had the book been well perused before their coming over, surely they had never return'd with so large a commission as they boast of, for the Parliament have punished divers persons for their blasphemies, and very like these should not have scaped scotfree.[2]

---

[1] This is not ingenuous. First and last, the seven petitioners were fined nearly a thousand pounds sterling.

[2] While Parliament's Commissioners for Plantations declined to disapprove the conduct of Massachusetts in the matter of the seven petitioners for enfranchisement, in the matter of Gorton they enjoined that government not to molest him and his companions further, so long as they behaved themselves peaceably.

CHAP. IV.

Of the second Synod holden at Cambridg in N. E. and the images of the Son [Sun] that appeared.

This year the General Court of the Mattachusets Government taking into consideration the many errors in point of doctrine that were daily broached by some of our English Nation, although the churches of Christ, and the people under this Government were free,[1] at least in open profession; yet to declare to all the world, and render an accompt of their faith and profession wherein they walk, it was thought meet, that the churches of Christ should meet together in a Synod, by their Elders and Messengers, to hold forth the doctrine and discipline of Jesus Christ, according to the rule of the New Testament, with the grounds of Scripture from which they hold the same; and further to make trial of them by the said rules and none other: accordingly at the time appointed they assembled together. Their disputation was plain and easie to be understood of the meanest capacity, clearing up those points that were most dubious.[2] They having agreed on all matters, with a full concurrence of the assembly, did appoint them to be put in print, that they might be the better scanned and tried of every particular person in the several congregations or churches, many churches approving thereof for the generality, others there be that have not yet fully viewed the same; the books are extant,[3] and shew that the churches of Christ in N. E. are not ashamed to make confession of their faith to all the world, and are yet ready to receive any further light shall be made known unto them from the Word of God, and none other, nor do they receive this because a Synod hath said it, but because the Lord hath spoken it by his Spirit, and

[1] *I. e.*, free from such doctrinal errors.

[2] The point in which New England Congregationalism differed most from English Independency was in the use of occasional synods and councils of churches as a means of securing coherence among the churches.

[3] This is the document entitled *A Platform of Church Discipline gathered out of the Word of God and agreed upon by the Elders and Messengers of the Churches assembled in the Synod at Cambridge in New England* (Cambridge, 1649), commonly called the "Cambridge Platform."

witnessed by the same Spirit to their souls that he hath so done; some sorts of persons have been much opposite to this Synod, first those that are so inured with the broad beaten path of liberty, that they fear to be confined in the straight and narrow path of truth; the second are such as have their wills wedded to some singular rare conceited opinion, for which they have been admired of many, and now they fear their gain will be gone, if this spirit be cast out; the third and last sort are more honest then the two former, and only scared with their big words, who tell them of the Popish and Prelatical Synods, what a deal of trash and cannon Laws they have brought in, and that if they will fall to receiving books once, they shall have more and more thrust upon them: As also if any shall say its only to declare the doctrine and discipline the churches of N. E. hold, its enough, quoth they, that our faith concerning these things is contained in the Bible, and this is all the accompt we need to give to any; but for all these scare-crows, N. E. hath through the blessing of the Lord received much peace and truth from the former Synod, we wish our countrymen and our selves may receive the like, and much more from this, which ended not with this year.[1]

This year, about the latter end thereof, appeared two Parelii, or images of the Sun, and some other strange apparitions of light about her, like a Rainbow, with the heels upward, which unwonted sights have been interpreted by the provident passages since shewed, among those who have had an outside of profession and name, to be singular for understanding the mind of God, who would overthrow all the Ordinances of Christ, under the name of New-light, and that there can be no restoration of Religion, till new Apostles come: This desperate opinion doth so fitly resemble these wonderful apparitions, that seemed to be another Sun, yet indeed had no light in them, but vanished away no man knew how; so these opinionists would make men believe they had found out another Sea from their phantastical revelations.

[1] The synod sat in 1646, 1647, and 1648.

Chap. V.

Of the great pains and care taken by those in Authority, for the compiling of Lawes for this little Commonwealth.

This year [1] the General Court appointed a Committee of divers persons to draw up a Body of Laws for the well-ordering of this little Commonwealth; and to the end that they might be most agreeable with the rule of Scripture, in every County there was appointed two Magistrates, two Ministers, and two able persons from among the people, who having provided such a competent number as was meet, together with the former that were enacted newly amended, they presented them to the General Court, where they were again perused and amended; and then another Committee chosen to bring them into form, and present them to the Court again, who the year following passed an Act of confirmation upon them, and so committed them to the Press, and in the year 1648. they were printed, and now are to be seen of all men, [2] to the end that none may plead ignorance, and that all who intend to transport themselves hither, may know this is no place of licentious liberty, nor will this people suffer any to trample down this Vineyard of the Lord, but with diligent execution will cut off from the city of the Lord the wicked doers, and if any man can shew wherein any of them derogate from the Word of God, very willingly will they accept thereof, and amend their imperfections (the Lord assisting); but let not any ill-affected persons find fault with them, because they suit not with their own humour, or because they meddle with matters of Religion, for it is no wrong to any man, that a people who have spent their estates, many of them, and ventured their lives for to keep faith and a pure conscience, to use all means

---

[1] The date in the margin is 1646. The first Massachusetts code, the "Body of Liberties," was passed in 1641. In response to a strong popular movement, a fuller code was prepared by four successive committees of the General Court in 1646 and 1647, of two of which Captain Johnson was a member.

[2] Of *The Book of the General Lawes and Libertyes concerning the Inhabitants of the Massachusets* (Cambridge, 1648) six hundred copies were printed. Yet it was supposed till 1906 that not a single copy was extant. In that year a copy was found in England. It is now in a private library in New York.

that the Word of God allows for maintenance and continuance
of the same, especially they have taken up a desolate Wilderness to be their habitation, and not deluded any by keeping
their profession in huggermug, but print and proclaim to all
the way and course they intend, God willing, to walk in.   If
any will yet notwithstanding seek to justle them out of their
own right, let them not wonder if they meet with all the opposition a people put to their greatest straits can make; as in all
their undertaking, their chiefest aim hath been to promote
the Ordinances of Christ, so also in contriving their Laws,
Liberties, and Priviledges, they have not been wanting,
which hath caused many to maligne their civil Government,
and more especially for punishing any by a Law, that walk
contrary to the rule of the Gospel, which they profess, but to
them it seems unreasonable, and savours too much of hypoc-
risie, that any people should pray unto the Lord for the
speedy accomplishment of his Word in the overthrow of
Antichrist, and in the mean time become a Patron to sinful
opinions and damnable errors that oppose the truths of
Christ, admit it be but in the bare permission of them.

Chap. VI.

Of the Lords wonder-working Providence, in fitting this people
with all kind of Manufactures, and the bringing of them
into the order of a commonwealth.

On the day of Election for Governor and Magistrates,
(which are new chosen every year) the honored John Winthrope Esquire was chosen Governor, and the like honored
Thomas Dudly Esquire Deputy Governor, John Endicut
Esquire was chosen Major-General, which is an Officer the
Freemen make a yearly choice of, all other Military Officers
stand for term of life, unless any be out for misdemeanour;
the number of freemen added this year were about 85.[1]   The
Land affording very good iron stone, divers persons of good
rank and quality in England were stirred up by the provident

---

[1] In fact, 61.

hand of the Lord to venture their estates upon an iron work,[1]
which they began at Braintree, and profited the owners little,
but rather wasted their stock, which caused some of them to
sell away the remainder, the chief reason being the high price
of labour, which ordinarily was as much more as in England,
and in many things treble; the way of going on with such a
work here, was not suddainly to be discerned, although the
Steward had a very able eye, yet experience hath out-stript
learning here, and the most quick-sighted in the Theory of
things, have been forced to pay pretty roundly to Lady Experience for filling their heads with a little of her active after-
wit; much hope there is now, that the owners may pick up
their crums again, if they be but made partakers of the gain,
in putting off England commodities at N. E. price, it will
take off one third of the great price they gave for labour, and
the price of their iron; it is supposed another third is taken
of the abundance of wood had for little, will surely take off
the residue, besides land at easie rates, and common land free
for their use; it were to be desired that those Gentlemen who
have undertaken the work, would consider the place where
their works are, namely in N. E. where the Lord Christ hath
chosen to plant his Churches in, to hide his people under the
covert of his wings, till the tyranny of Antichrist be over-
passed, and any that have disbursed pence for the furthering
of his work, shall be repayed with thousands: Besides, the
Gentlemen that govern this Colony are very desirous to be
helpful in what they may, and had rather take any burthens
upon themselves and the Inhabitants, that in justice they
ought, then that those Gentlemen should be any wayes dam-
nified. The Lord is pleased also to compleat this Common-
wealth abundantly beyond all expectation in all sorts of needful occupations, it being for a long time the great fear of many,
and those that were endued with grace from above also, that
this would be no place of continued habitation, for want of a
staple-commodity, but the Lord, whose promises are large to
his Sion, hath blest his peoples provision, and satisfied her poor
with bread, in a very little space, every thing in the country

[1] A company formed by John Winthrop the younger and supplied with
English capital obtained from the colony large privileges, and began work success-
fully at Lynn, and then at Braintree. But soon the business languished.

proved a staple-commodity, wheat, rye, oats, peas, barley, beef, pork, fish, butter, cheese, timber, mast, tar, sope, plank-board, frames of houses, clabboard, and pipestaves, iron and lead is like to be also; and those who were formerly forced to fetch most of the bread they eat, and beer they drink, a hundred leagues by Sea, are through the blessing of the Lord so encreased, that they have not only fed their Elder Sisters, Virginia, Barbados, and many of the Summer Islands that were prefer'd before her for fruitfulness, but also the Grandmother of us all, even the firtil Isle of Great Britain, beside Portugal hath had many a mouthful of bread and fish from us, in exchange of their Madeara liquor, and also Spain; nor could it be imagined, that this Wilderness should turn a mart for Merchants in so short a space, Holland, France, Spain, and Portugal coming hither for trade, shipping going on gallantly, till the Seas became so troublesome, and England restrain'd our trade, forbidding it with Barbados, etc.[1] and Portugal stopt and took our ships; many a fair ship had her framing and finishing here, besides lesser vessels, barques, and ketches, many a Master, beside common Seamen, had their first learning in this Colony. Boston, Charles-Town, Salem, and Ipswitch, our Maritan[2] Towns began to encrease roundly, especially Boston, the which of a poor country village, in twice[3] seven years is become like unto a small City, and is in election to be Mayor Town suddainly,[4] chiefly increased by trade by Sea, yet of late the Lord hath given a check to our traffique, but the reason may be rendred hereafter; nor hath this Colony alone been actors in this trade of venturing by Sea, but New-haven also, who were many of them well experienced in traffique, and had good estates to mannage it. Canectico did not linger behind, but put forth to Sea with the other; all other trades have here fallen into their ranks and places, to their great advantage; especially Coopers and Sho-

---

[1] An act of Parliament passed in October, 1650, prohibited trade with Barbados, Antigua, the Bermudas, and Virginia, because of their course in holding out for the royalist cause against the Parliament.

[2] Maritime.   [3] Read "thrice."

[4] This fixes the date of writing this part of the book. Boston petitioned the General Court in June, 1650, to be made a corporation; the petition was not granted, but avoided, at the session of May, 1651.

makers, who had either of them a Corporation granted,[1] in-
riching themselves by their trades very much, Coopers having
their plenty of stuff at a cheap rate, and by reason of trade
with forraign parts abundance of work; as for Tanners and
Shomakers, it being naturalized into these occupations, to
have a higher reach in mannaging their manifactures, then
other men in N. E. are, having not chang'd their nature in this,
between them both they have kept men to their stander
hitherto, almost doubling the price of their commodities,
according to the rate they were sold for in England, and yet
the plenty of Leather is beyond what they had their [there],
counting the number of the people, but the transportation of
Boots and Shoes into forraign parts hath vented all however:
as for Tailors, they have not come behind the former, their
advantage being in the nurture of new-fashions, all one with
England; Carpenters, Joyners, Glaziers, Painters, follow
their trades only; Gun-smiths, Lock-smiths, Black-smiths,
Naylers, Cutlers, have left the husbandmen to follow the
Plow and Cart, and they their trades; Weavers, Brewers,
Bakers, Costermongers, Feltmakers, Braziers, Pewterers, and
Tinkers, Ropemakers, Masons, Lime, Brick, and Tilemakers,
Cardmakers to work, and not to play,[2] Turners, Pumpmakers,
and Wheelers, Glovers, Fellmungers,[3] and Furriers, are or-
derly turn'd to their trades, besides divers sorts of Shop-
keepers, and some who have a mystery beyond others, as have
the Vintners.

Thus hath the Lord been pleased to turn one of the most
hideous, boundless, and unknown Wildernesses in the world
in an instant, as 'twere (in comparison of other work) to a
well-ordered Commonwealth, and all to serve his Churches,
of which the Author intends to speak of three more, which
came to be gathered in the compass of these years.

---

[1] The coopers and shoemakers of Boston were incorporated in October, 1648.
[2] Makers of wool-cards, not playing-cards.
[3] Dealers in peltries.

Chap. VII.

Of the three last Churches that were gathered in the compass of these years, namely Haverhil [Andover], Malden, and another Church gathered in the Town of Boston.

This year 1648. John Winthrope Esquire was chosen Governor, and Thomas Dudly Esquire Deputy Governor, and John Endicut Esquire Major General, all three as they were the former year, the number of freemen added were about 94.[1] About this time there was a Town founded about one or two mile distant from the place where the goodly river of Merrimeck receives her branches into her own body, hard upon the river of Shawshin, which is one of her three chief heads; the honored Mr. Simon Broadstreet taking up his last setling there, hath been a great means to further the work, it being a place well fitted for the husbandmans hand, were it not that the remoteness of the place from Towns of trade, bringeth some inconveniencies upon the planters, who are inforced to carry their corn far to market; this Town is called Andover, and hath good store of land improved for the bigness of it, they soon gathered into a Church, having the reverend Mr. Whodbridg[2] to instruct them in the wayes of Christ, till he returned to England, and since have called to office the reverend Mr. Deynes, for whose further incouragement the promises of the Lord for protecting, providing, increaseing, and continuing, even the very least of his Churches, going on according to his precepts, are abundantly manifested in his Word.

> Thou Sister young, Christ is to thee a wall
>   Of flaming fire, to hurt thee none may come,
> In slipp'ry paths and dark wayes shall they fall,
>   His Angels might shall chase their countless sum.
> Thy Shepheard with full cups and table spread,
>   Before thy foes in Wilderness thee feeds,
> Increasing thy young lambs in bosom bred,
>   Of Churches by his wonder-working deeds:

[1] In fact, 32.
[2] John Woodbridge, Dudley's son-in-law. His successor was Francis Dane.

To countless number must Christ's Churches reach,
    The day's at hand, both Jew and Gentile shall
Come crowding in his Churches, Christ to preach,
    And last for aye, none can cause them to fall.

About this time the Town of Malden had his first foundation stones laid by certain persons, who issued out of Charles-
Town, and indeed had her whole structure within the bounds
of this more elder Town, being severed by the broad spreading river of Mistick the one from the other, whose troublesome
passage caused the people on the North side of the river to
plead for Town-priviledges within themselves, which accordingly was granted them; the soyl is very firtile, but they are
much straitned in their bounds, yet their neerness to the chief
Market Towns, makes it the more comfortable for habitation.
The people gathered into a Church some distance of time
before they could attain to any Church-Officer to administer
the Seals unto them, yet in the mean time at their Sabbath
assemblies they had a godly Christian named M. Sarjant,
who did preach the Word unto them, and afterwards they
were supplied at times with some young Students from the
Colledg, till the year 1650. one Mr. Marmaduke Mathews,[1]
coming out of Plimouth Patten, was for some space of time
with a people at the Town of Hull, which is a small Port-town
peopled by fishermen, and lies at the entrance of the Bays
mouth, where this Mr. Mathews continued preaching, till he
lost the approbation of some able understanding men, among
both Magistrates and Ministers, by weak and unsafe expressions in his teaching, yet notwithstanding he was called to the
office of a Pastor by the brethren of this Church of Christ at
Malden, although some neighbour-churches were unsatisfied
therewith, for it is the manner of all the Churches of Christ
here hitherto, to have the approbation of their Sister-churches,
and the civil Government also, in the proceedings of this
nature, by the which means Communion of Churches is con-

---

[1] Marmaduke Mathews was a Welshman, and a graduate of All Souls
College, Oxford. He preached at Yarmouth, Hull, and Malden. His call to
Malden without the approval of the neighboring churches was investigated by
the General Court, through a committee of which Captain Johnson was a member; the Court fined the church £50 and Mathews £10.

tinued, peace preserved, and the truths of Christ sincerely acknowledged, yet the Author will not miss to mind him in the following Meeter.

> Mathews! thou must build gold and silver on
>> That precious stone, Christ cannot trash indure,
> Unstable straw and stubble must be gone,
>> When Christ by fire doth purge his building pure.
> In seemly and in modest terms do thou
>> Christs precious truths unto thy folk unfold,
> And mix not error with the truth, lest thou
>> Soon leave out sense to make the truth to hold:
> Compleating of Christs Churches is at hand,
>> Mathews stand up, and blow a certain sound,
> Warriours are wanting Babel to withstand,
>> Christs truths maintain, 'twill bring thee honors crown'd.

The last Church that compleated the number of 30. was gathered at Boston, by reason of the popularity thereof, being too many to meet in one assembly; the North-east part of the Town being separated from the other with a narrow stream cut through a neck of land by industry, whereby that part is become an Island, it was thought meet, that the people inhabiting the same should gather into a Church-body,[1] and build a Meeting-house for their assembly, the which they have already done, but not as yet called any one to office; for since the people of Christ in some other places, both in England and elswhere, have through the goodness of God obtained like liberty with our selves, the Ministers of Christ have had their labours taken up in other places as well as here, which hath caused this Church as yet to be destitute. The beginning of this year was sad to the people of N. E. by reason of the death of their honoured Governour, John Winthrope Esquire,[2] whose indefatigable paines in this Wilderness-work

---

[1] The Old North Church, afterward famous as the church of Increase, Cotton, and Samuel Mather, was organized in 1650.

[2] Governor Winthrop died March 26, 1649. To have had as its chief magistrate at the beginning that wise, unselfish, righteous, and noble statesman was to Massachusetts a good fortune comparable to that which the presence of Washington brought to the early history of the United States. His *Journal,* or *History of New England,* a record of incomparable value and merit, occupies two volumes in this series.

is not to be forgotten, nor indeed can it be; his Funeral was very sadly and solemnly performed, by a very great concourse of the greater part of this Colony, whose mournful looks and watry eyes did plainly demonstrate the tender affection and great esteem he was in with the people.

Chap. VIII.

Of the death of divers personages, who were in great esteem with the people of New-England, famous for their godliness, and eminent parts, both for Magistracy and Ministery, and of the correcting hand of the Lord upon his N. E. people.

This year, after the death of this godly Governour, was chosen to succeed in the place Jo. Endicut Esq. and Tho. Dudly Esq. to be Deputy Governor, to the place of Major-General Edw. Gibbons; and seeing that the Lord is pleased to call this people to mourning, the Author will proceed to relate what further occasion this people have had to lament their miscarriages, that have caused the rod to be stretched out toward them, for of a truth they are no Antinomians.[1] The next loss was the death of that famous Preacher of the Lord M. Hooker, Pastor of the Church of Christ at Hartford, and M. Philips, Pastor of the Church of Christ at Watertown, and the holy heavenly, sweet-affecting, and soul-ravishing Minister M. Tho. Shepheard, Pastor of the Church of Christ at Cambridg, whose departure was very heavily taken by all the people of Christ round about him.[2] And now N. E. that had such heaps upon heaps of the riches of Christs tender compassionate mercies, being turn'd off from his dandling knees, began to read their approaching rod in the bend of his brows and frowns of his former favourable countenance toward them; their plenty of all things, which shold have cheared their hearts, and quickned their spirits in elevating both soul and body to a thankful frame, through the work of his blessed Spirit; on the contrary, it brought a fulness on many, even to loath the very honey-comb, insomuch that good whole-

---

[1] *I. e.*, do not profess to be exempt from the operation of the Law.
[2] Hooker died in 1647, Phillips in 1644, Shepard in 1649.

some truths would not down, yet had the Lord those that were precious unto him, who were not wanting to help one another out of this distemper, and with more warmer affections exhort one another, Come let us go up unto the house of the Lord, and he will teach us his wayes. Also the Lord was pleased to awaken us with an Army of caterpillers, that had he not suddainly rebuked them, they had surely destroyed the husbandmans hope; where they fell upon trees, they left them like winter-wasting cold, bare and naked; and although they fell on fields very rarely, yet in some places they made as clear a riddance, as the harvest mans hand, and uncovered the gay green Medow ground, but indeed the Lord did by some plats shew us what he could have done with the whole, and in many places cast them into the high-wayes, that the Cart-wheels in their passage were painted green with running over the great swarms of them; in some fields they devoured the leaves of their pease, and left the straw with the full crop, so tender was the Lord in his correction; this minded all these Jacobites of the end of their coming over, but chiefly the husbandman, whose over eager pursuit of the fruits of the earth made some of them many times run out so far in this Wilderness, even out of the sweet sound of the silver Trumpets blown by the laborious Ministers of Christ, forsaking the assembly of the Lords people, to celebrate their Sabbaths in the chimney-corner, horse, kine, sheep, goats, and swine being their most indeared companions, to travel with them to the end of their pilgrimage, or otherwise to gather together some of their neerest neighbours, and make a preachment one unto another, till they had learn'd so much, that they could away with none other teaching. As also the Lord was pleased to command the wind and Seas to give us a jog on the elbow, by sinking the very chief of our shipping in the deep, and splitting them in shivers against the shores; a very goodly Ship called the *Seaforce*[1] was cast away, and many N. E. people put to hard shifts for their lives, and some drowned, as the godly and dearly beloved servant of Christ, Mr. Tho. Coitmire, a very able Seaman, and also a good Scholar, one who had spent both his labour and estate for the helping on of this Wilder-

---

[1] Of the wreck of the *Seafort* on the coast of Spain, in 1645, there is a vivid account in Winthrop, II. 248, 249.

ness-work: as also another ship set forth by the Merchants of New-haven, of which the godly Mr. Lamberton went Master, neither ship, persons, nor goods ever heard of;[1] another ship also built and set forth by the inhabitants of Cambridg, split and cast away neer the same place where the *Seaforce* was lost; as also another Barque mostly set forth by Dorchester men, sunk in the Sea, and never heard of the manner how, with divers others which might be here inserted; this seemed the sorer affliction to these N. E. people, because many godly men lost their lives, and abundantly the more remarkable, because the Lord was pleased to forbid any such things to befal his people in their passage hither; herein these people read, as in great capital letters, their suddain forget-fulness of the Lords former received mercy in his wonderful preservation, bringing over so many scores of ships, and thousands of persons, without miscarriage of any, to the wonderment of the whole world that shall hear of it, but more especially were the Merchants and traders themselves sensible of the hand of the Lord out against them, who were in some of the ships, and had their lives given them for a prey; as also Vintners, and other men of trade, whose gain is increased by Merchants men, being so taken up with the income of a large profit, that they would willingly have had the Common-wealth tolerate divers kinds of sinful opinions to intice men to come and sit down with us, that their purses might be filled with coyn, the civil Government with contention, and the Churches of our Lord Christ with errors; the Lord was pleased after all this, to let in the King of Terror among his new-planted Churches.

For this year 1650. Tho. Dudly Esquire was chosen Gov-ernor, and John Endicut Esquire Deputy Governor, Major-General Edward Gibbons, continued in his office still; the number of freemen added were about 55.[2] This year was the first noted year wherein any store of people died, the ayr and place being very healthy naturally, made this correction of the Lord seem the greater, for the most that died were chil-dren, and that of an unwonted disease here, though frequent

---

[1] See p. 178.   [2] In fact, 31.

in other places, the Lord now smiting many families with death in them, although there were not any families wherein more then one died, or very rare if it were otherwise, yet were these pilgrim people minded of the suddain forgetfulness of those worthies that died not long before, but more especially the little regard had to provide means to train their children up in the knowledg of learning, and improve such means as the Lord hath appointed to leave their posterity an able Minister; as also to stir them up to prepare for the great work of the Lord Jesus in the overthrow of Antichrist, and calling of the Jews, which in all likelyhood is very suddainly to be performed; as also in stirring up all the young ones that remain, to consider for what end the Lord hath spared their lives, when he cut off others by death, namely, to prosecute the work that he hath given them to do in the power of his might, with the greater zeal and courage.

[1651.] This year the honored and much desired servant of Christ, John Endicut Esquire was chosen to be Governour of the English, inhabiting the Colony of the Mattachusets, and the antient honored and long continued Champion for the truth, as it is in Jesus, Tho. Dudly Esquire was chosen Deputy Governour, by the major Vote of these wandering Jacobites, with heart and good will the honored Major-General Edward Gibbons continued in place this year. The Government shewed their desire to be assisting to the State of England, in making orders for establishing their Edict for these Western parts of the world among our N. E. people; the Lord in his infinite wisdom saw meet to continue his correcting hand among his N. E. Churches, somewhat more then ordinary in a sore disease, of which many [died] (in comparison of what used to do) and yet not so many as ordinarily use to do in other plantations of this Western world; and whereas the former year young children died most, this year those of grown years died also, and although so small a sickness might not be taken notice of in other places, yet the rareness of it in so healthy a country as is this, cannot but speak loud in the ears of God's people, who desire to hear the rod, and who hath appointed it, and perceive plainly many of them, that the Lord will have us to know, that if his own people tread in the same steps of riot and excess in the plenty he hath given them, with the men of this world, he will lay the same sicknesses and diseases upon them; and further they perceive, according to the ordinary dispensation of his providences toward them, he hath some further great work to do with his N. E. people, that he is beginning again to awaken, rouze up, and quicken them with the rod of his power: For thus they begin to reason with themselves, when the Lord was pleased to expose them, their wifes, and little ones to the troubles of a tempestuous Sea in so long a voyage, and the wants of a barren Wilderness in great penury of food, he brought forth by his mighty power, and stretched-out arm, the glorious fabrick of his New-E. Churches; and therefore now again they look for some farther extraordinary great work of his, if he shall once again be pleased to refine them in this furnace of his, and would the Lord Christ would confirm our brethren in England in like faith by our example, yea, and far beyond many degrees, as the Wonder-working providence of Sions Saviour toward them hath more abundantly exceeded, and that as this in three seven years is comprised, though very weakly, in this little book, there's in one seven year would require volumes, and as this is wonderful, there is almost miraculous, and wonderful to the whole world, as if the Lord Christ did intend to make his power known more abundantly then ever the sons of men saw Kings and Kingdoms strengthened, with affinity and consanguinity, the valiant of the world, men skil'd in feats of war, as Goliah from a child, fierce and pampered horses, whose necks are covered with strong neighing, and cunning Engenires, men skilful to destroy with all the terrible engins of war, together with swarms of souldiers flocking together to swallow up the poor remnant of Gods people; all these hath the Lord caused to fall before your eyes, and our ears have heard the noyse of this great fall; and beloved countrymen, and our dear brethren in Christ, step into the closet of your own hearts with us, and see if there will not be some things in this following verse that may suit your condition as well as ours, that having sown in tears, we may reap with joy the glorious harvest of our Lord Christ, which is hard at hand, for assuredly the Lord is tyed neither to us, nor you, but may, if it please him, cast off both, and raise up new instruments for his following work, but if he be pleased to give us melting hearts for our former miscarriages, and renew us with a more zealous courage and earnest contending for the faith, it is very like he hath more glorious works by far for us yet to do.

CHAP. IX.

Of the wonder-working providences of Christ, wrought for his people among our English Nation, both in our Native country, and also in N. E. which should stir us up to mourn for all our miscarriages much the more.

From silent night, true Register of moans,
　　From saddest soul consum'd in deepest sin,
[*A*] From heart quite rent with sighs and heavy groans,
　　My wailing muse her woful work begins,
And to the world brings tunes of sad lament,
Sounding nought els but sorrows sad relent.

Sorry to see my sorrows cause augmented,
　　And yet less sorrowful were my sorrows more,
[*A*] Grief that with grief, is not with grief prevented,
　　Yet grief it is must ease my grieved sore;
So grief and sorrow, care but how to grieve,
For grief and sorrow must my cares relieve.

The wound fresh bleeding must be stanch'd with tears,
　　Tears cannot come unless some grief proceed,
[*A*] Grief comes but slack, which doth increase my fears,
　　Fear, lest for want of help I still shall bleed;
Do what I can to lengthen my lifes breath,
If Christ be wanting, I shall bleed to death.

Thou deepest searcher of each secret thought,
　　Infuse in me thy all-affecting grace,
[*A*] So shall my work to good effect be brought,
　　While I peruse my ugly sins a space,
Whose staining filth so spotted hath my soul,
That nought can wash, but tears of inward dole.

A The consideration of the wonderful providence of Christ in planting his N. E. Churches, and with the right hand of his power preserving, protecting,

favouring, and feeding them upon his tender knees: Together with the ill re-
quital of his all-infinite and undeserved mercies bestowed upon us, hath caused
many a soul to lament for the dishonor done to his Name, and fear of his casting
of this little handful of his, and the insulting of the enemy, whose sorrow is set
forth in these four first staffs of verses.[1]

How soon, my soul, hast thou the Lord forgot,
    [B] Who thee and thine through troublous Seas hath lead,
On earth thy parts should praise him, suddain rot,[2]
    Why dost neglect his glorious Kingdom spread.
Thy eyes have seen the Mountains mov'd with's hand,
And sunk in Seas to make his Sion stand.

No wonder then thy works with Eastern wind
    [B] On Seas are broke, and thy best Seamen slain,
Sith thou thy gain, and not Christs work dost mind,
    Lord stay thy hand, I see my works are vain.
Our ships they shall thy Gospel forth convey,
And not bring home strange errors here to stay.

Instead of home-oppression, they shall now
    Thy Saints abroad relieve, by Sea them send;
No riot shall our Merchantmen allow,
    Time in exchange-walks, not in Taverns spend;
Godly grief and good purpose comes from thee,
Lord Christ command, and then to work go we.

B   The Rod of God toward us in our Maritine affairs manifested, not only
to our own shipping, but strangers; as the *Mary Rose* blown up in Charles River,
and sunk in a moment, with about thirteen men slain therein: As also one Capt.
Chadwicks Pinnace, and about four men slain therein;[3] beside what hath been
formerly said touching our own shipping.

O thou my soul how weak's thy faith become,
    With scatter'd seed of man and beast, thou hast
Seen thy great God increase thy little sum,
    C Towns close compact in desart land hath plac't:
In Wilderness thy table richly spread,
Thy poor therein hath satisfi'd with bread.

    [1] These notes A, B, C, D, E, and the letters in square brackets referring
to them, occur thus in the original.
    [2] Thy parts which should praise him suddenly rot.
    [3] See Winthrop, II. 9, 153.

While firtil lands with hunger have been pined,
  C Thy harvest hath with heaps on heaps come in;
Oh mourn, that thou no more thy God should'st mind,
  His gentle rod to teach thee doth begin;
Then wonder not that swarms of Locust fly,
And that earths fruits for want of moysture die.

A countless crew of Caterpillers craul,
  To rob the earth of her green mantle quite;
Wolves, only wont on lesser beasts to fall,
  C On great ones prey by day, and eke by night:
Thy houses are consum'd with much good store,
By fearful fires, which blustering winds blow o're.

Lord stay thy hand, and stop my earthly mind,
  Thy Word, not world, shall be our sole delight,
C Not Medow ground, but Christs rich pearl wee'l find,
  Thy Saints imbrace, and not large lands down plight.
Murmure no more will we at yearly pay,
To help uphold our Government each way;

Not strive who least, but who the most shall give,
  Rejoyce will we, our hearts inlarged are,
C Those wait on th' Altar, shall on Altar live,
  Nor shall our riches their good doctrine mar;
Our pride of parts in thought of clear discerning,
No longer shall disgrace their godly learning.

Our meaner sort that metamorphos'd are,
  With womens hair, in gold and garments gay,
C Whose wages large our Commonwealths work mar,
  Their pride they shall with moderation lay:
Cast off their cloaths, that men may know their rank,
And women that with outward deckings prank.

  C Of the Lords hand against our Land affairs, as is heretofore expressed; and also in the suddain taking away many mens estates by fire, and chiefly by a most terrible fire which happened in Charles-Town, in the depth of Winter, 1650. by a violent wind blown from one house to another, to the consuming of the fairest houses in the Town. Under the pretence of being unequally rated, many men murmure exceedingly, and withdraw their shoulders from the support of Government, to the great discouragement of those that govern, 1651. Pride and excess in apparrel is frequent in these daies, when the Lord calls his people to humiliation and humble acknowledgment of his great deliverances; and that which is far worse, spiritual pride, to shew our selves to be somebody, often step out of our ranks, and delight in new fangled doctrines.

The worlds imbrace, our longing lust for gain,
    D No longer shall us into corners draw,
Nor our large herds us from Gods house detain
    From fellowship of Saints, who learn thy Law:
Thy righteous Judgments Lord do make me tremble,
Nor word, nor rod, but deep in this dissemble.

Two Masters, Lord, we will professed serve;
    How can we, Christ, united be to thee,
D When from thy Law learn'd we so greatly swarve,
    With watry tears unclued[1] we will be.
From creature-comforts, Christ thou art our stay,
Work will and deed in us we humbly pray.

D An over-eager desire after the world hath so seized on the spirits of many, that the chief end of our coming hither is forgotten; and notwithstanding all the powerful means used, we stand at a stay, as if the Lord had no farther work for his people to do, but every bird to feather his own nest.

Oh thou, my soul, and every part in me
    Lament, the Lord his worthies from the earth
Takes to himself, and makes our earth to be
    E A mourning place left destitute of mirth;
Are these the daies wherein that Beast shall fall?
Lord leave us means, though thou be all in all.

What courage was in Winthrope, it was thine;
    Shepheards sweet Sermons from thy blessing came,
[*E*] Our heavenly Hooker thy grace did refine,
    And godly Burr receiv'd from thee his frame:
Philips didst thou indue with Scripture light,
And Huet had his arguings strong and right.

Grave Higginson his heavenly truths from thee,
    [*E*] Maveruck was made an able help to thine;
What Herver had thou[2] gavest, for's people free;
    Follow Green full of grace, to work thou didst assign:
Godly Glover his rich gifts thou gavest,
Thus thou by means thy flocks from spoiling savest.

[1] Undone.   [2] Harvard.

But Lord, why dost by death withdraw thy hand
   From us, these men and means are sever'd quite;
Stretch forth thy might, Lord Christ do thou command,
   Their doubled spirit on those left to light:
Forth of their graves call ten times ten again,
That thy dear flocks no damage may sustain.

Can I forget these means that thou hast used,
   To quicken up my drowsie drooping soul?
Lord I forget, and have the same abused,
   Which makes me now with grief their deaths condole,
And kiss thy rod, laid on with bowels tender,
By death of mine, makes me their death remember

Lord, stay thy hand, thy Jacobs number's small,
   Powre out thy wrath on Antichrists proud Thrones;
Here [hear] thy poor flocks that on thee daily call,
   Bottle their tears, and pity their sad groans.
Where shall we go, Lord Christ? we turn to thee,
Heal our back-slidings, forward press shall we.

Not we, but all thy Saints the world throughout
   Shall on thee wait, thy wonders to behold;
Thou King of Saints, the Lord in battel stout
   Increase thy armies many thousand fold.
Oh Nations all, his anger seek to stay,
That doth create him armies every day.

E   The Lords taking away by death many of his most eminent servants from us, shewes, that either the Lord will raise up another people to himself to do his work, or raise us up by his Rod to a more eager pursuit of his work, even the planting of his Churches the world throughout.   The Lord converts and calls forth of their graves men to fight his battels against the enemies of his truth.

Chap. X.

Of the endeavours of this people of Christ, to inlarge his Kingdom the world throughout, and first of their preaching Christ to the Indians, among whom they live.

These brood of Travellers having thus through the good hand of their God upon them, thus setled these Churches, according to the institution of Christ, and not by the will of man; they now endeavour to be assisting to others. The reverend Mr. Hugh Peters, and his fellow-helper in Christ Mr. Wells [1] steered their course for England, so soon as they heard of the chaining up of those biting beasts, who went under the name of spiritual Lords; what assistance the Gospel of Christ found there by their preaching, is since clearly manifested; for the Lord Christ having removed that usurping power of Lordly Prelates, hath now inlarged his Kingdom there, and that not onely by the means of these men, but by divers others, both godly and eminent servants of his, who never saw New-England; and by divers other godly Ministers of Christ, who have since gone from hence, both young Students and others, to the number of twenty, or thereabout, in the whole; besides some who were eminent in the civil Government here, both gracious and godly servants of Christ, and some who have been Magistrates here, to the number of five or six. The Lord Christ grant they may all endeavour the advancement of his truths, both in Churches and civil Government. But before the Author cease to speak of England, he is bold to say, that the Lord Christ will overturn, overturn, overturn, till he hath caused such a Government to be set up, as shall become nursing fathers to his new-planted Churches.

The Indian people in these parts at the English first coming, were very barbarous and uncivilized, going for the most part naked, although the country be extreme cold in the winter-season: they are onely clothed with a Deers skin, and a little bit of cloth to cover their privy part. The Women for the most part are very modest, although they go as naked as the Men: they are generally very laborious at their planting time, and the Men extraordinary idle, making their squawes to carry their Children and the luggage beside; so that many times they travell eight or ten mile with a burden on their backs, more fitter for a horse to carry then a woman. The men follow no kind of labour but hunting, fishing and fowling, in all which they make use of their Bowe and Arrowes to shoot the wilde creatures of the Trees, as Squirrells, gray and black Rockoones: as for Deer, they ordinarily catch them in traps, with a pole bent down, and a Cord at the end, which flyes up

[1] Weld.

and stayes their hasty course. Bever, Otter, and Moose they catch with Traps also; they are very good marks-men, with their Bowe and Arrows. Their Boyes will ordinarily shoot fish with their Arrowes as they swim in the shallow Rivers, they draw the Arrow halfe way, putting the point of it into the water, they let flye and strike the fish through; the like they do to Birds lesser and great: onely the Geese and Turkies being strong of wing, sometimes flee away with their Arrowes sticking in them; this is all the trade they use, which makes them desititute of many necessaries, both in meat, drink, apparell and houses.

As for any religious observation, they were the most destitute of any people yet heard of, the Divel having them in very great subjection, not using craft to delude them, as he ordinarily doth in most parts of the World: but kept them in a continuall slavish fear of him; onely the Powawes, who are more conversant with him then any other, sometimes recover their sicke folk with charmes, which they use, by the help of the Divell; and this makes them to adore such; one of them was seen, as is reported, to cure a Squaw that was dangerously sick, by taking a snakes skin and winding it about her arm, the which soon became a living snake crawling round about her armes and body; another caused the sick patient, for healing, to pass bare footed through many burning coals; those that cannot cure them they call *Squantams powwons:* but if the patient live, he is had in great admiration, and then they cry, *Much winnit Abbamocho,* that is, very good Divell: for Squantam is a bad Divel, and Abbamocho is their good Divell. It hath been a thing very frequent before the English came, for the Divell to appear unto them in a bodily shape, sometimes very ugly and terrible, and sometimes like a white boy, and chiefly in the most hideous woods and swamps: they report that sometimes he hath come into their wigwams, and carryed away divers of them alive: and since we came hither, they tell us of a very terrible beast for shape and bigness, that came into a wigwam toward the North-east parts, remote from any English plantations, and took away six men at a time, who were never seen afterward. The English at their first coming did assay and endeavour to bring them to the knowledge of God: and in particular the reverend, grave, and godly Mr. John Wilson, who visited their sick, and instructed others as they were capable to understand him.   But yet very little was done that way, till in process of time they by continuall coming to the English, became better able to understand them; and now of late yeers the reverend Mr. Eliot [1] hath been more then ordinary laborious to study their language, instructing them in their own Wigwams, and Catechising their Children.   As also the reverend Mr. Mayhewe one who was tutored up in N. Eng. and called to office by the Church of Christ, gathered at a small Island called Martins Vineyard: [2] this man hath taken good pains with them: but the particulars of our godly Ministers labours, together with the good hand of our God upon their indeavours, being already published, [3] no further need be spoken.

[1] John Eliot the apostle, whose preaching to the Indians appears to have begun in 1646. The margin adds: "Also Mr. William Leveriry [Leveridge] Pastor of Sandwich Church, is very serious therein, and with good success."

[2] Thomas Mayhew, the minister's father, had in 1641 bought Martha's Vineyard from the representative of Lord Stirling. Soon afterward he and his son, Rev. Thomas Mayhew, went there to live, and the latter began preaching to the numerous Indians of the island. In a letter of October, 1651, about the time when Johnson was writing, the son reports, "Through the mercy of God, there are an hundred ninety-nine men, women and children that have professed themselves to be worshippers of the great and ever-living God." He died in 1657, but his work was continued by his aged father, the proprietor, governor, and patriarch of the island.

[3] Of the early Massachusetts tracts relating to the conversion of the Indians, tracts which are now famous rarities, those which would have been known to Johnson at this time were *New Englands First-Fruits* (London, 1643), *The Day-Breaking if not the Sun-Rising of the Gospell with the Indians in New England* (1647), *The Clear Sunshine of the Gospell breaking forth upon the Indians of New England* (1648), and *The Glorious Progress of the Gospell amongst the Indians in New-England* (1649). The interest aroused in England by these publications led Parliament in 1649, through the efforts of Edward Winslow, then in London, to incorporate the Society for Propagating the Gospel in New England.

CHAP. XI.

*Of the gratious goodness of the Lord Christ, in planting his
Gospel in the purity of it, in Virginia: and of the first
Church gathered there according to the rule of the Gospel.*

About the yeer 1642 the Lord was pleased to put it into the
heart of some godly people in Virginia, to send to N. E. for
some of the Ministers of Christ, to be helpfull unto them in
instructing them in the truth, as it is in Jesus. The godly
Mr. Philip Bennit coming hither, made our reverend Elders
acquainted with their desires, who were very studious to take
all opportunities for inlarging the kingdome of Christ: and
upon serious consideration, the reverend Mr. Knowls of Water-
towne, and Mr. Tompson of Braintree were sent unto them,
who arriving there in safety, preached openly unto the people
for some good space of time, and also from house to house exhorted the people dayly, that with full purpose of heart they
would cleave unto the Lord; the harvest they had was plentifull for the little space of time they were there, till being opposed by the Governour and some other malignant spirits,
they were forced to returne to N. E. again.[1] It were much to
be desired, that all people would take notice of the hand of
God against this people, after the rejection of these Ministers of
Christ: and indeed it was none other but the thrusting Christ
from them; and now attend to the following story, all you
Cavaliers and malignant party the world throughout, take
notice of the wonderworking providence of Christ toward his
Churches, and punishing hand of his toward the contemners
of his Gospel. Behold ye dispisers, and wonder. Oh poor
Virginia, dost thou send away the Ministers of Christ with
threatning speeches? No sooner is this done, but the barbarous, inhumane, insolent, and bloody Indians are let loose
upon them, who contrive the cutting them off by whole
Families, closely carying their wicked counsells till they had

[1] An act of the Virginia assembly of March, 1643, forbade non-conformists
to teach or preach publicly or privately in that colony, and required the governor,
Sir William Berkeley, to compel all non-conformists to depart. The massacre
mentioned below was that of April, 1644.

effected their desires, their bloody designe taking place for
the space of 200 miles up the River: the manner of the English Plantations there being very scattering, quite contrary
to N. E. people, who for the most part desire society. The
manner of the Indians proceeding was thus, they divided
themselves into severall companies, and beset the English
houses a little before break of day, waiting for the first person
that should open the doore and come forth, whom they cruelly
murdered, beating out their brains, and then forthwith
entred the house and slew all they found within, sometimes
firing the houses, and leaving the living children miserably
to be consumed with their dead Parents in the fearfull flames;
some people fleeing from this barbarous massacre, as they passed
by a fired house, heard a pitifull out-cry of a poor Child, crying, I burn, I burn: although they could willingly have made
haste away, yet the miserable out-cry of this poor babe,
caused them to hast to the house, and rescue it forth the flames,
that was even almost ready to scorch it. This cruell and
bloody work of theirs put period to the lives of five or six
hundred of these people, who had not long before a plentifull
proffer of the mercies of Christ in the glad tidings of peace
published by the mouth of his Ministers, who came unto them
for that end: but chusing rather the fellowship of their drunken
companions, and a Preist of their own profession, who could
hardly continue so long sober as till he could read them the
reliques of mans invention in a common prayer book; but
assuredly had not the Lord pittied the little number of his
people among this crooked generation, they had been consumed
at once, for this is further remarkable in this massacre, when
it came toward the place where Christ had placed his little
flock,[1] it was discovered and prevented from further proceeding, and the Lord by this means did so allay their spirits of
malignity toward his people, they gathered in a Church in
presence of the very governour himself, and called to office one
Mr. Harrison, who could not long continue among them, by
reason of their fresh renewed malignity, who had formerly an
evil eye toward them, and could no better refraine from op-
pressing them, then Pharoah after he had rest from the

---

[1] Mostly in Upper Norfolk or Nansemond County.

plagues under which he was. After the departure of Mr.
Harrison, one Mr. Duren became an help unto them; but he
and his people also were forced to remove many hundred
miles up into the country,[1] where they now remain; but assuredly the Lord hath more scourges in store, for such as
force the people to such sufferings; and therefore let this
Church of Christ continue in the way of his truth according
to the rules of his Gospel, and without doubt the Lord will
preserve and continue them, let the adversaries of his Truth
be never so potent. As also about this time, the Lord was
pleased to gather a people together in the Isle of Bermoodas,
whose hearts being guided by the rule of the word, they
gathered into a Church of Christ according to the rules of the
Gospel, being provided with able persons, indued with gifts
from the Lord to administer unto them the holy things of
God;[2] and after thcy began to be opposed, their reverend
elder Mr. Goulding came into these parts, and from hence he
went to England: but this little flock of Christ not long after
being banished from thence, went to one of the Southern
Islands, where they endured much hardship; and which the
Churches of Christ in these parts understanding, about six or
eight of them contributing toward their want, gathered about
800 *l.* to supply their necessity: the which they shipped in a
small vessell hired for that end, and sent by the hands of two
brethren both corne and other necessaries: they arriving in
safety by the blessing of God upon their labours, were well
welcomed by their brethren, who abundantly blessed the
Lord for them, and with godly and gratious expression
returned a thankfull acknowledgement of the present good
hand of the Lord Christ, in providing for them: so that as
this book began with the wonderworking providence of Sions
Saviour, in providing so wonderfull gratiously for his Churches
the World throughout; so it here endeth with the same; and

---

[1] Of all this episode of Puritanism in Virginia a clearer account may be seen
in Winthrop, II. 73, 94–95, 351–353. It appears that Elder William Durand
was banished before Thomas Harrison. The latter finally retired to Ireland,
after a sojourn in Massachusetts. By removal " many miles up into the country" the Puritan immigration into Maryland is probably intended.

[2] A marginal note gives their names, "Mr. Nathaniel White, Mr. Patrick
Copeland, Mr. William Golding."

it were to be desired, that the Churches of Christ in Europe would gather up the wonderfull providences of the Lord toward them also, and more especially those in our native Country: for assuredly it would make much for the magnifying of his glorious works in this day of his power: and although the malignant and antichristian party may say, they can shew the like wonders (as Jannes and Jambres that withstood Moses) [1] yet were the worke of Christ for his poor Churches, within these few yeers, gathered together by some able instrument whom the Lord might be pleased to stir up for that end, and laid open the view of all, they would be forced to confess, this is the very finger of God, and no doubt but they would be a great strengthening to the faith of those, who are appointed of the Lord, for the overthrow of Antichrist (the Lord helping) for assuredly, the time of his having mercy upon Sion is come.

Chap. XII.

Of the time of the fall of Antichrist, and the increase of the Gentile Churches, even to the provoking of the twelve Tribes to submit to the kingdom of Christ.

It hath been the longing expectation of many, to see that notable and wonderfull worke of the Lord Christ, in casting down that man of sin who hath held the whole world (of those that profess any Christ) under his Lordly power, while the true professors of Christ have hardly had any appearance to the eye of the world; first, take notice the Lord hath an assured set time for the accomplishment of this work, which is set down in his word,[2] although more darkly to be understood; wherefore the reverend Ministers of Christ, for these many yeers have studied and laboured for the finding it out, and that holy man of God Mr. John Cotton, among many other, hath diligently searched for the Lords mind herein, and hath declared some sudden blow to be given to this blood-thirsty monster: but the Lord Christ hath unseparably joyned the time, meanes, and manner of this work together,

---

[1] II Timothy iii. 8.
[2] The margin gives the reference, Revelation xvii. 14.

and therefore all men that expect the day, must attend the means: for such hath been and is the absurdity of many, that they make semblance of a very zealous affection to see the glorious work of our Lord Christ herein, and yet themselves uphold, or at least side with those that uphold some part of Antichrists kingdome: and therefore the lordly Prelacy may pray for his fall till their lungs are spent, and their throats grow dry, But while they have a seeming shew (and hardly that) to oppose his doctrines, they themselves in the mean time, make use of his power to advance themselves to honour: as also in these dayes there are divers desperate, blasphemous, and erronious persons whose consciences and their own self-will are unseparable companions; these are very hot in their own apprehensions to prosecute the work; but in the mean time, they not only batter down the truths of Christ, and his own Ordinances and Institutions, but also set up that part of Antichrists kingdom, which hath formerly had a great blow already, even his deceiveable and damnable doctrines: for as one badg of the beast is to be full of blasphemies, so are they, and these take unto themselves seven spirits worse then the former, making the latter end worse then the beginning, as this story may testifie: and some stories in our native country much more. But to come to the time of Antichrists fall; and all that expect it may depend upon the certainty of it: yea it may be boldly said that the time is come, and all may see the dawning of the day: you that long so much for it, come forth and fight: who can expect a victory without a battel? the lordly Prelates that boasted so much of these great atcheivements in this work, are fled into holes and corners: Familists, Seekers, Antinomians and Anabaptists, they are so ill armed, that they think it best sleeping in a whole skin, fearing that if the day of battell once go on, they shall fall among Antichrists Armies: and therefore cry out like cowards, If you will let me alone, and I will let you alone; but assuredly the Lord Christ hath said, *He that is not with us, is against us:* there is no room in his Army for toleratorists. But some will say, We will never believe the day is come, till our eyes behold Babylon begirt with Souldiers. I pray be not too hasty; hath not the Lord said, *Come out of her my people?* etc., surely there is a little space left for this, and now is the time, seeing the Lord

hath set up his standerd of resort: now, *Come forth of her,
and be not partakers of her sins:* now is the time, when the
Lord hath assembled his Saints together; now the Lord will
come and not tarry. As it was necessary that there should
be a Moses and Aaron, before the Lord would deliver his
people and destroy Pharaoh lest they should be wildred
indeed in the Wilderness; so now it was needfull, that the
Churches of Christ should first obtain their purity, and the
civill government its power to defend them, before Antichrist
come to his finall ruine: and because you shall be sure the day
is come indeed, behold the Lord Christ marshalling of his in-
vincible Army to the battell: some suppose this onely to be
mysticall, and not literall at all: assuredly the spirituall fight
is chiefly to be attended, and the other not neglected, having
a neer dependancy one upon the other, especially at this time;
the Ministers of Christ who have cast off all lording power
over one another, are created field-Officers, whose Office is [1]
extravagant in this Army, chiefly to encourage the fighting
Souldiers, and to lead them on upon the enemy in the most
advantagious places, and bring on fresh supplies in all places
of danger, to put the sword of the spirit in their Souldiers
hands: but Christ (who is their general) must onely enable
them to use it aright: to give every Souldier in charge that
they watch over one another, to see that none meddle with
the execrable things of Antichrist, and this to be performed
in every Regiment throughout the Army: and not one to
exercise dominion over the other by way of superiority: for
Christ hath appointed a parity in all his Regiments, etc. let
them beware that none go apart with rebellious Korah. And
further, behold, Kings, Rulers, or Generals of Earths Armies,
doth Christ make use of in this day of battell, the which he
hath brought into the field already also; who are appointed
to defend, uphold, and maintain the whole body of his Armies
against the insolent, beastly, and bloody cruelty of their in-
satiable enemies, and to keep order that none do his fellow-
Souldier any wrong, nor that any should raise a mutiny in
the hosts. Notwithstanding all this, if any shall say, they will

---

[1] Against this point is a marginal note reading, "Yea every Officer hath his
own proper Regiment." The word "extravagant" is used in the sense of "not
confined to any small locality"—a roving commission.

not believe the day is come till they see them ingage battell
with Antichrist; Verily, if the Lord be pleased to open your
eyes, you may see the beginning of the fight, and what success
the Armies of our Lord Christ have hitherto had: the Forlorne
hopes of Antichrists Army, were the proud Prelates of England;
the Forlorne of Christs Armies, were these N. E. people, who
are the subject of this History, which encountring each other
for some space of time, ours being overpowered with multitude,
were forced to retreat to a place of greater safety, where they
waited for a fresh opportunity to ingage with the main battell
of Antichrist, so soon as the Lord shall be pleased to give a
word of Command. Immediately upon this success, the Lord
Christ was pleased to command the right Wing of his Army,
to advance against the left Wing of Antichrist, wherein his
former forlorn hopes of proud Prelates lay: these by our right
Wing had their first pay (for that they had done to our forlorne before) being quite overthrown and cut in pieces by the
valiant of the Lord in our right Wing, who still remain fighting.
Thus far of the battell of Antichrist, and the various success:
what the issue will be, is assuredly known in the generall
already. Babylon is fallen, the God of truth hath said it;
then who would not be a Souldier on Christs side, where is
such a certainty of victory? nay I can tell you a farther word
of encouragement, every true-hearted Souldier that falls by
the sword in this fight, shall not lye dead long, but stand upon
his feet again, and be made partaker of the triumph of this
Victory: and none can be overcome, but by turning his back
in fight. And for a word of terrour to the enemy, let them
know, Christ will never give over the raising of fresh Forces,
till they are overthrown root and branch. And now you antient people of Israel look out of your Prison grates, let these
Armies of the Lord Christ Jesus provoke you to acknowledge
he is certainly come, I [ay] and speedily he doth come to put
life into your dry bones: here is a people not onely praying
but fighting for you, that the great block may be removed
out of the way, (which hath hindered hitherto) that they with
you may enjoy that glorious resurrection-day, the glorious
nuptials of the Lamb: when not only the Bridegroom shall
appear to his Churches both of Jews and Gentiles, (which are
his spouse) in a more brighter aray then ever heretofore, but

also his Bride shall be clothed by him in the richest garments
that ever the Sons of men put on, even the glorious graces of
Christ Jesus, in such a glorious splendor to the eyes of man,
that they shall see and glorifie the Father of both Bridegroom
and Bride.

1. Oh King of Saints, how great's thy work, say we,
　　Done and to do, poor Captives to redeem!
Mountaines of mercy makes this work to be
　　Glorious that grace by which thy works are seen.
　　　　Oh Jesu, thou a Saviour unto thine,
　　　　Not works but grace makes us this mercy find.

2. Of sinners cheife, no better men they be,
　　Thou by thy work hast made thy work to do:
Thy Captaines strength weak dust appears in thee,
　　While thou art brought such wondrous works unto.
　　　　Then Christ doth all, I [ay] all is done for his
　　　　Redeemed ones, his onely work it is.

3. Doth Christ build Churches? who can them deface?
　　He purchast them, none can his right deny:
Not all the world, ten thousand worlds; his grace
　　Caus'd him once them at greater price to buy.
　　　　Nor marvell then if Kings and Kingdomes he
　　　　Destroy'd, when they do cause his folke to flee.

4. Christ is come down possession for to take
　　Of his deer purchase; who can hinder him?
Not all the Armies earthly men can make:
　　Millions of spirits, although Divels grim:
　　　　Can Pope or Turke with all their mortall power,
　　　　Stay Christ from his inheritance one hour?

5. All Nations band your selves together now,
　　You shall fall down as dust from bellows blown:
How easie can our King your power bow?
　　Though higher you in mens accompt were grown.
　　　　As drop in bucket shall those waters be,
　　　　Whereon that Whore doth sit in high degree.

6. Christs wrath is kindled, who can stand before
　　His anger, that so long hath been provoked?
In moment perish shall all him before,
　　Who touch'd Mount Sinai, and it soundly smoaked.
　　　　New-England Churches you are Christs, you say,
　　　　So sure are all that walk in Christs way.

7. No such need fear fury of men or Divels,
   Why, Christ among you takes his dayly walk:
He made you gold, you keeps from rusting evils,
   And hid you here from strife of tongues proud talke.
      Amongst his he for their defence doth bide,
      They need no more that have Christ on their side.

8. Man be not proud of this thy exaltation:
   For thou wast dung and dogs filth when Christ wrought
In thee his work, and set thee in this station
   To stand; from him thy strength is dayly brought.
      Yet in him thou shalt go triumphant on:
      Not thou but Christ triumphs his foes upon.

9. You people whom he by the hand did lead
   From Egypt land through Seas with watry wall:
Apply your selves his Scriptures for to read:
   In reading do for eyes enlightned call,
      And you shall see Christ once being come is now
      Again at hand your stubborn hearts to bow.

10. Though scattered you, Earths Kingdoms are throughout
    In bondage brought, cheife by those make some shew
Of Jewish rights; they Christ with you cast out;
    Christ will their Cords for you in sunder hew.
       Through unbeliefe you were to bondage brought:
       Believe that Christ for you great work hath wrought.

11. He will your heart not member circumcise:
    Oh search and see, this is your Jesus sure,
Refuse him not, would God you were so wise:
    None but this King can ought your hope procure.
       Once doting on an Earthly Kingdom you
       Mist of your Christ; be sure be wiser now.

12. The day's at hand he will you wiser make
    To know Earths Kingdoms are too scant and base
For such a price, as Christ paid for your sake:
    Kings you shall be, but in a higher place;
       Yet for your freedom Nations great shall fall,
       That without fear of foes, him serve you shall.

13. You are the men that Christ will cause subdue
    Those Turkish Troops, that joyned Jews have been:
His Gentile Churches cast down Babels crue:
    Then you that brood of Mahumetts shall win,
       Destroy his seed 'mongst Persians, Turkes and Moores,
       And for poor Christians ope the Prison doors.

14. Your Nation prov'd too scant for his possession,
  Whose pretious blood was made a price for sin:
And Nations all who were in like transgression;
  Some of the whole Christ to his Crown will win,
    And now makes way for this his work indeed,
    That through the world his Kingdom may proceed.

15. Now Nations all I pray you look about,
  Christ comes you neer, his power I pray embrace:
In's word him seek; he's found without all doubt:
  He doth beseech with teares, Oh seek his face:
    Yet time there is, the Battel's but begun;
    Christ, call thy folke that they to thee may run.

16. Place them in thy strong Armies newly gather'd,
  Thy Churches, Lord, increase and fill withall:
Those blessed ones are given thee by thy Father,
  The wickeds Rod off from their backs recall.
    Breake off their yokes, that they with freedom may
    Tell of thy workes, and praise thee every day.

17. Lord Christ, go on with thy great wonders working,
  Down headlong cast all Antichristian power:
Unmaske those men that lye in corners lurking,
  Whose damned doctrines dayly seates advance.
    For why, thy Folke for this are dayly longing,
    That Nations may come in thy Churches thronging.

18. What greater joy can come thy Saints among,
  Then to behold their Christ exalted high?
Thy Spirits joy with ravishment stirs strong
  Thy Folke, while they thy Kingdomes glory eye.
    Angels rejoyce because their waiting is
    In Saints assembly, where thy name they bliss.

19. Thy workes are not in Israels Land confined,
  From East to West thy wondrous works are known
To Nations all thou hast thy grace assigned,
  Thy spirits breathings through the World are blown.
    All Languages and tongues do tell thy praise,
    Dead hear thy voyce, them thou dost living raise.

20. Oh blessed dayes of Son of Man now seen,
  You that have long'd so sore them to behold,
March forth in's might, and stoutly stand between
  The mighties sword, and Christs dear flock infold.
    Undaunted close and clash with them; for why?
    'Gainst Christ they are, and he with thee stands by.

21. No Captive thou, nor Death can on thee seize,
Fight, stand, and live in Christ thou dayly dost:
He long ago did lead as Captives these,
And ever lives to save thee where thou goest.
His Father still, and Spirit shall with thee
Abide, and crowne thy Head with lasting glee.

For thy words sake, and according to thine own heart, hast thou done all these great things, to make thy servant know them, 2 *Sam.* 7. 21.

FINIS.

INDEX

Aberginian, 41, 41 n.
Adams, C. F., *Three Episodes of Massachusetts History*, 40 n., 124 n.
Aggawam, *see* Essex County.
Agissawam, 41 n.
Allen, Bozoan, 229.
Allen, Rev. John, 171, 171 n., 179, 215.
Allen, Thomas, 215.
Allin, John, Jr., 202, 202 n.
America Painted to the Life, 3.
American Antiquarian Society, 4.
Ames, Rev. William, 202, 202 n.
Anabaptists, 31, 31 n., 132 n., 269.
Andover, 231, 249.
Anne, Cape, 205.
Antigua, 247 n.
Antinomians, 31, 31 n., 50, 67 n., 68 n., 83 n., 102 n., 124 n., 134 n., 179 n., 197 n., 252, 269.
Apollonius, Rev. William, 104 n.
Aquidneck, 186 n.
Arbella, ship, 51 n., 56, 63 n., 65.
Arber, Edward, *English Reprints*, 13.
Arians, 50.
Arminians, 50.
Atherton, Capt. Humphrey, 142 n., 143, 229.

Baillie, Rev. Robert, 125, 137; *Dissuasive from the Errors of the Time*, 125 n., 137 n.
Ball, Rev. John, 137; *Trial of the New Church Way in New England and in Old*, 137 n.
Barbados, 55, 247, 247 n.
Barnard, Tobias, 202, 202 n.
Batchellor, Rev. Stephen, 73, 188 n., 189.
Bellingham, Gov. Richard, 37, 37 n., 97, 97 n., 101, 192, 205.
Bennet, Philip, 265.
Berkeley, Sir William, 265 n.
Bermudas, 55, 247 n., 267.
Blackstone, *see* Blaxton.
Blaxton, Rev. William, 46, 46 n., 64.

Blaxton's point, 64.
Blinman, Rev. Richard, 205, 206 n.
Body of Liberties, by Nathaniel Ward, 97 n., 244 n.
Boston, 191; defeated hopes of being a city, 9, 247; situation of, 11; church of Christ, 70, 88; frontier town, 90; trade of, 96; petition of church, 174 n.; fifty-eight persons disarmed, 175; farms kept from being part of Braintree, 197, 197 n.; foundation of, 212 n.; forts of, 227–232; growth of, 247; petition to be made a corporation, 9, 247 n.; coopers and shoemakers of, 248 n.; founding of the Old North Church, 251, 251 n.
Bradford, *History of Plymouth Plantation*, 14, 42 n., 46 n.
Bradstreet, Gov. Simon, 65, 141, 249.
Braintree, 117 n., 171 n., 197, 236, 246, 246 n.
Branford, Conn., 195 n.
Brewster, Nathaniel, 202, 202 n.
Bridges, Capt. Robert, 231.
Brigham, Sebastian, 231.
Bright, Rev. Francis, 46 n.
Brooke, Nathaniel, 3, 10, 11, 21.
Brooke, Lord, 106, 118 n.
Browne, Rev. Edmund, 171, 171 n., 182, 196.
Brownists or Separatists, Errours of the Sect called, by Wm. Rathband, 137 n.
Bulkley, Rev. Edward, 111 n., 202, 202 n.
Bulkley, Rev. John, 111 n., 202, 202 n.
Bulkley, Rev. Peter, 110.
Burr, Rev. Jonathan, 192, 192 n., 215 n.
Burrough, Rev. Jeremiah, 138, 138 n.

Cambridge, founding of, 90; church of, 93, 93 n., 252; plan of certain people to remove to Connecticut, 105–107; first synod held at, 170–175; printing-press of, 183 n.; selected as a site for Harvard College, 200; second synod held at, 242–243.

Cambridge Platform, 242 n.

Cambridge Synods, 25 n.; first, 152 n., 170–175; second, 242–243.

Canonicus, 161–163, 235.

Canterbury, 5, 6, 50 n.

Carter, Rev. Thomas, 117, 117 n., 135, 215, 217, 217 n.

Castle Island, 33 n., 69, 93 n., 170 n., 232, 232 n., 234.

Charles I., 23 n., 37 n., 38 n., 157 n., 158 n., 208 n.

Charles River, 38, 63 n., 64, 65, 67, 68, 74, 84, 90.

Charlestown, Johnson settled in, 6; founding of town and church, 7; establishment of civil government, 65; meeting of Court of Assistants at, 66, 66 n.; church divided into two, 67, 67 n.; situation and description of, 68–69; another church founded, 70, 70 n.; Rev. Thomas James, pastor of church of, 82, 82 n.; frontier town, 90; helpers in the church of, 100; two persons disarmed in, 175; foundation not due to definite acts of the General Court, 212 n.; church appointed seven men to supervise new settlement of Woburn, 212, 213 n.; forts of, 227–232; growth of, 247; the fire of 1650, 259 n.

Charter of Freedom, 208.

Chauncy, Rev. Charles, 180 n., 181, 192 n., 194.

Chelmsford, 227 n.

Chelsea, 64.

Child, Dr. Robert, 141 n., 240 n.

Church covenant, 216.

Church Discipline, Platform of, agreed upon by the Synod at Cambridge, 242 n.

Church-Discipline, Survey of the Summe of, by Thomas Hooker, 91 n.

Church-Government exercised in Presbyteriall, Classicall and Synodicall Assemblies, by John Paget, 137 n.

Church of England, 154–160, 240 n.

Church of Scotland, 240 n.

Church officers, 26–30, 34, 35, 38.

Churches, rules for governing, 25–26; conduct of members, 28–29; government in, 98.

Churches of Christ in New England, The Way of the, by John Cotton, 125 n.

Churches, *see also* St. Botolph's and St. George's.

Clap, Roger, 229.

Cod, Cape, 176, 176 n.

Coddington, William, 185 n.

Coitmore, Thomas, 253.

Colonial Society of Massachusetts, Publications of the, 162 n.

Comet of 1618, 39.

Commissioners of Plantations, 37 n., 241 n.

Commonwealth, *see* Massachusetts.

Concord, 110, 111, 115 n., 195.

Congregational churches, general councils or synods of, 152 n., 170–175, 242–243.

Congregationalism, democratic methods of, 7; principles and practices of, 10; polity of, 25–26, 26 n; theory regarding churches, 27 n.; essential features in Massachusetts Bay of, 46 n.; classical exposition of polity in New England of, 91 n.; controversy respecting merits of systems of Presbyterianism and, 137, 138, 172; imposition of hands, 217 n.; use of synods and councils, 242 n.

Connecticut, migration to, 91 n., 105–106, 193 n.; Samuel Stone removed to, 93 n.; settlement of Saybrook transferred to the colony of, 118 n.; Pequot country, 148 n.; New Haven Colony absorbed by, 178 n.; confederation to assist other colonies, 219.

Connecticut River, 147.

Cook, Col. George, 230.

Copeland, Rev. Patrick, 267 n.

Cotton, Rev. John, 63 n., 67 n., 87–89, 125, 174, 215, 268; *The Way of the Churches of Christ in New England*, 125 n.

Cotton, Rev. Seaborn, 9, 63, 202, 202 n.

Covenant of Grace Opened, 111 n.

Cradock, Matthew, 10, 12, 38.

Cutter, William R., 8.

Dalton, Rev. Timothy, 188 n., 189.

Dane, Rev. Francis, 249.

Danforth, Samuel, 202, 202 n.

Davenport, Rev. John, 46 n., 171, 171 n., 176 n., 177, 177 n.

Davenport, Capt. Richard, 170, 232.

Deacons, 25 n., 27 n., 68.
Dedham, 171 n., 179.
Dennison, Major-Gen. Daniel, 230.
Denton, Rev. Richard, 193 n., 194.
Deputies, election of town, 141, 142; principal ones, 143, 144.
Discipline, rules of, for the people of Christ, 33–35.
Dissuasive from the Errors of the Time, by Robert Baillie, 125 n., 137 n.
Doctrines, 26, 27, 29, 36, 50, 99, 123–136, 147, 220.
Dodge, Prof. R. E. Neil, Johnson's metres, 12.
Dorchester, description of, and organization of church of, 69, 69 n.; Rev. Richard Mather called to the church of, 105, 105 n.; emigration to Connecticut, 106; Rev. Jonathan Burr called to, 192, 192 n.; foundation not due to definite acts of the General Court, 212 n.
Dover, 206, 207, 207 n.
Downing, George, 202, 202 n.
Draper, John, 17.
Dudley, Gov. Thomas, 9; elected deputy-governor, 65, 77, 81, 85, 139, 182, 188, 240, 245, 249, 252, 255; elected governor, 81 n., 93, 192, 234, 254; elected major-general, 228; death of, 81 n.
Dummer, Richard, 99.
Duncan, Nathaniel, 142 n., 143.
Dunkirk men-of-war, 56, 56 n.
Dunster, Pres. Henry, 198, 202, 204, 215.
Durand, Rev. William, 267, 267 n.
Dutch, 59, 71, 76, 101, 148, 150, 219.
Duxbury, 118 n., 119.

Eagle, 51, 56.
Earthquakes, 160, 160 n., 185, 225.
East Greenwich, manor of, 37.
Eaton, Rev. Samuel, 192 n., 193.
Eaton, Theophilus, 171, 171 n., 176, 176 n., 177 n., 178.
Eclogues, Spenser's, 14.
Elders, 26, 27, 27 n., 28, 68, 70 n., 99, 108, 216, 217.
Elegy, Gray's, 13.
Eliot, Rev. John, 72, 215, 264.
Endicott, Gov. John, 9, 12; governor of colony at Naumkeag, 44 n.; elected deputy-governor, 205, 209, 219, 245,

254; elected governor, 225, 252, 255; elected major-general, 234, 249.
Endicott Rock, 37 n.
English Independency, 242 n.
English nation, 23, 24, 40, 49, 59, 154–161.
English Reprints, Arber's, 13.
Essex County, 96, 96 n., 229, 231.

Familists, 31, 31 n., 50, 249.
Farrett, James, 195 n.
Fenwick, George, 118, 118 n.
Fisk, Rev. John, 171, 171 n., 182, 226, 227, 227 n.
Flint, Rev. Henry, 117 n., 197.
Flint, Thomas, 117.
Fordham, Rev. Robert, 195, 195 n.
Formalists, 50.
France, 55.
Frederick V., 158 n.
Freemen, 66, 141; number admitted in successive years, 66, 77, 81, 85, 93, 101, 118, 139, 182, 188, 192, 205, 209, 219, 225, 240, 245, 249, 254.
French, 59, 71, 76, 219.

Gabriel, ship, 61 n.
Gardiner, Sir Christopher, 10, 163 n.
Gardiner, Lion, 163 n.; *Relation of the Pequot Wars*, 165 n.
Gassendi, 39 n.
General Court, 8, 9, 140, 141 n., 228, 228 n.; gift of Dr. Wilson acknowledged by, 33 n.; meetings of, 65, 65 n. 66, 66 n.; rules for election of governor and deputy-governor, 81 n.; counties organized by, 96 n.; laws passed to restrict wages, 200 n.; committee to examine state of Harvard College, 204 n.; order relating to salt-petre, 218; fuller code of laws prepared, 244, 244 n.
Geneva Bible, 52 n.
Germans, 59.
Gerrish, William, 231.
Gibbons, Major-Gen. Edward, 64, 161 n., 229, 235, 252, 254, 256.
Gloucester, 45, 205, 206, 231.
Glover, John, 143.
Glover, Rev. Jose, 183, 183 n.
Goffe, Thomas, 38 n.
Golding, Rev. William, 267.
Goodenow, Edmund, 230.

Goodwin, Rev. Thomas, 138, 138 n.
Gookin, Major-Gen. Daniel, 5, 142 n., 143, 230.
Gorges, Sir Ferdinando, 3, 4.
Gorges, Ferdinando, Esquire, 3, 4.
Gorges, Robert, 46 n.
Gorton, Samuel, arrest of, 9, 224; reports injurious to the Massachusetts plantation, 10; theology of, 31 n.; leader of the so-called heretics, 220, 220 n.; relations with the Indians, 222–223; *Simplicities Defence against Seven-Headed Policie*, 223 n.; government not to molest, 241 n.
Gortonists, theology of, 31, 50, 122; heresies of, 128, 129; incite the Indians, 220; seek to defraud Indians of their land, 222–223; numbers increase, 224; arrest and imprisonment of members, 224–225; government not to molest, 241, 241 n.
Gospel Covenant, The, by Peter Bulkley, 111 n.
Gospell breaking forth upon the Indians of New England, The Clear Sunshine of the, 264 n.
Gospell with the Indians in New England, The Day-Breaking if not the Sun-Rising of the, 264 n.
Government, civil, 90, 123 n.; rules relating to, 30–32; Plymouth, 43; establishing of, 63–65; election of officers and their duties, 139–140; members, 140–141; sectaries not to be tolerated, 144–145; kind of men to be chosen to uphold the, 145–146.
Gray's *Elegy*, 13.
Great Britain, 36, 247, *see also* English nation.
Green, Rev. Henry, 226.
Green-Harbor, *see* Marshfield.
Greenleaf, Edmund, 231.
Griffin, ship, 63 n.
Guilford, 177 n., 193 n.

Hampton, 74 n., 188, 189, 190, 231.
Harlackenden, Roger, 103.
Harrison, Rev. Thomas, 266–267, 267 n.
Hartford, 91 n., 93 n., 105, 118, 149.
Harvard, Rev. John, 187, 187 n., 201, 201 n.
Harvard College, 90, 105 n., 180 n., 187, 198 n., 200–205, 228 n.

Hathorne, Capt. **William, 142 n., 143,** 231.
Haverhill, 231, 234.
Hawkins, Jane, 132 n., 187 n.
Hawthorne, *see* Hathorne.
Haynes, Gov. John, 87, 101, 106.
Hempstead, Long Island, 193 n., 195 n.
Hewett, Rev. Ephraim, 193 n., 194.
Higginson, Rev. Francis, 46, 47, 109; *New England's Plantation*, 47 n.
Higginson, Rev. John, 161 n.
Hill, Joseph, 142 n., 143, 230.
Hingham, 115, 115 n., 116, 116 n., 193 n.
Hobart, Rev. Peter, 115, 116 n.
Holland, 32, 247, *see also* Dutch.
Hooke, Rev. William, 192 n., 193, 193 n.
Hooker, Rev. Thomas, 87, 90, 93, 106, 118, 252; *Survey of Church-Discipline*, 91 n.
Hopkins, Gov. Edward, **171, 171 n.,** 178, 178 n.
Hough, Rev. Samuel, 226.
Hour-glass, 136 n.
Hubbard, Rev. William, 142 n., 143.
Hull, 250.
Husbandmen, Company of, 73 n.
Hutchinson, Mrs. Anne, 68 n.; popularity of, 28 n.; doctrine of, 31 n.; John Cotton's position toward teachings of, 88 n.; leader of Antinomians, 124 n.; women as preachers, 127; removal to Pelham Neck and subsequent murder, 186, 186 n.
Hutchinsonian party, 152 n., 174 n, *see also* Antinomians.

Igoshaum, 41.
Independency, in England, 242 n.
Indians, 45, 76, 85, 87, 90, 92, 108, 109, 114, 159, 195; reception of the first settlers, 39–40; Massachusetts, 41, 41 n.; attack against Plymouth settlers, 42; stories of Samoset and Squanto, 43, 43 n.; trading for beaver-skins with the, 64; John Eliot's missionary work among the, 72 n., 264; complaint against the Tarratines, 78; attack on Saugus, 79; small-pox plague, 79–80; peaceful agreement for purchase of Concord, 110 n., 111, 112; paths of, 113; beginning of Pequot war, 147–150; embassy to Canonicus, 161–163; con-

duct of the Pequots, 164; war with the, 167–170; murder of Anne Hutchinson and daughters, 186–187; battle between the Narragansetts and Mohegans, 219–222; preparations for second war against, 234–236; preaching to the, 261–264; massacre of 1644, 265–266.

Ipswich, 74 n., 100, 143; organization of church at, 95–96; description of, 96; ministers of church of, 119; two people disarmed in, 175; growth of, 247.

Ireland, 55, 78, 108.

Ireland, Deputy of, 92.

Jackson, Edward, 143.

Jacobites, 74, 90, 113, 147, 160, 238.

James I., 23 n., 158 n.

James, Rev. Thomas, 82, 82 n., 100.

Jenners, Rev. Thomas, 180 n., 181.

Jennison, William, 230.

John, Sagamore, 79, 80 n.

Johnson, Lady Arbella, 56, 64.

Johnson, Capt. Edward, 43 n., 45 n., 49 n., 50 n., 52 n., 58 n., 63 n., 100 n., 134 n., 143 n., 162 n., 222 n., 229 n., 230 n., 264 n.; *Wonder-working Providence*, 4–5; emigration to Massachusetts, 6; account of the settling of Charlestown, 7; service in the colony, 8–9; reasons for publishing book, 10; typographical errors and style of book, 11–14; character and personal qualities of, 15–16; editions of his book, 17; accusations against the Anabaptists, 31 n.; commissioner to survey Merrimac River, 37 n.; passenger on the *Eagle*, 51 n.; description of Charlestown, 69 n.; exploration of Woburn, 74, 74 n.; account of so-called Antinomians, 124 n.; election of magistrates, 141 n.; probable member of embassy to Canonicus, 161 n.; member of committee of the General Court to examine the state of Harvard College, 204 n.; supervised new settlement of Woburn, 213 n.; appointed surveyor of military stores, 231 n.

Johnson, Hon. Edward F., 8.

Johnson, Isaac, 56, 65, 229.

Johnson, John, 144, 231, 231 n.

Johnson, William, of Canterbury, 5.

Johnson, Major William, 7, 18.

Jones, Rev. John, 110, 112, 202, 202 n.

Kent, 5.

Kepler, 39 n.

Kieft's war, 186 n.

Knowles, Rev. John, 190, 191, 191 n., 215, 265.

Lamberton, Capt. George, 178, 178 n., 254.

Laudian persecution, 94.

Lawes and Libertyes concerning the Inhabitants of the Massachusets, The Book of the General, 244 n.

Laws, 97 n., 244, 244 n.

Legend of Gaveston, 14.

Leveridge, Rev. William, 264 n.

Long Island, 195.

Lothrop, Rev. John, 98.

Lothrop, Thomas, 231.

Ludlow, Roger, 93.

Lusher, Eleazar, 143, 229.

Lynn, 195 n.; churches of, 70 n.; description of, 73; attack of the Indians, 79; Rev. Samuel Whiting welcomed by church of, 120; iron work at, 246 n.

Magistrates, not to open gates of forts, 32; election by the freemen in General Court, 81, 81 n., 140, 141 n.; not to do evil, 145–146; duty to be present at church, 215.

Magnalia, by Cotton Mather, 14.

Maine, 73 n.

Malden, 230, 249, 250.

Manufactures, 245.

Marshfield, 206 n.

Martha's Vineyard, 38 n., 49 n., 264.

Mary Rose, ship, 258 n.

Mason, Hugh, 230.

Mason, Capt. John, 167 n., 168 n.; *Brief History of the Pequod War*, 165 n.

Massachusetts, *History of New-England, from the English planting in the Yeere 1628 until the Yeere 1652*, 3; relations between Sir Ferdinando Gorges and, 4; arrival of Capt. Johnson in, 6; reports injurious to plantation of, 10; distinguished founders and their principles, 15–16; doctrine of the government of, 31 n.; claim to New Hampshire and Maine, 37 n.; the pestilence of 1616–1617, 40, 40 n.–41; number of churches in, 49 n.; relations of Samuel Maverick with, 64 n.; counties of, 96 n.; first code of laws of, 97 n.; government maintained right to punish for infractions of the "First Table," 123 n.; public worship in, 135 n.; arrest of Thomas Morton by the magistrates of, 155 n.; expedition against the Indians by a body of troops, 164 n.; levy of men in war against Indians, 165, 165 n.; Wm. Coddington banished from, 185 n., authority extended over New Hampshire, 207 n.; emigrants to island in Caribbean Sea, 208 n.; confederation to assist other colonies, 219; jurisdiction extended over the Shawomet region, 222 n.; relations of the Gortonists and, 223–224; drilling of soldiers, 228; military officers, 228–232; Wm. Pynchon named in patent of, 236 n.; petition against the government of, 240; another code of laws prepared, 244, 244 n.

Massachusetts, Chronicles of, by Alexander Young, 94.

Massachusetts History, Three Episodes of, by C. F. Adams, 40 n., 124 n.

Massachusetts Bay, 67, 179.

Massachusetts Company, 4, 37 n.

Massachusetts Historical Society, 17.

Massasoit, 41.

Mather, Rev. Cotton, 251 n.; *Magnalia*, 14.

Mather, Rev. Increase, 105 n., 251 n.

Mather, Rev. Nathaniel, 202.

Mather, Rev. Richard, 105, 215.

Mather, Rev. Samuel, 202, 202 n., 251 n.

Mathews, Rev. Marmaduke, 250, 250 n.

Matthews, Albert, 162 n.

Maude, Rev. Daniel, 207, 207 n.

Maverick, Rev. John, 70, 105, 240 n.

Maverick, Samuel, 63, 64, 105, 240 n.

Mawhiggins, *see* Mohegans.

Mayhew, Rev. Thomas, 264, 264 n.

Mayhew, Thomas, Sr., 38 n., 264 n.

Medfield, 179 n.

Mennonites, 31 n.

Mercurius Politicus, 4.

Meritorious Price of Our Redemption, The, by Wm. Pynchon, 237.

Merrimac River, 37n., 38, 90, 99, 189, 214.

Mexanino, 235 n., 236.

Miantonomoh, 161, 220–222.

Middlesex County, 96 n., 229.

Milford, Conn., 177 n.

Military affairs, 227–233.

Miller, Rev. John, 184, 215 n.

Ministers, duties of, 27, 27 n.; banishment to the New World, 53; work of the, 142; encouragement to people of Hartford by, 165–166; members of Cambridge Synod, 171–173; churches edified by the, 182.

Mixan, *see* Mexanino.

Mohegans, 148, 219–222.

Morton, Thomas, 10, 69, 154; *New English Canaan*, 155 n.

Mount Wollestone, *see* Braintree.

Moxon, Rev. George, 237, 237 n.

Münster, 132.

Mystic, Conn., 167 n., 250.

Mystic River, 167 n., 214, 250.

Nanepashemet, 80 n.

Nantasket, 93 n.

Narragansetts, 41, 148, 161, 219, 222.

Natick, 72.

New England, 21, 23, 24, 30, 53; origins of town and church government in, 7; ecclesiastical and civil polity of, 10; first published history of, 14; people shipped to, 25; gift of Dr. Wilson to, 33 n.; Puritan emigration to, 37 n.

New England, Briefe Discription of, by Samuel Maverick, 64 n.

New England, Chronological History of, by Thomas Prince, 4.

New England, Council for, 37 n., 73 n.

New England, Good News from, by Edward Winslow, 42.

New England, History of, by Palfrey, 167 n., 193 n.

New England Confederation of 1643, 178 n., 219 n.

New England Congregationalism, 242 n., *see also* Congregationalism.

New Englands First-Fruits, 264.

New England's Plantation, by Rev. Francis Higginson, 47 n.

New Englands Prospect, by William Wood, 91 n.

New English Canaan, by Thomas Morton, 155 n.

New Haven, Conn., 176–178, 219, 247, 254.
New Rochelle, N. Y., 186 n.
Newark, N. J., 195 n.
Newbury, 74 n., 98, 143, 175, 189.
Newfoundland, 58.
Newman, Rev. Samuel, 180 n., 181.
Newtown, see Cambridge.
Niantics, 41, 148, 162.
Noddle's Island, 63.
Norfolk County, 96 n., 229, 231, 266 n.
Norton, Francis, 143, 230.
Norton, Rev. John, 94, 94 n., 103, 104, 104 n.
Nowell, Increase, 7 n., 85, 85 n., 86, 215.
Noyes, Rev. James, 98, 98 n.

Old North Church, 251, 251 n.
Oyster Bay, 195 n.

Paget, Rev. John, 137 n.
Paine, Robert, 143.
Papists, 23, 31, 50, 144.
Parker, Rev. Thomas, 98, 98 n.
Parkes, William, 144.
Parliament, 240, 240 n., 247 n.
Partridge, Rev. Ralph, 118, 119, 119 n.
Pastors, see Ministers.
Peck, Robert, 193 n., 194.
Pelham, Herbert, 188.
Pelham, William, 230.
Pelham Neck, 186 n.
Pequod War, Brief History of the, by Capt. John Mason, 165 n.
Pequots, 161 n.; afflicted by the pestilence of 1616–1617, 41; beginning of war with the English, 147–149; council of war, 162–164; accounts of war, 165 n.; attack on fort of the, 167; battle between the English and the, 167–170.
Pequot Wars, Relation of the, by Lion Gardiner, 165 n.
Perkins, William, 229.
Pessacus, 235 n., 236.
Peters, Rev. Hugh, 109, 109 n., 262.
Philip, King, 41.
Phillips, Rev. George, 75, 191, 252.
Pierson, Rev. Abraham, 195, 195 n.
Pilgrim, 199, 199 n.
Pinnace, Capt. Chadwick's, 258 n.
Piscataqua River, 207, 207 n.

Plantations, Commissioners of, 37 n., 241 n.
Plough, Company of the, 73 n.
Plymouth, 32 n., 43, 49 n., 98, 193, 219.
Plymouth Plantation, History of, by Bradford, 14, 42 n., 46 n.
Pokanoket, country of, 40.
Pomham, 220, 222.
Poole, Dr. William F., 17.
Popery, 23, 31, 50, 144.
Portugal, 59, 71, 247.
Powwows, 41, 80, 168.
Prelacy, 71, 76; servitude under, 23; resolved to cast down false foundation of, 24; their pressure on the churches, 31; enemy to Reformation, 122; Puritans struggle against, 155 n.; petitioners for, 240.
Prelates, 147; lands in England, 96; war with Scotland, 157, 157 n., 158, 160; lordly power of, 171; defeat of, 269, 271.
Presbyterians, 122; accused of prostrating the authority of Christ, 131; controversy respecting merits of systems of Congregationalists and, 137 n., 138 n., 172; withdrawal of Saxton and Denton from New England on account of, 193 n.; petition for Presbyterian government, 240.
Presbyteries, Due Right of, by Rev. Samuel Rutherfurd, 137 n.
Prichard, Hugh, 229.
Prince, Thomas, Chronological History of New England, 4.
Printing, 182.
Proclamations, 23, 24, 26.
Providence, R. I., 185, 185 n.
Providence, Isle of, 208.
Psalms of Sternhold and Hopkins, 12.
Puritan emigration, 37 n.
Puritans, 10, 26 n., 155 n., 158 n.
Pynchon, William, 236, 236 n., 237 n.

Quinipiac, 176 n.
Quincy, 197 n.

Rathband, Rev. William, 137, 212.
Rawson, Edward, 142 n., 143.
Rayner, Rev. John, 192, 192 n.
Reading, 225.
Reformation, 49, 121, 132 n., 236–238.
Rhode Island, 185, 185 n.

Rogers, Rev. Ezekiel, 183, 183 n., 184.
Rogers, Rev. Nathaniel, 118, 119.
Rowley, 182.
Roxbury, church of, 70 n., 71; situation and description of, 71–72; calling of Rev. Thomas Welde to church of, 83, 83 n.; five people disarmed in, 175; story of maid lost in storm, 191.
Russell, Richard, 142 n., 143.
Rutherfurd, Rev. Samuel, *Due Right of Presbyteries*, 137 n.

Saco, Me., 180 n.
Sagamores, 41.
Saggamore, John, 79, 80 n.
St. Botolph's Church, Boston, England, 63 n., 88 n.
St. George's Church, Canterbury, 5–6.
Salem, 73; founding of, 45; first church of, 46, 46 n., 47–49; new arrivals at, 64; ministers of church of, 109; six people disarmed in, 175; foundation not due to definite acts of the General Court, 212 n.; growth of, 247.
Salisbury, 189, 231, 234.
Saltonstall, Sir Richard, 74, 102 n.
Saltonstall, Richard, Esquire, 74, 102 n.
Sargent, William, 250.
Saugus, 79, 120.
Savage, James, 17.
Savage, Thomas, 229.
Saxton, Rev. Peter, 193 n., 194.
Saybrook Fort, 106, 118, 148, 148 n., 163 n.
Saye, Lord, 106, 118 n.
Scituate, 98, 180, 193 n.
Scotland, 55.
Seafort, ship, 253, 253 n.
Sectaries, 31, 31 n., 144.
Sedgwick, Major-Gen. Robert, 7 n., 212 n., 230.
Seekers, the, 31, 31 n., 50, 269.
Seekonk, 180 n.
Sele, Lord, 118 n.
Sewall, Samuel, Judge, 45.
Shakespeare, William, *Venus and Adonis*, 14.
Shawshin, grant of, 90.
Shawshin River, 214.
Shepard, Rev. Thomas, 9, 103, 134 n., 135; plot against, 94; account of early life and emigration, 94 n.; character of, 107; work of, 201; death of, 252

Shepherd's Calendar, by Spenser, 14.
Shoals, Isles of, 96.
Simmes, *see* Symmes.
Simplicities Defence against Seven-Headed Policie, by Samuel Gorton, 225 n.
Skelton, Rev. Samuel, 46 n., 48, 48 n.
Smith, Henry, 193 n., 194.
Smith, Capt. John, 39 n.
Smith, Rev. Ralph, 194 n.
Socananoco, 220, 222.
Southampton, Long Island, 195, 195 n.
Southold, Long Island, 177 n.
Spain, 247.
Spaniards, 59.
Spenser, *Shepherd's Calendar*, 14; *Tears of the Muses*, 14.
Sports, Declaration concerning, 23 n.
Springfield, 237.
Stamford, Conn., 177 n.
Standish, Capt. Miles, 42, 69 n.
State-house, 162, 162 n.
Stone, Rev. Samuel, 87, 90 n., 93, 93 n., 106, 118.
Sudbury, 171 n., 195.
Suffolk County, 96 n., 229.
Sun, 242, 243.
Swedes, 76, 178 n., 219.
Symmes, Mrs. Sarah, 100.
Symmes, Rev. Zachary, 7 n., 100, 135 n., 215.
Synods, 25, 152, 153, 170–176, 242, 243.

Tears of the Muses, by Spenser, 14.
Thatcher, Rev. Thomas, 181.
Thompson, David, 63 n., 64.
Thompson, Rev. William, member of first Synod in New England, 171, 171 n.; called to the Weymouth church, 182; called to the church of Braintree, 197; character of, 198; appointed to preach during war with the Indians, 235–236; sent to preach in Virginia, 265.
Thompson's Island, 64 n., 69.
Torry, William, 143, 229.
Tottel's Miscellany, 13.
Trial of the New Church Way in New England and in Old, by John Ball, 137 n.
Tyng, Capt. William, 143, 229.

Uncas, 220–222.
Underhill, Capt. John, 129 n., 165 n., 167 n.

Vane, Sir Henry, 102, 118, 164 n.
Vassall, William, 240 n.
Venus and Adonis, by William Shakespeare, 14.
Virginia, 55, 247, 247 n.; Puritans in, 265–268.
Voyages, 25, 35, 39, 58, 61–63.

Wages, 200 n.
Walker, Lieut. Richard, 79, 230.
Walton, William, 117.
Ward, Rev. John, 97, 103, 235.
Ward, Rev. Nathaniel, 95, 97, 103, 235; *Body of Liberties*, 97 n.
Wareham, Rev. John, 70 n., 106.
Watertown, 90, 193, 252; church of, 70 n.; situation and description of, 74; George Phillips, pastor at, 75 n.; John Knowles, teaching elder at, 190–191; foundation not due to definite acts of the General Court, 212 n.
Weld, Edmund, 202 n.
Weld, Rev. Thomas, 82, 83, 262.
Wells, *see* Weld.
Wenham, 171 n., 225, 226, 227 n., 231.
Weymouth, 180, 180 n.
Wheelwright, Rev. John, 31 n., 68 n., 124 n., 197.
Whipple, John, 143.
White, John, 37, 37 n.
White, Nathaniel, 267 n.
Whitefield, Rev. Henry, 193 n., 194.
Whiting, Rev. Samuel, 119, 120, 120 n.
Whitingham, John, 230.
Willard, Capt. Simon, 5, 111, 230.
Williams, Roger, 31 n., 123 n., 161 n.
Wilson, Doctor, 33 n., 231.

Wilson, Rev. John, 80, 88; called to church of Charlestown, 67; return to England, 84; return to America for the third time, 104; went with the army against the Indians, 165; dedication of Woburn church, 215; work among the Indians, 264.
Wilson, John, Jr., 202, 202 n.
Windsor, Conn., 193 n., 194.
Winnipiseogee, Lake, 37 n.
Winnisimmet, 63 n.
Winslow, Edward, 241; *Good News from New England*, 42 n.
Winthrop, Gov. John, 6, 9, 38 n., 58 n., 80, 161; flag-ship, *Arbella*, 51 n.; elected governor, 65, 76, 81, 85, 139, 182, 188, 209, 219, 240, 245, 249; trip to island to consider fortifications, 92; involved in dispute relating to authority of magistrates, 116 n.; elected deputy-governor, 118, 225, 234.
Winthrop's *Journal*, 14; cited, 65 n., 78 n., 88 n., 93 n., 101 n., 113 n., 116 n., 119 n., 129 n., 132 n., 139 n., 160 n., 204 n., 208 n., 219 n., 251 n., 258 n., 267 n.
Winthrop, John, Jr., 246 n.
Witchcraft, 237, 237 n.
Woburn, 4–8, 17, 74 n., 117 n., 192 n.; planting of church and town of, 212–218.
Women, 28, 77, 262.
Wood, William, 91 n.
Woodbridge, Rev. John, 249, 249 n.
Worcester, Rev. Thomas, 190.

Yarmouth, 94, 184.

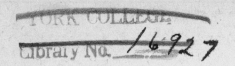